UNEMPLOYMENT

Cause and Cure

UNEMPLOYMENT

Cause and Cure

PATRICK MINFORD

with David Davies, Michael Peel
and Alison Sprague

Martin Robertson · Oxford

First published in 1983 by Martin Robertson & Company Ltd.,
108 Cowley Road, Oxford OX4 1JF.

British Library Cataloguing in Publication Data

Minford, Patrick
Unemployment.
1. Unemployment – Great Britain
331.13'7941 HD5765.A6

ISBN 0-85520-622-5

Typeset by Oxford Verbatim Limited
Printed and bound in Great Britain
by T. J. Press (Padstow) Ltd.
Padstow, Cornwall

Contents

Preface

This book was written in response to demands from various quarters sympathetic to our previously published work, for a comprehensive account of the unemployment problem in Britain and a properly worked out programme of measures to combat it. It embodies the results of the research programme of the Liverpool Research Group in Macroeconomics over the past six years, as well as practical insights gained from periodic policy commentary and forecasts published in the group's Economic Bulletin. It has been published with all possible speed in order to promote public debate of the wide issues involved. Decisions on these require wide public understanding of the side-effects of measures whose obvious impact is socially popular and desirable; at the same time, people must take into account the social dimension of measures which would have substantial effects on the country's purely economic performance.

During the past decade, increased understanding of the mechanism of inflation, due largely to the work of Professor Milton Friedman and those who have followed his pioneering research programme, has led to the political acceptability of apparently harsh measures to reduce and, it is hoped, eliminate inflation from many Western economies, and in particular, Britain. In Europe, and again particularly in Britain, unemployment has risen first steadily, then sharply. It has, however, been greeted with intellectual bewilderment on the part of the public and on the part of politicians, with a plethora of minor, cosmetic measures, as well as a refusal (correct in the authors' view) to abandon their anti-inflation programme. In our view, expounded in the following pages, there does exist a coherent anti-unemployment programme which could be embraced, though with a variety of different forms depending on the social preferences of the people in each given country. We hope that over the next decade there will be an increased understanding of the unemployment mechanism, which in its turn will lead to the embracing of such a programme, politically unacceptable as it may seem at present to many observers conditioned by the post-war period. We hope too that this book will be a contribution to that process.

We gratefully acknowledge crucial assistance and support from a number of sources. First, that of our colleagues in the Liverpool Research Group, who have been involved over a number of years in the development of the Liverpool model used in this book; Chris Ioannidis, Satwant Marwaha, Kent Matthews and David Peel. Secondly, that of the Social Science Research Council, which has financed our research programme since 1977. Third, that of officials in this country and overseas who have patiently answered our requests for often detailed information and analysis of tax/benefit system and other institutions. We are also grateful to George Brennan for setting up and running the UK labour market regressions before this book, reporting revised results, was begun, and to Professor George Bain of Warwick University for making available to us his unpublished estimates of unionization in individual industries. We have also had many illuminating conversations with Daniel Benjamin, whose work with Levis Kochin has pointed the way to a proper analysis of the operations of the British social security system. Finally, we thank Paula Banks, assisted by Jackie Fawcett, Chris Nash and Vivienne Oakes, for typing this manuscript expertly within our exacting deadlines.

Summary

INTRODUCTION

Unemployment in the United Kingdom fluctuated moderately within the range of 1–2 per cent of the labour force throughout the 1950s and early 1960s. From the middle of the 1960s it began a more or less steady rise, by 1970 to 3 per cent, by 1976 to 6 per cent, and by 1982 to 12 per cent. Part of the current higher unemployment rate is to be attributed to the extremely severe world recession, associated with US policies to reduce inflation, while insufficiently curbing public sector deficits. Another part is the effect associated with the Conservative Government's policies to reduce inflation in the UK. Both these effects are temporary in nature; in response to the Government's policies at home, and as a better balance in US fiscal and monetary policies allows world real interest rates to fall, recovery from the recession will occur, though at a rate and with a timing that is inherently hard to predict as world events over the past two years have repeatedly demonstrated.

However, these elements account for a limited part of the unemployment total. Precise calculations are difficult, but, assuming none of the proposals made here were to be carried out, unemployment at the next peak of the economic cycle, whenever that comes, would seem unlikely to fall below 2–2.5 million (8–10 per cent of the labour force). Some others would regard even the upper end of that range as optimistic, a view that would leave even more of the rise in unemployment to be explained by factors other than the recession at home and abroad.

In this book, we focus on these 'underlying' factors and remedies for them rather than on cyclical or 'demand-management' factors and policies. We fully accept the present framework of Government demand management and anti-inflation policy; and within that framework, discussion of details for the money supply and Public Sector Borrowing Requirement targets lies outside the scope of the book.

THE CAUSES OF UNEMPLOYMENT

It is a widespread opinion among economists – and one which we fully endorse – that the proximate cause of unemployment is excessively high wage costs, produced either by high wages or by low productivity. We have identified this as a strong mechanism in the UK.

However, one cannot stop at this point in the analysis and proclaim, as has from time to time been done, that government can, by direct intervention in the wage-setting process, reduce real wages or increase productivity. Such direct intervention (or incomes policy) has repeatedly failed to achieve anything of the sort in the UK, besides being inconsistent with the economic freedom that is this Conservative Government's aim. The reason for this failure is that there are market forces and distortions of considerable power driving real wages and productivity to the levels we observe. In order to modify these levels and so the level of unemployment, we have to understand these forces and modify the market distortions.

This book identifies two major distortions in the UK labour market which prevent real wages and productivity from adjusting naturally to shifts in technology, demand, and industrial structure, and relocating those freed from one sector into other sectors.

The first and most basic is the operation of the unemployment benefit system. The minimum flat rate benefit including any supplementary benefit 'top-up' is paid indefinitely to an unemployed man for as long as he remains unemployed; such a man will very naturally expect to be re-employed at a wage after tax and work expenses which is at least as high as this benefit, and probably somewhat higher because he may not wish to 'work for nothing', whatever his personal attitude towards work. His work even at this wage may well be poorly motivated because of his lack of reward, so that productivity also suffers. Hence wages cannot effectively fall below this level for even the most unskilled worker. This level then acts as a floor under the whole wage structure, and working practices accepted at this unskilled level may similarly affect higher levels of the occupational structure. It follows that shifts in economic conditions which would warrant a fall in real wage costs, will have only a limited effect on them and unemployment will result instead. This mechanism, in other words, substantially limits the wage flexibility of the UK economic system.

The second major factor is the power of unions to raise wages relative to non-union wages. Given the way the benefit rate sets a floor below the non-union wage, as unions raise wages for their members, the workers who then lose their jobs cannot all find alternative work in the non-union sector because wages there do not fall sufficiently; the overall effect is increased unemployment.

These are the fundamental causes isolated in the book. Other factors are contributory, but not fundamental, in the sense that were these causes to be withdrawn, the other factors would not add to unemployment. Such factors include changes in taxation, shifts in technology, adverse movements in the terms of trade and in world demand for UK products, and changes in population size and structure. Many of these are frequently cited in press and other commentary on unemployment as 'reasons' for unemployment. They are so only in the limited sense we have defined. To repeat, if wages and productivity adjusted without constraint, these factors would not alter unemployment, but would instead have their effect on real wages. We pay little attention to them accordingly in what follows.

The explanation of the labour market we have just given is not to be tested by any very simple relationships such as, for example, one between unemployment and the ratio of benefits to work-income. There are a number of complex interactions which need to be disentangled. The book details some work of this nature that we have undertaken; some 1100 observations of post-war UK behaviour have been used in this work and the analysis given emerges unrefuted from these tests. These were supplemented by analysis of the post-war experience in four Continental countries, West Germany, France, Italy and Belgium. These provided econometric support for the approach and useful institutional comparisons. In particular we found that the behaviour of Belgian wages and unemployment closely mirrored that of the UK, even in the size of its unemployment problem, because of its similar flat rate benefit system and powerful unions. In the other three countries with ratio systems, however, behaviour – as the approach predicts – was quite different. We also obtained estimates of the relevant relationships for the UK; these, approximate as they must be, form the basis of the estimated effects of policy changes shown below.

POLICY PROPOSALS

Our proposals fall into four parts:

(1) suggested changes in the benefit system;
(2) supporting changes in tax and income supplements for those in work;
(3) changes in the law and institutions regulating labour market behaviour;
(4) a number of other measures to improve the operation of labour and closely related markets.

Colloquially, (1) may be said to deal with the 'unemployment trap', (2) with the 'poverty trap', (3) with union monopoly power; and (4) deals with minimum wages, regional issues, and the housing market. Taken as a whole, our proposals are capable of reducing unemployment very substantially over a five-year period; politically we believe them to be well capable of implementation with public acceptance as a programme for reducing unemployment, though they will be strongly resisted by particular vested interests. They will increase incentives and get the labour market operating effectively once again.

The Benefit System

Wage flexibility is substantially reduced by the fixed ('flat rate') benefit level. This is because benefits do not vary with wage levels. This is to be contrasted with the practice in a number of Continental countries – for example, Germany, France, Italy and Denmark – where benefits are awarded essentially in a particular ratio to wages. Hence as wages fall, benefits fall in like proportion and do not act as a floor below wages, reducing their flexibility.

Our first proposal is therefore to introduce a maximum statutory ratio (or 'cap') of 70 per cent for total unemployment benefits to net income in work. This is similar to the ratio used on the Continent, for example 68 per cent in Germany, 67 per cent in Italy. This cap would be widely seen as fair in view of the need to maintain minimum work incentives. It would be simple to work (Continental practice shows it to be quite feasible), and it would, according to our estimates, bring about a sizeable reduction in unemployment: nearly 0.75 million over five years. It would also of course greatly increase the flexibility of wages, since for many workers (probably around half) benefits would vary proportionally with wages.

We also propose the introduction of a jobs pool, consisting of all available vacancies and other community work especially organized, in each area (as in the US 'workfare' scheme), together with tighter procedures for denying benefit. Benefits should be conditional on acceptance of a job from the pool – after three months for workers under 25, after six months for other workers. This proposal would reinforce the pressures for jobs to be taken at lower wages; it would also be regarded politically as a 'positive' effort to provide jobs for those unemployed people willing to work for benefits only.

Tax and the Support of Work Income

The introduction of the above measures will increase work incentives substantially for those in low-paid occupations. But a further contribution to reducing unemployment can be obtained by raising tax thresholds and child benefits (to cover families with children). This will increase incentives for those in higher paid occupations, whose benefits will not be affected by the cap. Furthermore it will also increase the social acceptability of the cap by raising the in-work incomes of those affected by it, so both mitigating the fall in their living standards when unemployed, and implying an absolute rise in living standards if they now choose to work even at a lower wage.

Our third proposal is therefore a rise in tax thresholds by 40 per cent and in child benefit by £2.15 per child (bringing it to £8 per child). The rise in tax thresholds should come in two phases, 25 per cent in the 1983 budget, 15 per cent in the 1984 budget. The rise in thresholds will save administrative resources by taking households out of tax; it will also carry out the Conservative manifesto pledge to cut taxes (offsetting the 1981 fall in real thresholds and raising them a further 25 per cent).

However, incentives to work are also damaged seriously for those *in* work at the lower end of the pay scale (the 'poverty trap'). Because of the interaction of tax, national insurance, Family Income Supplement (FIS), means-tested benefits in kind (such as free school meals and free prescriptions, often called 'passported benefits' because drawing of FIS is a 'passport' to receiving them), and rent/rate rebates, living standards barely rise and can actually fall as wages rise for low-paid workers. This is likely to affect work effort, training undertaken, and so productivity.

The raising of tax thresholds itself helps reduce this problem. It also gives an opportunity, because living standards are being raised, of modifying the support system to remove the poverty trap.

Our fourth proposal is to abolish means-tested benefits in kind and replace them by a more generous FIS calculated as two thirds of the shortfall in net income below new, higher 'poverty levels'. This administratively simple measure effectively removes the poverty trap, while substantially protecting the families currently being supported. Some 80,000 families would be worse off, but mostly to a very small extent (less that 3 per cent.) However, to prevent this without restoring the poverty trap would be very costly in either revenue or administrative resources.

Union Power

With labour legislation currently in place, though substantial rights exist to restrain union actions through the courts, enforcement of these rights is lacking. In many cases, the public sector is involved and the government should ensure that public sector bodies enforce their rights fully. Nevertheless, private sector bodies may for various reasons including intimidation and legal costs, be unwilling to pursue actions that it would be in the public interest to have pursued.

Furthermore, the law is by now extraordinarily complex and still fails in the original objective of eliminating labour market monopoly power; closed shop practices are still permitted and unions may still call out workers in breach of contract with their own employers with immunity from tort actions. A bolder approach which goes all out to eliminate labour monopoly power is required. This should be seen to be even handed between workers and employers; as such charges of discrimination against workers because of 'union bashing' would be turned aside.

Our proposals here are simple and threefold:

(a) to restore jurisdiction of the common law to all union actions;
(b) to legislate a 'status' provision such that any contract contingent on the union status of the employee would be invalidated; this would render closed shop agreements, explicit or implicit, null and void;
(c) to institute a Labour Monopolies Commission under the existing competition laws with independent power to investigate any apparent breaches of the public interest in labour market competition, and to bring actions under common law to obtain enforcement of the investigation's proposed remedies.

Proposal (a) would make all union strike action actionable unless expressly covered by a negotiated strike clause in a collective contract; this would give a stimulus to collective agreements, provided these were permitted by the Labour Monopolies Commission. Proposal (b) would give freedom for any person to enter into a contract with any employer; evidence of employment or dismissal because of union membership or lack of it would be actionable. Proposal (c) supplies an active agent to ensure that monopoly positions are broken up, regardless of whether the parties wish it or not, and regardless of whether the offence is by employer or unions. The activities of the Commission would build up a body of case law that should have over time in the labour market the same effect as the Restrictive Trade Practices Court and the Monopolies and Mergers Commission have had in the goods market under existing laws.

Up to now post-war governments have acted as if labour market monopoly was in the public interest; they have done so either because of the desire for political favour with the unions or out of fear. Labour market monopoly is not in the public interest. This Government could, both because of its popular mandate to deal with the problem and because of union weakness in the current labour market, finally deal with the problem once and for all. These proposals are a means to do so.

Other Measures

(1) that all remaining Wages Councils should be abolished; their activities are like those of unions, to raise wages with a consequent rise in unemployment;
(2) to improve mobility, council house rents should be raised to economic levels and private sector rentals should be decontrolled;
(3) to assist the cap proposal to reduce regional disparities in unemployment, a regional employment subsidy based on the unemployment rate of the region should be instituted using EEC regional fund finance.

ECONOMIC EFFECTS OF THE PROPOSALS

We estimate that (i) the cap and related tax proposals should reduce unemployment by around 0.9 million over a five-year period; (ii) the labour market monopoly proposals could reduce unemployment by around 1 million, over a ten-year period in view of the big build-up of case law required for it to be fully effective; (iii) the costs to the Exchequer, after allowing for higher net revenues from lower unemployment and higher output, would be about £2.5 billion in 1983–4 rising to a maximum of £3.25 billion in 1984–5, and falling back to £2 billion within five years. These costs would appear to be within reach, without jeopardizing the PSBR targets set out within the Medium-Term Financial Strategy, though clearly this judgment is a tentative one at this time and will have to be reviewed closer to the budget.

PART I

The Causes of Unemployment in the UK

ANALYSIS OF UK UNEMPLOYMENT

The facts of the 'unemployment trap' described below show how close to benefit levels wages are for very large numbers of workers with incomes less than the average. The implications of this situation are serious and twofold: first, falls in real wages will be hard to achieve (this is sometimes described as 'downward wage rigidity') and second, and as a result, adverse shocks to employment either from the supply or the demand side will have an effect on jobs rather than real wages.

Nevertheless, this is not the only factor in the situation (nor can unemployment be explained or predicted in the UK just by looking at the benefit/wage ratio). To obtain estimates of the likely trends in unemployment and the effects of different policy measures, we have endeavoured to set out a theory of unemployment which embraces the main relevant factors, and to obtain estimates of the relevant relationships for the UK in the post-war period.

The theory that is currently most popular among labour economists is 'search' theory. Suppose that a man has been made redundant or otherwise is out of work. He then searches for a new job for his particular skill. Extra time spent searching costs him extra; this cost includes the outlays on search net of a utility derived from leisure (which of course could be negative). He gets job offers at intervals with a wage attached to it, which is taken randomly from a distribution (which he knows) of potential wages for the job type. He accepts an offer when it is equal to or greater than the expected wage from the next offer minus the extra cost of search involved in waiting for another period.

This theory is undoubtedly suitable for individuals in certain labour markets, notably where the individual has a clearly defined job preference, and jobs of that type become available periodically, and have a wage distribution attached to them. For example, professional people, such as an economics lecturer, may be well described by it. However, the vast mass of jobs are manual or semi-skilled non-manual. Within these jobs, some are restricted by union entry conditions, others are in industries with little union intervention. There would seem to be for such jobs a 'going rate', one in the union sector where jobs are rationed, and one in the non-union sector (if there is one for that job type) where jobs are freely available at the rate. Take taxi-drivers, for example: there are areas such as Newcastle where there is close regulation of rates and attempted control of entry, and areas such as Liverpool which are effectively deregulated. An unskilled man could become a taxi-driver in Liverpool at will, or he could try to get a more profitable regulated job in Newcastle. But it is by no means clear that he will 'search' and remain unemployed. Rather, he may well decide whether it is worth his while to do either. If he concludes that the deregulated one is good enough, but the regulated one would be better if it came up, he may take the deregulated one and be ready to drop it and shift if and when the other comes up. It seems unlikely that he would remain unemployed, 'searching' the union or regulated sectors, unless he decided that the non-union rates were just not attractive at all. If he did so, he would lose income without necessarily enhancing his chances of a union job.

Such a person will furthermore be content to choose from a wide menu of jobs. Take, for example, the recent case of a Liverpool taxi-driver who had been made redundant from an engineering firm. He decided that, given the scarcity of union jobs, the taxi rate was acceptable; no doubt he is keeping engineering places under review as they come up.

These considerations suggest an alternative model of the work decision, which is 'new classical' in spirit. The worker has knowledge of 'going rates' in unregulated, or non-union sectors in which he has the necessary skills to work; he does not need to 'search' for this knowledge. He decides when to enter and when to withdraw from these sectors in a standard 'optimizing' manner, that is he maximizes the present value of his expected welfare, given these wage rates and other relevant prices, including benefits out of work, and taxes etc. in work. Though all workers would like to have a union job, it is assumed that the chances of getting one are not affected by taking a non-union job, so that the union wage does not affect his work decision.

It turns out in this model that the number of people willing to work at *union* wages is irrelevant to the determination of wages or jobs in either the union or the non-union sectors. The reason is straightforward: the union's mark-up over the non-union real wage is determined by its monopoly power interacting with technology and demand conditions; this monopoly power is precisely the power to ignore the desires of non-union members for the better wages within the controlled sector. In practice, of course, this ability would be eroded substantially, the larger the non-union sector. But this erosion depends not so much on the non-union members' frustration as on the enhanced ability of firms to hire non-union members beyond the reach of the union (as in the USA, with firms hiring in the South rather than the unionized North East).

The model therefore implies that the total supply of labour will be dependent on the level of current real wages in the non-union sector ('free market wages'), net of tax and expenses, relative to net out-of-work benefits, on the one hand, and expected future net real non-union wages on the other. In other words, the people who are 'on the margin' of supply in the labour market are in the non-union sector (in 'unprotected jobs'), typically on low wages and in unattractive jobs. Hence the importance in labour supply of replacement ratios (i.e. the ratio of benefits out of work to net in-work income) for low income households, for these are the ones most likely to withdraw into unemployment and swell the statistics under additional downward pressure on wages.

There are various ways in which the supply of labour could contract as real wages fell. Workers could decide to quit more frequently, taking longer periods between work. For manual men, for whom explicit part-time work is awkward, this would approximate to part-time working over the year as a whole. Workers could take spells of work abroad, and spells on benefits at home. They could do less actual work on the factory premises, so lowering productivity per hour. For example they could choose longer rest periods, hold meetings at work, go absent without leave or simply make less effort. Workers could decide not to work at all until real wages picked up again. They could, for instance, withdraw from the labour market in recessions and return in boom periods. Most drastically they could withdraw indefinitely and change their life style to one of living on benefits and casual, probably undeclared, earnings, on the assumption that real wages are never likely to be sufficiently attractive. To those accustomed to the ways of prosperous Southern areas of the country, such ideas may seem unfamiliar, even outrageous; but it has to be said that they are part of the everyday gossip and 'casual empiricism' of an area such as Liverpool.

Viewed in this way the distinctions between decisions on duration of unemployment, those on participation in work, and those on work effort or productivity become blurred. There is in essence a continuous decision on more or less no participation in work and work effort.

This decision is naturally viewed as taken for the fiscal year. For example, someone wanting to work half the time would be best advised to work half the year and be unemployed for the other half (in either order) – that way he uses up his tax allowances. Were he to work for one year and be unemployed for the whole of the next year, he would fail to use and subsequently lose his tax allowances in the second year under the UK tax system operating over our sample period.

In the UK we can distinguish three major groups in the bulk of our sample period, according to their benefit status as illustrated in Figure I.1. There are 'flat rate' benefits – that is effectively the minimum paid, shown as point *A*. People on net incomes to the left of *A* will face a relative price of work and leisure of unity – a replacement ratio of 100 per cent or more. (The point *A* is properly the wage at which the flat rate benefit level is just attractive enough to make 100 per cent leisure preferable. This point could occur at a replacement ratio lower than 100 per cent, for some possibly higher.) They are likely to be in a situation where they do no work at all and be unresponsive to benefit or wage changes.

Then there was an earnings related supplement (ERS, abolished in December 1981) which raised the benefit/wage ratio to 2/3 for those whose incomes relative to flat rate benefits otherwise put them below this ratio. Their related price of work will be somewhat more attractive therefore; they accordingly will react to changes in the replacement ratio because of a substitution effect. The group to the right of *A* includes these people as well as those with benefit/income ratios between 2/3 and 1.

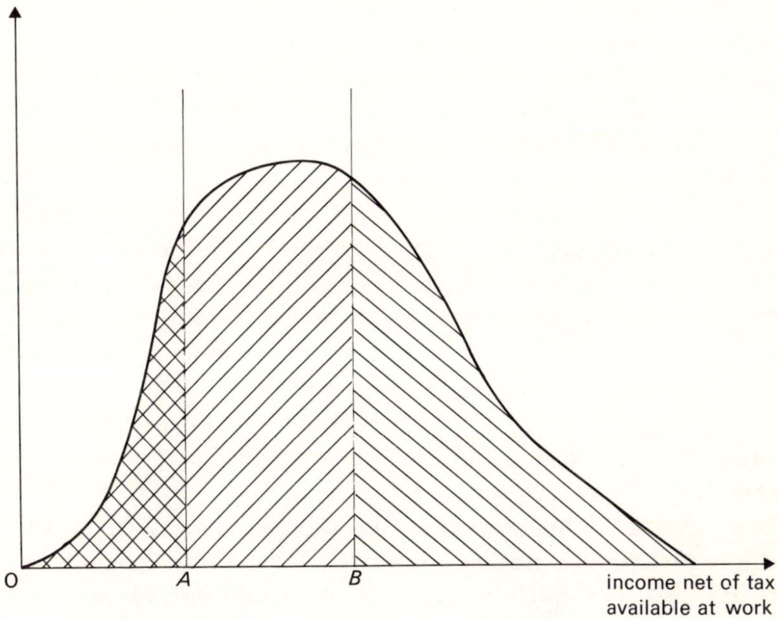

FIGURE I.1 *Distribution of Income and Benefit Status for a Typical Household Type*
(*A* = flat rate benefit 'cut off' point
B = earnings related benefit 'cut off' point)

Finally, there was a ceiling on ERS, that is, an income above which ERS became a flat rate supplement, shown as point *B*. Those to the right of *B* will have benefit/wage ratios progressively less than 2/3 as income rises; their substitution effect may therefore be smaller than those between *A* and *B*. (At very high incomes the relative price of work becomes lower again with the higher rate of tax. However, this is not of much concern for unemployment.)

Most importantly, as flat rate benefits rise, more people will be drawn into the area to the left of *A* where they may decide not to work at all. Since someone who does not work at all will be unemployed 12 times as long as someone who takes a two-month spell every two years, these people dominate the unemployment stock. In a time-series analysis, we may expect the elasticity of unemployment (under the UK system) to the benefit/income ratio to be very low for a low aggregate ratio (e.g. around 0.5), to rise as the ratio rises, reaching a peak and dropping again towards zero as the population becomes concentrated around or to the left of *A*.

This illustrates the important general point that while the cross-section studies of populations are undoubtedly of great value, they do not necessarily provide ready answers to questions about reactions of populations over time. In this case, to translate cross-section findings into time-series predictions of the effect of benefit changes, one requires to know the income distribution, the location of points *A* and *B*, the reservation wage levels and the elasticity between *A* and *B*. Such a translation is likely to be hazardous at best. A time–series relationship, for all its faults, provides a useful direct estimate of the reactions under investigation.

While labour supply and unemployment depend on non-union real wages in this way, non-union real wages in turn are determined at the level which set supply equal to demand in the non-union labour market. This market is like the free market in 'two-tier' markets, where one market is controlled, and one is free and unrestricted, for example the financial Belgian franc or any black market. It reacts sensitively to demand and supply factors in both markets. For instance, a rise in union monopoly power which raises the union mark-up over non-union wages, will raise union wages, non-union wages constant, and reduce demand for union labour. Those who lose their union jobs will be available for work in the non-union sector and depress wage levels there. As this non-union wage falls, so total labour supply contracts and unemployment rises.

As another example, suppose UK real costs of imported inputs rise, worsening the terms of trade. This has a substitution effect which raises the demand for labour, but an income (terms of trade) effect which lowers the demand for labour in conditions of external current account balance. Suppose, as is likely, the latter effect dominates. Then labour demand falls, probably in both union and non-union sectors. At constant real non-union wages, this will fall entirely on the non-union supply–demand balance; non-union real wages will drop, again lowering labour supply and raising unemployment.

EMPIRICAL WORK ON THE UK LABOUR MARKET – AN ACCOUNT OF THE ESTIMATING MODEL

Our analysis is concerned primarily with the long-run determination of employment, unemployment and real wages, and we assume that in the long run there is no excess supply or demand for labour or goods. Our long-run assumptions are captured in Figure I.2. It shows, first, a supply curve of labour to the UK economy associated with the average real non-union wage, W_c/P on the vertical axis; the quantity of labour (L) is on the horizontal axis. The supply curve is drawn flat at low wages because the ratio of real benefits (shown as B/P) to real wages becomes critically high for a large section of the population, but at high wages the benefit/wage ratios drop to irrelevance for the vast majority, so that the only effect of benefits is

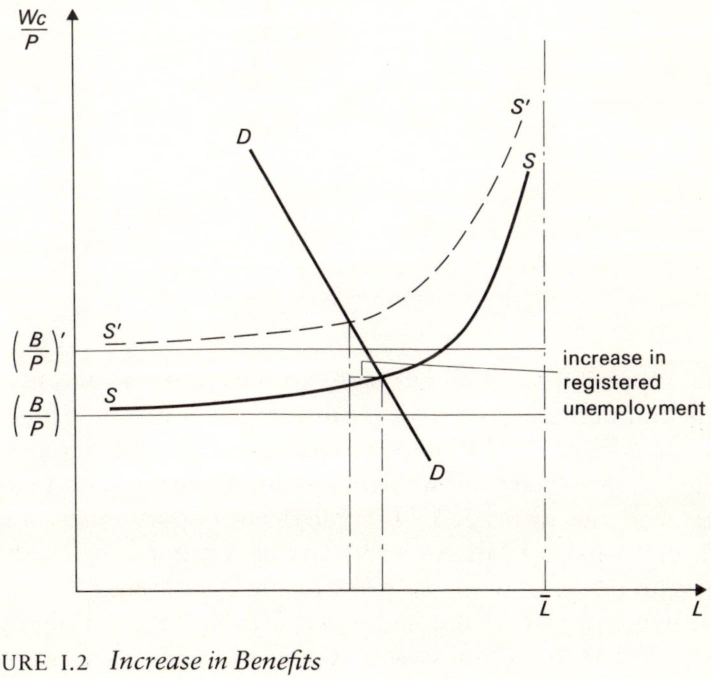

FIGURE I.2 *Increase in Benefits*

to raise somewhat the length of time spent between jobs in 'search'. At these high wages the supply of labour approximates to what we may call the 'labour force' shown as $\overline{L}$; those capable of working would wish to do so under appropriate terms, and would mostly register as desiring work at unemployment benefit offices.

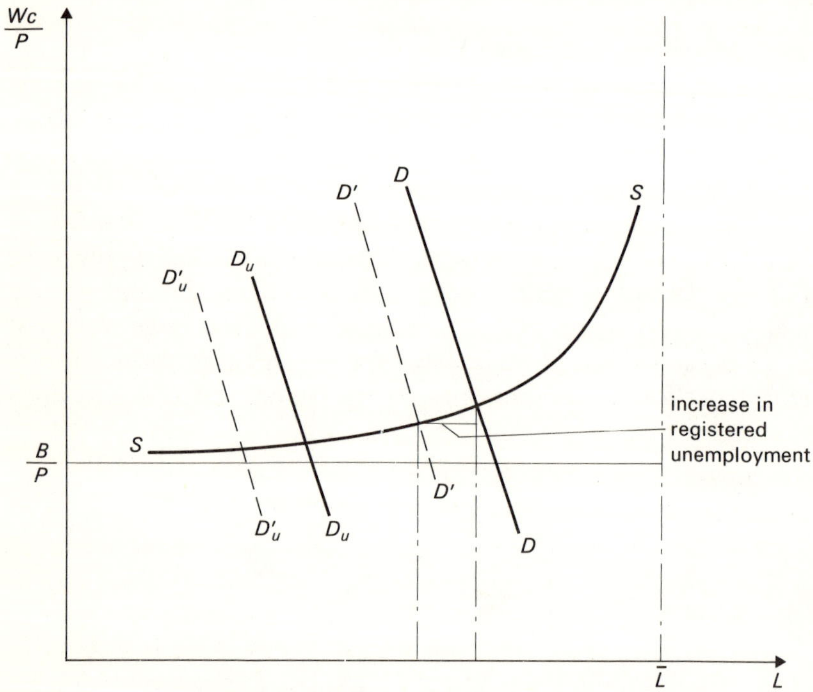

FIGURE 1.3 *The Effects of an Increase in Union Power*
(the dashed lines represent the situation after a rise in union mark-up)

This supply curve of labour shifts to the left if real benefits rise or if income tax rates rise (reducing disposable wages corresponding to the gross wage shown on the vertical axis), or if the labour force is reduced. We must allow also for the rigidity of the housing market and the dispersion of employment opportunities; a mismatch between population centres and opportunities will shift the *SS* curve to the left if mobility is obstructed by housing.

The demand side of the figure is drawn up on the simplifying assumption that there is a constant union 'mark-up' (the percentage by which unions raise unionized workers' wages above non-union wages) at all levels of non-union wages and other relevant variables. The expositional advantage of this clear over-simplification is that it allows union and non-union firms' demand curves for labour to be put on a single figure. With union real wages uniquely related to non-union real wages, demand for union labour, though truly related to the non-union real wage, is shown by the D_uD_u curve (Figure I. 3). The demand for non-union labour will be related straightforwardly to the non-union real wage. We can add the two demands for labour together to obtain the total demand curve *DD*.

The position of these demand curves – the 'level of demand' depends on four groups of factors. First there are the international ones: world trade and our terms of trade, which together dictate what domestic demand and output will be, consistent with current account balance at given non-union real wages. An expansion in world trade, for example, would increase demand for British goods from abroad. If these are supplied at higher real wages, the additional export earnings will be available for domestic demand to increase also, raising imports by the same amount. Both D_uD_u and *DD* curves shift to the right, and real wages rise, as will labour supply and employment.

Secondly, there are the technological factors which affect the productivity of labour and other costs. A rise in other costs, such as raw material or capital, both of which we assume to be set in international markets, will shift the *DD* curve to the left. A rise in the marginal product of labour will shift it to the right.

Thirdly, taxes on labour paid by firms and other implicit labour costs levied on employers (such as sickness benefits and redundancy costs) will shift the *DD* curve to the left.

Finally, we come to the union mark-up. A rise will shift the D_uD_u curve to the left, since a given non-union real wage will now correspond to a higher union real wage. The *DD* curve will be shifted to the left by the same amount (there will be no change in non-union labour demand at given real non-union wages).

What determines the union mark-up? Our analaysis is straightforward enough: each union is a maximizing monopoly which faces the problem of working out an optimal time-path of real wages for its members, given that actions it takes today will have effects far into the future. In principle, therefore, all the factors determining the demand for labour in both sectors and the total supply of labour will come indirectly into each union's analysis. Complicated as this problem is, the essentials of the solution are clear enough. In particular, the mark-up will rise the less easy the employer finds it to substitute other factors of production, including non-union labour, for union labour. 'Union power' is measured in principle by the difficulty of this substitution, but this is not helpful in practice since this difficulty is unobservable. In practice, we resort to the only available index of union power – the proportion of the labour force which is unionized – and suppose that it is likely to bear some rough relationship to the true measure.

We can put this whole framework together easily enough. Employment and real non-union wages are determined in the long run at the intersection of the supply curve, *SS* and the demand curve, *DD*. Unemployment is the difference between workers who register, $\bar{L}$, and those who are employed. This again is an over-simplification because not all in the labour force register for a variety of reasons – especially lack of eligibility and dislike of the unemployment status. But registered unemployment will be highly correlated with the difference between $\bar{L}$ and employment.

THE MECHANICS OF ESTIMATION

In the short run the economy will not jump quickly to any new long-run equilibrium, for the traditional reason that there are costs of adjusting labour demands (and possibly also labour supplies, though we do not find them important). These costs of adjustment cause both employment and union real wages (and so also average real wages) to move relatively sluggishly; our estimates suggest that adjustment takes about five years for 90 per cent to come through.

It is convenient for us to assume that in the non-union sector, day-to-day (as opposed to long-run) supply is always equal to day-to-day demand, hence our model assumes continuous labour market equilibrium, in the sense that this residual market always clears and there is no excess supply. However, this is less important than it seems. Our analysis still has the conventional characteristic; that it takes time to get to the long run. Other analyses which would share our long-run framework, but assumed short-run disequilibrium (excess supply or demand) could well produce similar results. So our analysis does not appear to rest crucially on the assumption of continuous market equilibrium.

What our analysis gives us are two basic equations and one group of equations.

(1) An equation for total average wages (union and non-union) which, using real wages as the supply price of labour, says it depends on the volume of unemployment, real benefits grossed up for direct taxes, the size of the labour force and the unionization rate. To allow for one-year nominal wage contracts over a proportion of employees, the size of inflation forecasting errors also enters the calculations. Unexpected inflation causes workers who contracted in advance to suffer an unexpected drop in real wages. Finally, the last period's real wages enter because of the adjustment costs noted earlier. This is the 'supply equation' in the analysis. (The unionization rate (and so the union mark-up) enters the supply equation though it entered the demand curves in the figure because the figure is in terms of the non-union wage, whereas the estimation is in terms of the (observable) total wage over all sectors.)

(2) An equation for unemployment, regarded as depending on the demand for labour; this is the demand equation in the analysis. Unemployment is related consequently to real wages grossed up for labour taxes on the employer, technological progress, the volume of output, and lagged unemployment.

(3) A group of equations determining the level of output. These are the equations of the Liverpool macroeconomic model. They have the property that, in the long run, output must be such that there is current account balance. Hence long-run output (and so employment) will depend, as in the figure, on world trade and the terms of trade, as well as on the other factors entering the *SS* and *DD* curves. Output in the short run depends on the fiscal, monetary and international shocks hitting the economy which cause fluctuations around the long-run equilibrium (discussed in our other work and not important here).

THE EMPIRICAL RESULTS – A BRIEF ACCOUNT

In all, we have 'fitted' the model described here to over 1100 pieces of data, a very large set indeed. Our primary work, since it is directly relevant to the estimates of UK policy effects, concerns wages and unemployment in the economy as a whole. But we have supplemented this with disaggregated work on 17 industries' wages and unemployment, and also with work on the regional behaviour of wages, unemployment and working days lost. For full details of these results, see Appendix A.

This body of work strongly supports the view that the level of benefits, direct tax rates, both paid by the employee and by the employer, and union power have major effects on the level of unemployment. These effects are substantial. We find that a 10 per cent rise in real benefits would, at current unemployment levels, raise unemployment by nearly 0.75 million; a rise in the fraction of labour force unionized by one percentage point would raise it 0.25 million; a rise in employer national insurance contributions by one percentage point would rise it by 0.15 million; a rise in the standard rate by one percentage point would raise it by 0.05 million. Table I.1 summarizes the principal results from each of our studies.

COMPARISON WITH PREVIOUS WORK ON THE UK

Unfortunately, it is impossible to compare these findings directly with previous work. The reason is that previous work has all been microeconomic in nature, and hence has supplied 'partial equilibrium' results. That is to say, no estimates have been derived, or for that matter were derivable, for total effects.

Nevertheless, we may compare to some extent the estimates of partial relationships embodied here with those found by others.

On benefits, our supply (wage) equation gives an implicit partial long-run elasticity of unemployment to the replacement ratio of 4.5; Nickell (1979a), Lancaster (1979) and Mackay and Reid (1972) have found elasticities of unemployment duration to the replacement ratio of around 0.6, in cross-section studies of samples of the unemployed. Lancaster went as far as to conclude that an 'elasticity

TABLE I.1

Percentage change of unemployment with respect to †*	*Percentage change in benefits*	*Percentage point changes in:* *Unionization rate*	*Personal tax rates*	*Employer tax rates*
From aggregate model	2.25	9	2.25	5
From average of industry models	4	9	4	9
From regional cross-section	n.a.	men 3 (union coverage) women 4	n.a.	n.a.

* Not percentage point change.
† Full effect, i.e. after all indirect effects (on output, real wages etc.) have occurred.

of this order could now be regarded as established beyond reasonable doubt'.

A detailed critique of all these studies cannot be undertaken here. The Mackay and Reid study is in any case somewhat dated and uses less powerful methods than those of Lancaster and Nickell. Nevertheless, there is one major issue to be raised with all these studies. They all assume, within a search model framework, that intended (or desired) duration is never long-term (or 'infinite'), or in terms of the search model that the offer–acceptance rate never tends to zero. We have suggested above that a person's optimal level of unemployment per fiscal year will depend sensitively on the relative price of work and leisure (as roughly measured by the replacement ratio). For high ratios he may decide to work not at all, or for only brief spells when market wages are exceptionally favourable. Such people are likely to exhibit a very low elasticity to changes in the ratio; this is Nickell's finding for those with long durations (six months or more). Yet the implication, if our suggestion is correct, is precisely the opposite to that which he draws (that there is little effect of the ratio on long-term unemployment). It is that at some ratio these people would cease to be below the margin and would participate 'properly' again in employment, having therefore at this ratio a very high ('switching') elasticity to it.

Furthermore, the total effect of the average replacement ratio on average duration across the sample would correspondingly be enormously higher. For suppose there were two equal groups, those with 'normal' duration of eight weeks at a ratio of 0.5, and those with 'medium' duration of 20 weeks at a ratio of 0.8. Their average duration and ratio would be 14 weeks and 0.65 respectively. Now suppose the ratios rise to 0.6 and 0.9; the first group, with an elasticity of 0.6, raises duration to nine weeks, the second responds by planning 'indefinite' duration, say two years (104 weeks) to allow for an occasional sampling of work. Average duration will eventually settle at 56.5 weeks, while the average replacement ratio will have only risen to 0.75; unemployment will have quadrupled in response to a 15 per cent (10 percentage point) rise in the average replacement ratio.

There are a number of potentially small points to be made, which may cumulatively add up to a severe problem for these studies. Nickell assumes that inflow rates on to the unemployment register are independent of replacement ratios; this is required both in his econometric procedure and in his conclusion that the duration elasticity to the ratio can be equated with the unemployment elasticity. He produces no evidence for this, other than that male inflow rate has 'hardly changed since 1967'. This is suggestive at best, since offsetting effects could be occurring. It certainly does not apply to the female inflow rate (outside his sample, but important in total unemployment) which has risen from around 80,000 per month in the late '60s to 118,000 in early 1982.

The specification of alternative earnings is important. Nickell uses an occupational earnings function estimated by Stewart (1976) to provide estimates of these. Lancaster uses actual reported earnings, which is surely an improvement. Neither, however, takes account of the union factor discussed above. Jobs in the union sector are rationed, those in the non-union sector are not. A person may hope for a unionized job 'wage offer', which may have the distribution characteristics posited by Lancaster and Nickell; but non-union jobs require alternative treatment. Earnings on these are likely to be a lot lower than union wages. In particular, these authors might have investigated the possibility of duration-dependence in the relevant earnings faced. Thus, a man made redundant from union employment may spend some weeks initially searching for union jobs at the higher wage to which he is accustomed, and then switch his attention to the lower wage non-union sector.

Details, such as the treatment of wife's income and of tax liability, can also be criticized in Nickell's study. Tax liability on potential work income varies with duration during any given fiscal year; but this is ignored by Nickell. Wife's income is included in both work income and benefit income; yet the marginal tax rates on wives of unemployed men are high and increase with his unemployment duration (since as he loses ERS and becomes increasingly dependent on supplementary benefit, her income risks loss of benefit).

Finally, we may note a general problem which, judging from an interesting (1982) paper by Lancaster and Chesher appears to be of increasing concern to Lancaster himself. This is that a large number of statistical assumptions are required to estimate these search models of duration, and sensitivity of the results to variations in these assumptions is largely unknown. Illustrating this, Lancaster and Chesher's paper uses an alternative technique on Lancaster's original sample. It is based on the reservation wage mentioned by the respondents. Using this and a variety of assumptions about the form of the wage offer distribution and the respondents' risk-aversion, leisure-valuation, etc, Lancaster and Chesher are able to show that:

(1) the data are consistent with a rising elasticity of duration to the replacement ratio;
(2) risk-aversion raises this elasticity;
(3) leisure-preference also raises it – possibly very substantially;
(4) substitution of the log normal for a Pareto distribution of wage offers lowers it.

We may also note that 'reservation wages' are close to (i.e. in the same frequency class of approximately 15 per cent width) 'expected earnings in a new job' for 46 per cent of their sample. For 0.5 per cent they were actually greater than expected earnings. Hence, a significant percentage is close to, at, or beyond the point where planned duration would become infinite. These final considerations point at the very least to great caution in interpreting the results from the earlier cross-section studies as a guide to the time-series response to changes in policy regime.

Maki and Spindler (1975), in a time-series analysis of the UK in the post-war period, found a partial elasticity of unemployment to the replacement ratio of 0.6. This estimate is flawed by the use of the ERS benefit ratio, which only applied to a minority of unemployed, and by the ambiguous status of the estimating equation, which is neither a structural equation nor a reduced form. Also, the most recent re-working of their data by Junankar (1982) shows too that the equation is fairly vulnerable to shifts in estimation period. Holden and Peel (1981) have estimated reduced form equations on UK post-war time series using benefits paid to a married man on average earnings with two children, which find an elasticity of around 0.4 to the replacement ratio. However, since other exogenous variables, such as world trade and unionization, have been omitted and rolled into the error process, the coefficient estimate may be biased. Similar problems and comments arise in the context of the work on the inter-war period by Benjamin and Kochin (1979) and others (see Benjamin and Kochin *et al*, 1982). This type of time-series work has been stimulating and suggestive, but it would appear that it has established only that benefits probably matter for unemployment, but to an undetermined degree.

Hence, the work reported here is for better or worse rather different from any of these studies, time-series or cross-section. Of the time-series studies, none has been based on a detailed market model as used here, while the cross-section studies appear to have paid inadequate attention to the problem of non-participation, which could well account for the high benefit elasticity we have found.

Whatever is true of benefits is also true of personal direct taxes, since these are included in the replacement ratios.

On unionization, the previous literature has estimated union mark-ups. These estimates have varied substantially, and have given rise to substantial controversy. Most recently, Treble (1982) has pointed out the tenuous basis for the majority of these estimates, which use a methodology originated by Lewis (1963). If one averages available estimates of this type for the UK mark-up (Parsley (1980)), it comes out around 25 per cent with a high variance. Insofar as any tentative estimate of this union mark-up emerges from our work, it is of the order of 70 per cent.

Treble (1982) reworked, using a sounder method, the data of Mulvey (who obtained estimates for the UK around 30 per cent) and obtained an estimate of about 40 per cent. This is closer to our implicit figure, but there is still reason to believe it is downward biased. This is because both the union mark-up and the level of non-union wages are likely to vary with the density of unionization. This variation would reduce the estimated coefficient in Treble's work. A proper treatment of the data used by Treble and Mulvey would require an additional equation to be estimated, in order to disentangle this effect from the true union mark-up estimate.

At this stage, we must regard estimates derived by methods such as those of Mulvey (i.e. all those for the UK, as cited in Parsley, 1980) and even Treble as inadequate and downward biased, pending a reworking with a full model. Our own time-series work here is based on the use of a full model, and there is no reason to believe the results are biased: they do not appear to be challenged by these previous estimates.

Lastly, on employer labour taxes there appears to be no directly comparable work for the UK post-war period. However, there appears to be little controversy over the employment effects of cuts in the national insurance contribution.

CONCLUSIONS

We can use the estimated annual relationships within the Liverpool model to compute the effects on the natural rate of unemployment, real wages and output of various permanent changes in taxation, benefits and unionization – shown in Table I.2. (All tax and benefit changes are offset notionally by lump-sum transfers, leaving net government revenues unchanged. These, which include the effect of changes in output, are noted in Column 5.)

TABLE I.2 *Effects of Regime Changes*

Fall of	*Unemployment** *('000)*	*Real (%) Wages*	*Output (%)*	*Available for lump-sum transfers (£ billion p.a. 1982 prices)†*
10 per cent in benefits	− 700	− 1.2	+ 1.5	+ 2.3
0.01 in T_F	− 150	+ 0.6	+ 0.5	− 0.6
0.01 in T_L	− 60	− 0.2	+ 0.2	− 0.9
0.01 in *UNR*	− 260	− 1.3	+ 0.85	+ 0.9

Source: Appendix A.
Notes: * Computed at $U = 2.8$ million.
† Includes extra revenue from rise in output. Negative figure denotes net drain on Exchequer. Assumes marginal overall tax rate of 0.4.
T_F = employment tax rate; T_L = personal rax rate; *UNR* = unionization rate.

It can be seen that per unit of revenue cost, cuts in national insurance charges paid by firms are more effective in reducing unemployment than cuts in the standard rate, while to equal the effect on unemployment of a 10 per cent cut in real benefits, it would require cuts in NI charges costing the Exchequer a net £5 billion per annum more. However, the effectiveness of a cut in taxes on employees in reducing unemployment would presumably be increased the more it was concentrated on the lower paid. One may presume

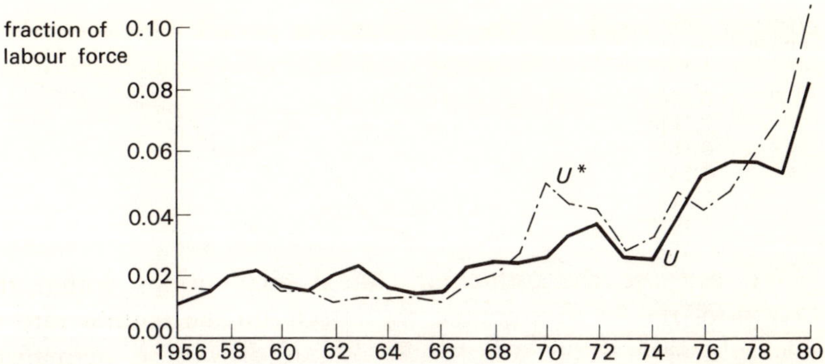

FIGURE 1.4 U *(unemployment) and* U* *(equilibrium unemployment)*

that, if totally concentrated on those at the bottom end, each £ of tax cut would have an effect on unemployment comparable with that of a £ of benefit cut. At present most of those in the 'unemployment trap' would pay significant tax if they were working (Howell, 1981).

Finally, we may use these equations to compute the natural rate of unemployment. Figures I.4 to I.9 show the model's 'prediction' for this from 1956 to 1980, as well as the behaviour of the 5 key determining variables. The natural rate of unemployment in particular is set at 7.25 per cent in 1979 (about 1.75 million). The date at which it began its dizzying rise can be set fairly precisely at 1966, that is at the beginning of Labour government after 13 years of Conservative government. This led to a sharp rise in union power, in benefits and taxation. In 1970–3 taxes were cut and the

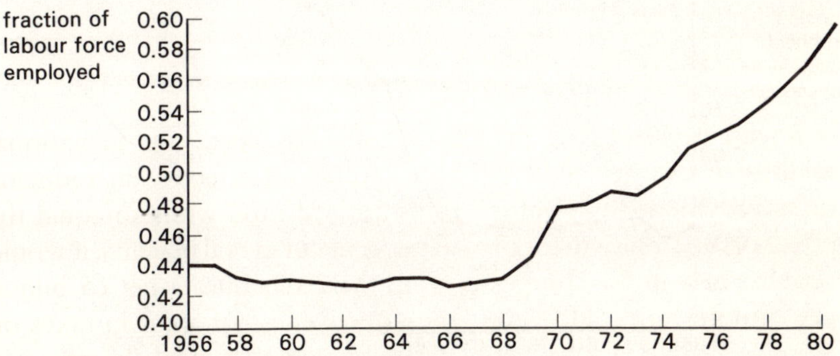

FIGURE I.5 UNR *(unionization rate)*

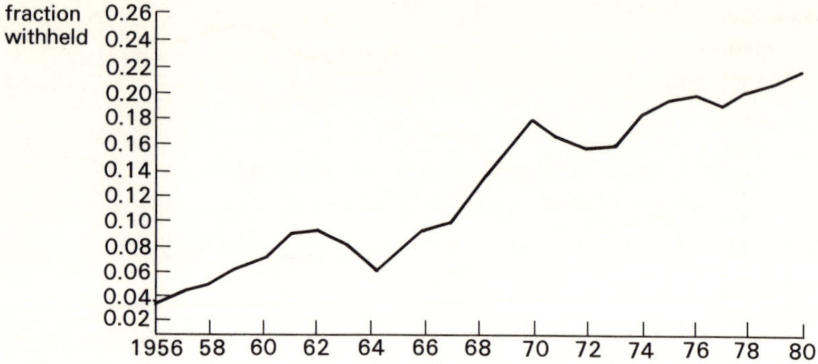

FIGURE I.6 T_L *(direct tax rate)*

rise in real benefits halted by the previous Conservative administration. However, the cut in taxes was unsustainable because it led to very large budget deficits, and has subsequently been more than reversed, while real benefits began to climb again in the mid-1970s as Labour rule resumed. Union power rose steadily during the 1970s and finally world trade growth collapsed in the second half of that decade. So the upward trend was resumed from 1973.

We have set out above a theory of the 'natural rate' of unemployment for the UK, and described our results based on over 1100 post-war observations of British economic behaviour.

Naturally, we would expect that future research will be able to refine these estimates and modify them perhaps in many details. Nevertheless, these future changes seem unlikely to alter the major thrust of our findings, judging from the similarity of the results

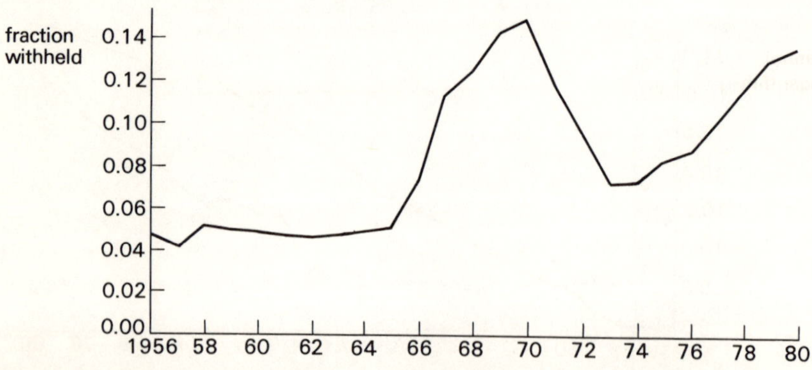

FIGURE I.7 T_F *(employers' tax rate on labour)*

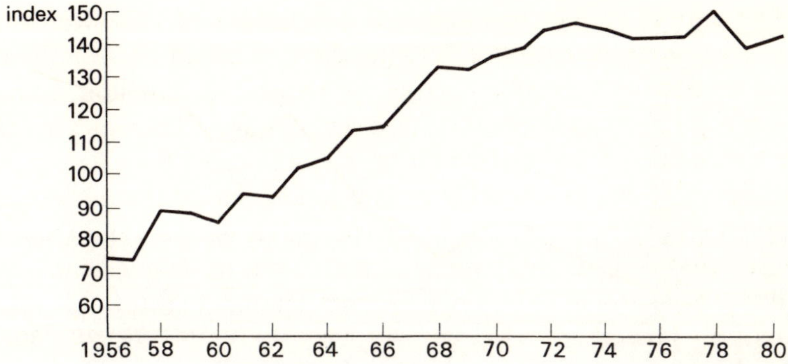

FIGURE I.8 b *(real benefits)*

which we have obtained from the different parts of our study, i.e. the whole economy (quarterly and annual data), industrial data and regional data.

These findings were that there is a significant and powerful total elasticity of real benefits on unemployment (operating through higher real wages) of the order of 2.25. This is substantially higher than other post-war estimates insofar as these are comparable. Tax rates on employers and employees have analogous impacts, though the elasticities are much lower. Finally, and perhaps most strikingly, we find that in the past two decades, union monopoly power has increased significantly and caused a substantial rise in real wages, with corresponding unemployment. The total elasticity of unemployment to the unionization rate (our index of union monopoly power) is no less than 4.5.

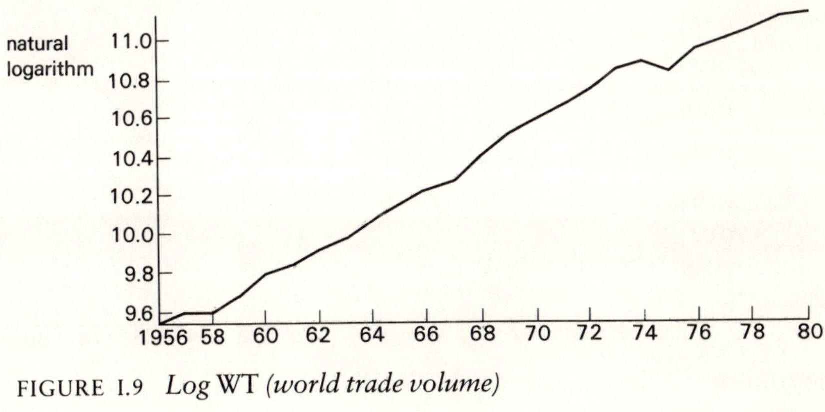

FIGURE I.9 *Log* WT *(world trade volume)*

The natural rate of unemployment in the UK in 1979 was estimated to be of the order of 7.25 per cent, or around 1.75 million. Since then it has probably risen to the range 2–2.5 million, owing to a further rise in unionization (the statistics for 1980 indicate that job losses have been higher among non-unionized than unionized members); to the fall in real tax thresholds; and to the rise in real supplementary benefits to compensate for rising rates and council house rents. Our analysis suggests that it can be lowered substantially by measures to reduce real benefits, labour tax rates and union monopoly power.

In the parts that follow, we go in detail into the facts relating to each of these major policy areas and suggest policy proposals to remedy the problems.

PART II

Policy Analysis and Proposals

CHAPTER 1

The Tax Benefit System

THE 'UNEMPLOYMENT TRAP'

Estimates of Replacement Ratios as of November 1982

The calculation of replacement ratios is bedevilled by the problem of non-take-up. Non-take-up of benefit entitlements may occur for a variety of reasons, including stigma effects, ignorance, and the transactions costs of take-up. However, it seems wrong to allow for non-take-up by simply recording benefits actually taken on average. The reason is that economic analysis is concerned with decisions by people on the margin, that is weighing benefit and costs which are finely balanced. It seems likely that such substitution effects as we observe – actions by those on the margin – will be carried out by people conscious of the marginal choices confronting them; for if they are not conscious of them, why should they move at all?

It seems better to calculate *entitlements*, as if everyone is rational and well informed, and then to allow the data to determine, through the estimated elasticities of response, how far these entitlements affect decisions. This has the advantage of consistency with the assumptions of the economic models typically used, based on maximizing behaviour. Take-up rates can then be regarded as reflecting people's decisions, given their tastes and attitudes, just as their unemployment duration and labour force participation reflects those decisions.

On the basis, then, of full entitlements we have calculated the November 1982 replacement ratios for single persons and for married men with non-working wives, by size of family and income. We present two calculations.

The first calculation is short term, assuming the person or married man is unemployed only for six months of the tax year (and is employed at the stated work income for the rest). The ratio shows additional benefits *net* of extra tax liability if unemployed, divided by additional earnings net of extra tax liability if employed. Tax is computed on a marginal basis, i.e. the year's allowances are counted as 'used up' by the six months of work income, and the residual allowances only are credited to the six months of unemployment. Work expenses of £8.25p. per week are deducted from, and Family Income Supplement with rent/rate rebates (based on £12 per week rent, £3 rates) added to, work income. Since supplementary benefit rates exceed unemployment benefit rates, the former are used to evaluate benefit entitlements – other 'passported' benefits are added as applicable.

There are elements in this calculation which are somewhat arbitrary. On work expenses, a DHSS study of those unemployed in 1978 indicates a weighted average of about £1.90 per week on travel to work costs related to the period of work (i.e. 1977). However, this includes 42 per cent who 'paid less than 50p per week', an incredibly low figure which presumably largely relates to young workers living with their parents and in many cases getting a lift from them. If so, it is hardly to be regarded as an economic cost of travel. Disregarding these, the weighted average figure is about £3.25, but something must be deducted for the 14 per cent with free travel provided by their employer. In the five years from late 1977 to November 1982 the transport price index will have arisen around 90 per cent. Hence for travel costs, something of the order of £5–6 seems reasonable. We have also allowed £2–3 for other work costs: additional expenditure on clothing and on food taken outside the home. This may well err on the low side, but there is no firm information. A notional allowance is made in these figures for fringe benefits. Subsidized canteen meals are frequently provided by an employer (15 per cent of the DHSS study obtained them); this is reflected in our low cost of food outside the home. Free travel provided by the employer to 14 per cent has also been mentioned. Notes on the other elements are to be found in Appendix B.

The second calculation presented is long term. This assumes the person has been unemployed for all or part of the preceding year. The ratio compares his net benefits should he remain unemployed for the whole of the current tax year, with his net income should he work for the whole tax year at the stated wage.

The picture presented by these calculations is a grim one from the point of view of incentives to participate in employment. The replacement ratios are such that, should a person 'work the system', incentives to have a job are on the whole rather small for the family man. Even for the single person, the replacement ratio reached 0.8 at just under 60 per cent of average earnings. Since the bulk of single persons are young (45 per cent of single person householders were under 25 in 1979 according to the General Household Survey (GHS), Table 2.5) and so have earnings well below the average, this is more damaging than it might sound.

It is difficult to estimate how many workers are affected by high replacement ratios, since so many different factors interact. However, we can use the Family Expenditure Survey (FES) 1980 to obtain an estimate of the distribution of gross weekly income across each (non-retired) household type. Assuming that the distribution of the earnings of the household head in each category matches that of household incomes, we reach the calculations shown in Table II.1.1. Using the FES shares for these households, the proportion of workers whose long-term replacement ratio is around unity or above is 15 per cent, while over 30 per cent have a ratio of more than 0.8. This must be only a rough approximation; however it indicates that there is a substantial proportion of the workforce with high replacement ratios. This picture is virtually unaltered both on balance and in detail if one looks at the short-term replacement ratios.

The Position of Married Women

The picture presented above assumes that in family households married women do not work. However, in 1979 (GHS) 27 per cent of wives of working men had full-time jobs, and another 34 per cent had part-time jobs; far fewer wives of unemployed men had jobs (only 14 per cent full-time, 18 per cent part-time).

The optimizing problem faced by the household is clearly a complex one, involving the work/home time preferences of each partner and total household income at each combination of full- and part-time work by each. Nevertheless, it may be reasonable to divide the problem into two separate stages: the husband's decision to work, assuming his wife does not work, and secondly, the wife's decision to work, full- or part-time, given the husband's decision. The justification would be that the wife is likely to move in and out

TABLE II.1.1 *Percentage of Workers by Household type with Replacement Ratios higher than those shown in November 1982*[a]

Replacement ratio	*Single men and women*[b]	M	*Married men*[c] M + 1	M + 2	M + 3	*Weighted average*
A. Long-term ratios						
0.5	62	51	n.a.	n.a.	n.a.	n.a.
0.6	(52)	41	n.a.	71	n.a.	n.a.
0.7	42	29	48	(55)	69	45
0.8	(32)	20	30	39	(58)	32.5
0.9	22	11	(23)	(30)	(48)	23.5
1.0	(10)	(5)	16[d]	21	38[d]	15
Percentage of working households shown in each category	21.5	26.8	17.4	25.5	8.8	100
B. Short-term ratios[e]						
0.5	61	51	n.a.	n.a.	n.a.	n.a.
0.6	(51)	41	48	71	n.a.	n.a.
0.7	41	29	(39)	(55)	69	43.5
0.8	(31)	20	30	39	(58)	32
0.9	22	(16)	(23)	(30)	(48)	25
1.0	(10)	11	16[d]	21	38	16.5

Source: *FES*, 1980 (for non-retired households) and Liverpool calculations of replacement ratios (Appendix B).

Notes: [a] Interpolated figures shown in brackets.

[b] Average earnings assumed to be £110 in 1979. Single person households had income of £91 approx. (0.83 of average). Average single person's earnings in November 1982 set at 0.83 × £140 = £116.

[c] Average weekly earnings of married men in November 1982 set at £160, i.e. approx. average earnings of all full-time male employees aged 21 years or over (excluding the effects of absence). Wife assumed not to be working.

[d] Percentage with replacement ratio in range 95–100 per cent.

[e] Assumes unemployed for second six months of tax year only.

of the labour market at different times in her lifecycle. A typical pattern would be full-time when just married, not at all when the children are young, part-time when they are at school, and finally full-time when they leave home. The husband has to take a decision about participation on a full-time job for a long period of time. Therefore the household's average life-time income is likely to be dominated by the husband's earnings.

On this basis, the replacement ratios for married men used in Table II.1.1 would not be seriously misleading.

We now turn to the choices facing married women, the remaining section of the potential labour force. Table II.1.2 documents the retention ratios they face, that is the proportion of extra gross income retained by wives. The top half deals with the situation when the husband is working. The retention ratios for full-time work are around 50 per cent with dependent children, but rise to around 60 per cent without children. In the calculations, we have made a notional allowance for child-minding of £5 per week for each child under five when both parents are working full-time; this

TABLE II.1.2 *Retention Ratios of Married Women November 1982*[a]

	Number of children				
	0	*1*	*2*	*3*	*4*
Husband working					
Husband and wife[b] both on average manual earnings, full-time	62.2	56.3	56.3	56.3	56.3
Both on 75 per cent of average manual earnings, full-time	60.3	51.0	49.6	49.3	20.7
Husband on average earnings, wife part-time £50 per week	74.5	64.5	64.5	64.5	42.1
Husband unemployed					
Wife on average manual earnings £85 per week	15.3	5.6	10.0	10.8	6.4
Wife on 75 per cent of average earnings £64 per week	2.6	11.9	7.9	8.7	2.5

Source: Liverpool calculations, Appendix B.

Notes: [a] Additional income kept by wife as a result of working, long-term, i.e. compares net income with net benefits after one year.

[b] Average weekly manual earnings: male £140, female £85.

may be on the low side. But most importantly, we cannot know what premium households place on wives' home time when there are dependent children. It seems quite possible that these ratios provide insufficient incentive for wives with children, especially those with low incomes. According to the GHS, they push wives with children mainly into part-time work where retention ratios are higher (because of no expenses for child-minding); 37 per cent of these wives had part-time work in 1979, only 14 per cent had full-time work, leaving 47 per cent who did not work at all. Working wives are most common, as one would expect, among families with no dependent children, where 40 per cent worked full-time, 26.7 per cent part-time, leaving only 30 per cent who did not work at all.

The bottom half of Table II.1.2 shows how the retention ratios fall dramatically when the husband is unemployed; the reason lies in the loss of the husband's supplementary benefit. Consistently with this, we saw earlier that 67 per cent of unemployed men's wives did not work in 1979.

POLICY PROPOSALS FOR THE UNEMPLOYMENT TRAP: A CEILING (OR 'CAP') ON BENEFIT INCOME RATIO

There are two aspects to the policy debate over benefits. There is on the one hand the understandable and widespread desire to provide an income 'safety net' for the least well off in society. On the other hand, there is the objective of maintaining incentives to work, so that society should not unnecessarily support those who could support themselves.

As economists, we restrict ourselves to comments on efficiency in meeting these potentially conflicting objectives. The obvious point is that income support can be given to *both* employed and unemployed, with a minimum differential in favour of income in work. For example, higher benefits to (or lower taxes on) the lower paid can be achieved, at some cost to those on average earnings and above, by changes in tax structure, without cutting benefits to the unemployed. The question is whether people will vote for the higher tax burden necessary for this to be done.

It would seem therefore right to separate two issues very clearly:

(1) minimum support levels;
(2) appropriate minimum differentials between in- and out-of-work income.

If one could obtain agreement that, as a matter of principle on efficiency grounds, the benefit ratio to net work-income should for no individual exceed, say, 68 per cent (as in West Germany) or some such figure, it would then be possible to have a rational discussion of appropriate tax and support levels, trading off the welfare of the less well-off (including those likely to remain unemployed) against that of the average and better paid. One would visualize this as a running discussion, with support levels altering according to general social welfare.

The crucial policy point to make is that the current system of unemployment support is dangerously inefficient because it does not limit replacement ratios as work-incomes fall. The minimum reform to it that we would wish to see is the introduction of a 'maximum replacement ratio' override (a benefit ratio ceiling) on the level of total net benefits paid out (similar to, but we would hope administratively simpler than, the old 'wage stop'). This could in principle be combined, if people wish it, with a more generous provision for the low paid in work which enables the living standards of the unemployed not to be seriously damaged.

The use of benefit ratio ceilings, our central proposal, is widespread in Europe. In Germany, the replacement ratio is universally fixed at 68 per cent for the first year out of work, dropping to 58 per cent thereafter. In Denmark, there is a standard replacement ratio of 80 per cent, as well as a maximum absolute amount (roughly equal to 80 per cent of average earnings). This ratio lasts for two years but it is effectively renewable indefinitely, by arranging short spells of re-employment. In Italy, the replacement ratio is 2/3rds indefinitely.

The closest parallel to Britain is Belgium where the unemployed can obtain 60 per cent of *gross* income with a set minimum absolute amount. As taxes on persons have risen, so the replacement ratio has risen with no upper bound set on low-income families. It is perhaps instructive that the two countries without ratio ceilings have had the worst unemployment experience in the past decade.

Simulations of the Effects of a Cap on the Benefit Ratio

The introduction of a 'cap' on the benefit ratio would change the operation of benefits on the labour market quite fundamentally. The effect is illustrated in Figure II.1.

Under the flat rate regime, the supply curve of labour is flattened substantially (or 'truncated') as wages fall towards the flat rate benefit level B/P. Hence as demand falls for the economy ('demand' being defined as the output sales the economy can sustain, without going into external current account deficit), so unemployment rises and wages fall little.

Under the capped regime, the supply curve shifts to the left of the no-benefit supply, because workers now receive some ratio of benefits to wages which induces them to work less; as wages fall, a higher proportion of workers receive the maximum ratio and so the leftward displacement becomes greater. But the displacement never

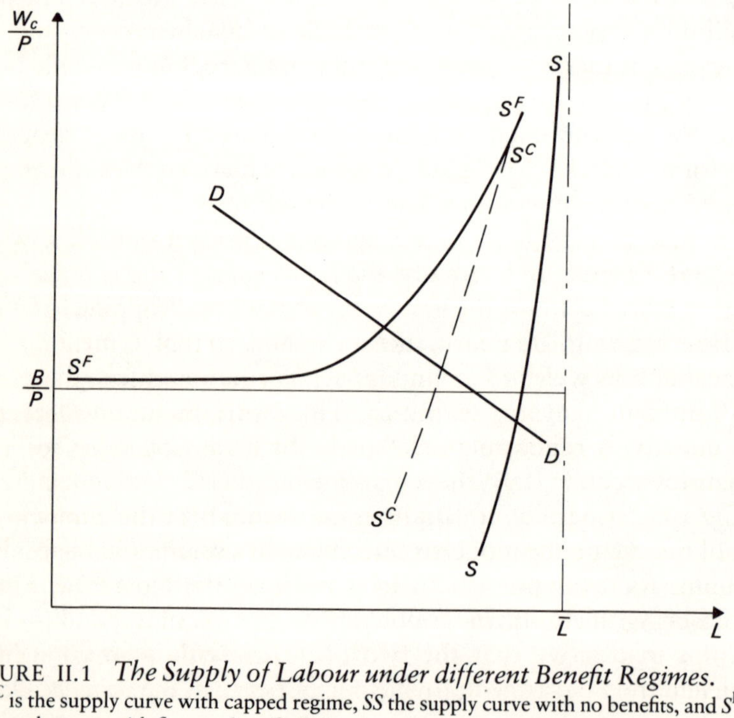

FIGURE II.1 *The Supply of Labour under different Benefit Regimes.* $S^C S^C$ is the supply curve with capped regime, *SS* the supply curve with no benefits, and $S^F S^F$ the supply curve with flat rate benefit B/P.

becomes a truncation as with the flat rate regime, because, as wages fall, so benefits fall too (if not, in the aggregate, quite in proportion). Hence the downward pressure on wages as demand falls encounters very much less resistance from benefit levels than in the flat rate case, and there is correspondingly very much less effect on employment and unemployment.

Our estimates for the UK are derived for a flat rate regime and are unlikely to be fully appropriate for a capped regime. Nevertheless, we may get some notion of the order of magnitude by using them, provided that we treat them cautiously. Table II.1.3 shows estimated *total* long-run effects on unemployment, real wages and output (using as a basis the quarterly equations shown above together with the Liverpool macroeconomic model).

TABLE II.1.3

	Long-run effect compared with present situation, on			
Maximum benefit ratio or 'cap' set at	*Unemployment ('000)*	*Real wages %*	*Output %*	*PSBR* (£bn 1982 prices)*
0.7	– 700	– 2.0	+ 2.4	3.8 (1.2)
0.8	– 375	– 1.1	+ 1.3	2.1 (0.7)
0.9	– 140	– 0.4	+ 0.5	0.8 (0.2)

Note: * The effect on the PSBR is assumed to be eliminated by lump-sum transfers back to the taxpayer; the column shows the 'tax cuts' made possible and assumed to take place. The bracketed figures are the direct saving on benefit payments.

These are long-run effects, and it can be seen that a cap at 0.7 has a sizeable effect, reducing unemployment by nearly 0.75 million, and contributing nearly £4 billion to the PSBR, money available for tax cuts to ameliorate the distributional consequences of this measure.

The time for these effects to come through on unemployment would be, taking the model at face value, as shown in Table II.1.4.

Hence for example a 0.7 cap if instituted in November 1982, would bring unemployment down by 0.25 million by March 1984 and 0.6 million by November 1986. These lags arise within the model entirely because of firms' adjustment costs in taking on extra labour. There seems no particular reason to believe that these costs

TABLE II.1.4

No. of years	*Percentage of effects*
1	20
2	50
3	70
5	90

would alter significantly when the benefit regime changed or to alter these lag estimates therefore.

We defer consideration of distributional consequences until we have considered all the policy measures which may be necessary. At that stage we evaluate how it may be necessary to handle distributional aspects in this overall package.

ADMINISTRATIVE ASPECTS OF THE CAP

The proposal is made here to limit total individual social security benefits so that, in all cases, out-of-work net income would be noticeably below in-work net income. In the past somewhat similar schemes became known as 'wage stops'.

In the past, schemes relating one form of income such as, for example, out-of-work or a social security based one, to another, such as past earned income, have existed. All have now been terminated except one aspect of one scheme which continues today. The National Assistance and Supplementary Benefit schemes contained a wage stop and this was abolished in 1975. Unemployment Benefit (UB) did have an earnings related supplement which augmented UB in the short term for middle and higher income earners, but this scheme terminated in 1981. The present Family Income Supplement (FIS), which is an addition paid to earned income for low wage workers is set for a year on a previous month's earnings, and so relates one set of earnings with another. Rent and rate rebates have somewhat similar linkages. There are, of course, difficulties and objections to such schemes, but many of these arise because of the complications built into them. If the proposal is kept simple and fair, many difficulties disappear. The concept under review here is quite simply a proposal to limit total net social security benefits to 70 per cent of previous net earned income. A similar and successful, system has existed in Denmark for some years now as well as West Germany, Italy and France.

The proposed scheme would be to place a ceiling on the total net unemployment benefits package, so that it did not exceed 70 per cent of recent in-work net income. Recent acceptable evidence of pay slips would be combined, if relevant, with other benefits, for example FIS, rent rebate, rate rebate, child benefits and other FIS 'passported' benefits, so as to arrive at a net in-work income figure. Mandatory tables similar to those for PAYE or a set tariff would assist here in establishing the FIS and other potential additions, and also in relating to the out-of-work income, starting with UB and Child Benefit (CB), and if appropriate Supplementary Benefit (SB) and other 'passported' benefits, as well as a credit for not having work expenses. These would then be established on a tax-paid basis, so as to reach a net out-of-work income figure, which would be subject to a 70 per cent maximum of the relevant in-work income level. This maximum would then be indexed to the Retail Price Index (RPI) with annual upratings as for other social payments.

Those unemployed at the time the cap came into force would have their work-income computed as follows. Previous pay slips would be produced to establish previous gross income. This would be uprated to the present by the RPI, and also adjusted for *current* tax rates, work expenses etc. This would then be used to set the 70 per cent ceiling.

Some workers currently unemployed, particularly those long-term unemployed, would probably be unable or unwilling to produce acceptable evidence of previous pay (e.g. a payslip, a letter from a previous employer, evidence of occupation and colleagues' earnings). In these cases, some simple fall-back procedure is required. We suggest that net previous wages be deemed equal to current benefits plus 10 per cent (corresponding to the approximate effect of the tax cuts). Benefits for these people could thus drop 20 per cent, creating an incentive to produce acceptable evidence.

Wives' earnings, if any, would be disregarded in the calculation of the husband's in-and out-of-work income, and the cap amount. The wife's benefits would similarly be subject to the cap, disregarding the husband's earnings or benefits. This will ensure that the incentive for each partner to work is maintained, in general. The only exception could be where the man is unemployed and loses supplementary benefit when his wife works. In this case, even though the wife's benefits out of work may be low, the loss of household income when she gives up work may be small; i.e. her 'retention ratio' is low. The incidence of this case, however, should be substantially reduced by the cap, since many unemployed men will receive less supplementary benefit than they do now, so the loss of it caused by the wife working will be correspondingly lower for them.

Young people and others joining the labour force will not be subject to the cap, since they have no previous earnings. However, as argued below under the 'workfare' and denial of benefit scheme, they should be subject to tougher conditions for benefit receipt after a short period of, say, three months on the dole; for their benefit at this point should be conditional on taking a workfare job.

The administrative advantages of such a scheme would be:

(1) it would be fair, plain and simple;
(2) it would relate to an individual's own circumstances; his incentive to rejoin the active workforce would rise;
(3) in-work benefits, some of which relate to family size and circumstances, would continue to exercise a significant influence on income received;
(4) there would be no undue discrimination against those with large families or high housing costs;
(5) the use of the most recent work-income figures would avoid some major disadvantages in past wage-stop schemes, e.g. relationship to an individual's potential earning capacity, its high error rate, forecasting future income, etc.
(6) there would be little scope for dispute as to figures etc. and therefore no need for any burdensome appeal procedure.

Possible administrative disadvantages would be:

(1) the scheme fails to cope with any particular hardship, physical or mental handicap problems or any exceptional needs;
(2) for the unemployed without evidence of pay the relevant base income would be arbitrary;
(3) it could increase civil service staff numbers and costs;

(4) it could arouse some controversy as wage-stop did for a decade (1965–75) and activate or divert pressure groups to fight the scheme.

The Danish scheme limits unemployment benefit, which is taxable, to the lower of either 80 per cent of previous gross earnings or 80 per cent of average wages. It is index linked to their retail price index and adjusted twice yearly. It lasts for two and a half years (now reduced notionally to 21 months) and then anyone still unemployed is transferred to supplementary benefit rates which are lower. However in practice it is possible to arrange an 'employment spell', so that receipt continues indefinitely. The scheme is reckoned to be most generous (in our view excessively so) and a major contributory factor to Denmark's rapidly rising PSBR – 10 per cent of GDP in 1981; many of the beneficiaries have reputedly been housewives. The benefit systems of Germany, France, and Italy are described elsewhere in the book. Each of these countries computes either all or the major part of benefits as a ratio to past earnings.

Previous wage-stop schemes have been terminated for various reasons, but the climate may now be judged right for the introduction of a similar measure, namely a ceiling on benefits. There are considerable economic advantages in terms of the labour market and public expenditure. There are administrative advantages and disadvantages of such a proposal, but the balance here clearly lies in favour.

A 'WORKFARE' SCHEME AND THE PROCEDURES FOR DENIAL OF BENEFIT

The placing of a cap on benefit ratios is designed to exert market pressure on unemployment by making people willing to take jobs at lower pay. Hence it has its effect via the general level of wages (or equivalently of productivity and work practices input by workers for the same wage). The only way to bring unemployment down is to alter the general market situation in some such way.

There is a case, however, for strengthening these pressures by tightening up the procedures for obtaining benefits, and in particular making benefits contingent on accepting, if no other is offered, a job designated by the state (from a 'workfare' pool of community and other jobs). In principle, the state should only provide benefits where the unemployed can get *no* job, however unpleasant or low paid. The practice however appears to be very different and this difference has been especially marked since the separation of job centres from benefit offices. The worker 'shops' for a job in the 'job centre'; if he cannot find one he likes, he claims benefits and typically gets them (the rate of denial is extremely low – in 1980 about 0.5 per cent of the unemployed).

It has been suggested that the state sets up 'community work schemes' and that the unemployed be offered places on such schemes, benefit being conditional on acceptance of such places if offered. The problem with such ideas is that they are expensive to the state – involving supervision, equipment and other costs – and that the jobs involved have a very low value to society (otherwise they would already have been undertaken). However, as a last resort component in a pool of jobs which *must* be accepted as a condition of benefit, they are of some use.

Let us designate such a pool of jobs 'workfare' jobs. It would then seem useful to include all existing jobs notified to job centres (often private sector but also public sector), in this pool; the 'community' jobs would then be there as a last resort, in the total absence of normal jobs. A private firm refunds the state at the market rate for the job. If benefits are greater than the market rate plus in-work benefits, then after six months on the job they should fall to this level.

The denial procedures in each area of the country could become tougher the longer the individual's period of unemployment; beyond six months it could become sufficient for benefit denial to refuse any job offered by workfare. Furthermore, repeat spells of unemployment, however short, could also attract such criteria. Finally, there could be the differentiation of these criteria by age – for workers below 25 years of age, acceptance of a workfare job after three months of unemployment could be a condition of further benefit. There would be a demonstration effect on low-wage vacancies; as firms got to hear of people filling them, more would come on to the market. At present it is a pointless expense to advertise jobs at low wages which are marginally competitive with benefits.

In general, new instructions should be given to benefit officers to keep close liaison with Manpower Services Commission (MSC) job centres and evolve from their experience operating procedures which implement these tougher denial provisions. The objective should be to open up the low-wage non-union employment sector, so reinforcing the downward pressure on real wage costs.

Administratively, such a workfare denial procedure will require the re-integration of MSC job centres (where the workfare pool of jobs will be primarily located) and unemployment benefit offices. Their separation now is clearly seen as an error. The simplest way to do this would be to place DHSS officials currently dealing with unemployment (and supplementary) benefits in the job centres. The unemployed must attend regularly at this job centre as well as whenever required by the workfare scheme.

THE 'POVERTY TRAP'

Effects

Strictly speaking, it is possible to consider the poverty trap – the very high marginal tax rates (MRTs) on low-paid workers – as an issue with no bearing on unemployment. For the poverty trap only affects those already working.

However, this is too narrow a view for several reasons. First, such high MRTs may will affect the supply of hours and so the level of under-employment. Second, they may affect the quality of the labour supply by discouraging training which would raise earnings. Third, they will tend to hold people at lower income levels, where they will have higher replacement ratios than otherwise. So more people than otherwise may elect to remain unemployed, for any given benefit system, because the population is more skewed towards those with higher ratios. In practice, therefore, there is a high coincidence between those 'at risk' from the two traps.

Estimates of the effects of the poverty trap on labour supply are, however, hard to come by. We survey the evidence briefly in Appendix C. There we find that there is evidence of incentive effects among workers facing high MRTs, but that the substitution elasticities to marginal real wages are typically small, in our view quite implausibly so. In the context of MRTs between 80 and 200 per cent, as occur in the povery trap, they are virtually useless.

Few people, in any case, regardless of political views would disagree that these MRTs must be reduced. Disagreement only arises as to the distributional effects that should be accepted as a consequence of reduction.

Facts About the UK Trap

In Appendix B we set out the MRTs for single persons and married men with non-working wives. The problem is most acute for married men with children. Figure II.2 shows the MRT for a married

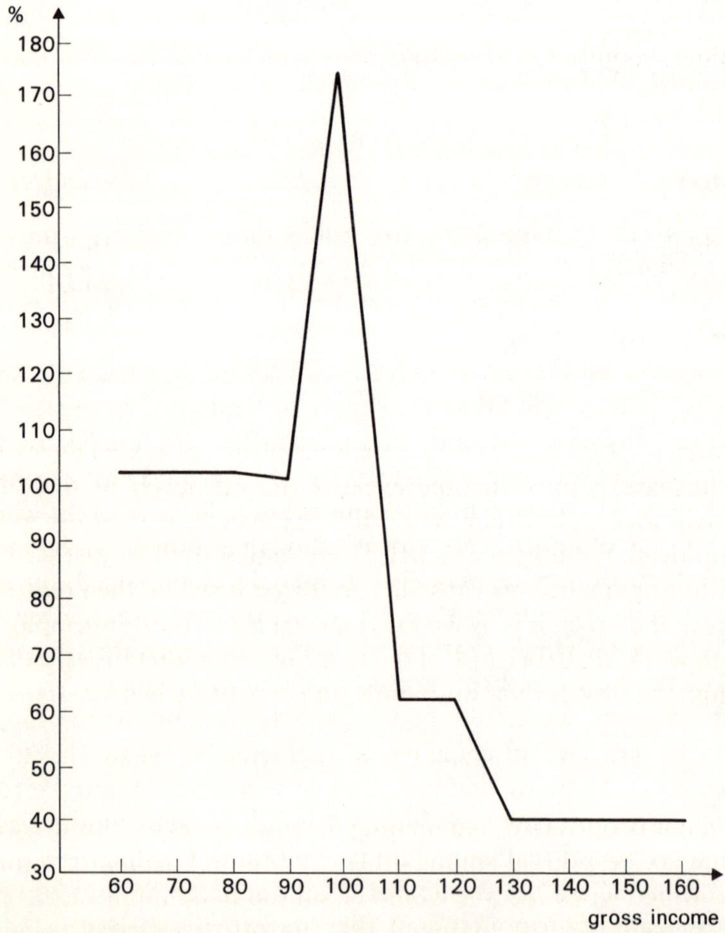

FIGURE II.2 *Marginal Tax Rate for a Married Man with Two Children*

man with two children. Net income remains static between £50 and £90 per week and then dips before starting finally to rise above this level at £120 per week. Here the MRT falls at last to 38.8 per cent (standard rate plus NI) having reached 170 per cent at £100 per week.

The problem arises because of the interaction of FIS (with 'passported' benefits), rent/rate rebates, and the tax system. Each of these is 'means-tested' in a different way, and it is the unintended overlap of the three means tests that creates the problem. Table II.1.5 shows this summarily.

TABLE II.1.5 *Certain Sources of Income of Married Men with Two Children, Wife not Working (£ per week)*

Wages	*FIS and passported benefits*	*Rent/rate rebates*	*Taxes and NI*
80	16.30	7.72	16.91
100	–	4.36	24.66
120	–	–	32.41

Married women do not face such problems, provided their own and husband's joint income exceeds the FIS level; in this case, they will face a 38.8 per cent MRT. However, if the husband is unemployed, then the wife's MRTs are similar to those just seen, as her additional earnings cause her to forfeit first FIS, then rent/rate rebates; of course, it is as we saw unusual for wives of unemployed men to work at all, because of the very low retention ratios they face through the loss of their husband's supplementary benefit.

POLICY PROPOSALS FOR THE POVERTY TRAP

The major proposal for eliminating the poverty trap is the 'negative income tax' (espoused among others by Milton Friedman), according to which work-income would be substantially supplemented by some percentage (the marginal tax rate) of its shortfall below a defined 'poverty level'. This percentage is not typically proposed to be the same as the marginal tax rate on income above the poverty level.

NIT abolishes the high MRTs while retaining acceptable distributional effects. Figure II.3 illustrates one such case where the NIT is 66 per cent below, 33 per cent above, this level.

Objections have been of two sorts. First, some people have a preference for transfers in kind rather than in cash to the poor, to ensure consumption patterns are constrained in a 'desirable' way. Secondly, NIT has been argued to be administratively impossible before the tax system is computerized. The previous Conservative administration abandoned it for this reason.

In practice, FIS and rent/rate rebates, which are both cash transfers, dominate the current UK system; passported benefits are

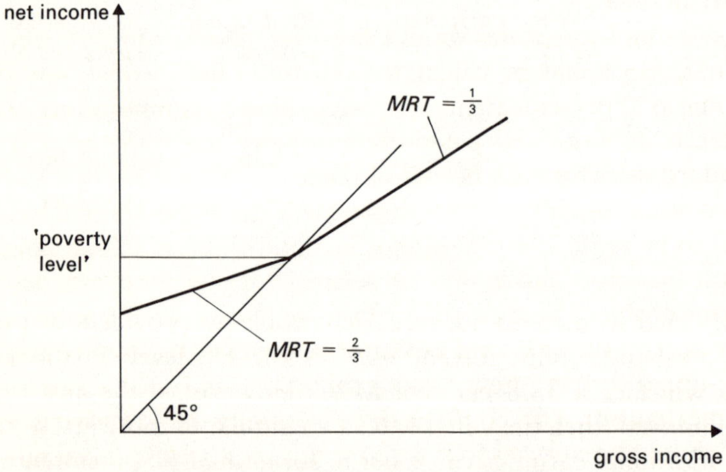

FIGURE II.3 *Negative Income Tax Illustrated*

significant but have very low take-up rates. Even if they were retained on the grounds that money for prescriptions, dental work etc. should be tied to these things, the replacement of FIS, rent/rate rebates and tax/NI by NIT would be a very substantial improvement.

However, the administrative objections could be still binding, the Inland Revenue now claiming computerization cannot occur before the very late 1980s. This raises the issue of transitional measures which are administratively possible and yet approximate to the NIT structure. We assume in this discussion that the benefit ratio ceiling is in place, so that the effects on replacement ratios are of second order.

What is needed in transition is to make one or more elements in the tax/transfer jigsaw act to *compensate* for other elements and create a smooth MRT structure. The choice of element to perform this task has clearly to be one of administrative convenience, since the economic effect will be identical whichever is chosen.

Administratively, all are costly. Rent/rate rebates are administered by local authorities, which are not well placed to monitor net incomes. The Inland Revenue already claim to be stretched in tax administration. FIS is calculated by the DHSS, and calculations involving more declarations and checking of income would also be costly in staff.

Two simple measures should, however, give substantial help.

First, FIS could be calculated on (fully) net income, not gross income as at present. Such net income could be computed net of tax, rent/rate rebates and passported benefits according to a set of standard rules for each household type.

Second, though the spikes in the MRT due to passported benefits need to be removed, this cannot be done without abandoning the simple 'passport' link to FIS. Of course, this may not in practice be a serious problem because of low take-up. However, if it were politically acceptable, it would be better in any case, because of this low take-up, to convert these passported benefits into cash terms via the FIS mechanism. This could be done by raising the FIS poverty level.

It should be noticed that we have not suggested reduced rate tax bands. The reason is partly administrative cost, but partly economic. The FIS proposal has a substantial effect. This could be enhanced by reduced rate bands for those subject to FIS; however, these bands could also lower MRTs too far (requiring correspondingly higher MRTs on *other* tax bands) for those not subject to FIS, such as single people on low incomes. An MRT of 38.8 per cent is not unreasonable when the average tax rate is of similar order for the population as a whole.

An Overall Tax Package Designed to Approximate to NIT While Being Distributionally Acceptable

Our proposals to this point have been to:

(1) introduce a cap on benefits;
(2) compute FIS on net income;
(3) abolish passported benefits and replace them with FIS.

Proposals (2) and (3) are intended as transitional measures to an eventual negative income tax. However, we have not yet discussed the rates and poverty levels for FIS. Nor have we paid attention to the distributional effect. Yet clearly these are of great importance.

Our proposals are completed as follows:

(4) Raise tax thresholds by about 40 per cent, i.e. roughly to the supplementary benefit levels for single persons and for a man and wife, shown in Appendix B Table B.2 (currently at £42.20 and £59.70 per week respectively). Hence the MRT *upwards* will be 0.388 from this point.
(5) To alleviate the position of families with children, raise child benefits by £2.15 per child.
(6) Set the FIS marginal tax rate at 2/3. Hence the MRT *downwards* will be, inclusive of NI, about 0.7.
(7) Set the FIS poverty levels so that families currently receiving FIS are in the aggregate, after the tax cut, about as well off as before. We have chosen £86 for married +1 child, £97 for m+2, £108 for m+3, somewhat above the current supplementary benefit levels.

Notice that (4) and (6) are roughly approximate to NIT with 0.388, 0.7 as the up and down MRTs. It should make the transition to a full NIT easy.

We now compute the effects of these changes:

(a) on the economy, and
(b) on the distribution of income.

EFFECTS OF THE POVERTY TRAP PROPOSALS ON THE ECONOMY

We compute the effects, *assuming* that the capped replacement ratio regime is in place with a cap of 0.7. This assumption is important, because those whose ratios are held down by the cap will be affected in their supply behaviour by the tax change only if it takes their ratio below 0.7. Hence the population affected is, to a first-order approximation, those with ratios already below 0.7; according to our earlier calculations this will be around 45 per cent of the working population. (We assume, for want of a better basis, that this percentage is also true of those in the non-union sector). The effects of tax on the supply behaviour of these people will depend on how far it changes their replacement ratios.

To estimate this, we take the position of those who are in the next group above the 0.7 replacement ratio. It turns out (see below) that this group's net income in work rises about 6 per cent (the fall in their 'tax rate'). The long run effects of this change are: on unemployment – 175,000, average real wages – 0.5 per cent, output + 0.6 per cent, the PSBR (excluding direct cost of tax cut) + £0.6bn (1982 prices). The rate at which these effects are felt is as above: 20 per cent (by year 1), 50 per cent (year 2), 70 per cent (year 3), with virtually all through by year 5.

It is clear that, taken on top of the cap, these proposals do not reduce unemployment much further. They are important because:

(a) they reduce the MRT below 100 per cent at all points of the income scale (see Table II.1.6); we are unable to quantify the effect of this, but we can be sure it is worthwhile;

(b) they distribute a larger proportion of the surplus generated through higher output towards the bulk of those in the bottom half of the income scale, provided they are working. This distributional impact is of immense social and political importance, for it becomes possible to say that, while the rewards of unemployment have been reduced for low-income workers – in the case of the lowest paid substantially so – the rewards of employment, even should they take a less well paid job, are generally raised, significantly in most cases. To this impact we now turn.

TABLE II.1.6 *Effects on Household Income of Package, for Low Incomes by Household type (non-retired only, £ per week)*

Gross income of household	Net income[a] before package	Change in tax and child benefits	Change in FIS and passport benefits	Net income corresponding to gross income[c] after package	η	% total effect on[b] real net income of household	Estimated number ('000)[dij] of households with net incomes less than shown (cumulative)
Single							
50	41.1	3.7	–	44.8	0.46	6.9	n.a.
64	46.3	3.7	–	50.0	0.53	5.7	700
96	59.9	3.7	–	63.6	0.85	3.1	1300
130	80.4	3.7	–	84.1	0.99	1.1	1900
Total households							3200
Married[e]							
100	69.5	5.7	–	75.2	0.63	5.6	450
130	85.5	5.7	–	91.2	0.93	3.4	800
Total households							4000
Married + 1[k]							
50	78.1	3.1	– 4.8	76.5	0.19	3.5	4
66	77.3	7.85	– 4.6	80.6	0.17	2.9	20
80	77.2	7.85	– 2.3	82.8	0.21	5.8	41
100	76.3	7.85	–	84.1	0.55	7.9	n.a.
130[f]	91.3	7.85	–	99.1	0.87	5.4	430
160[f]	105.5	7.85	–	113.3	0.93	4.1	790
Total households							2600
Married + 2[k]							
50	91.4	5.2	– 9.7	86.9	0.16	6.3	5
66	90.9	10.0	– 10.9	90.0	0.14	– 2.4	14
80	90.6	10.0	– 7.9	92.7	0.18	– 0.6	41
110	87.1	10.0	–	97.1	0.50	9.3	50
130[g]	92.9	10.0	–	102.9	0.86	7.6	340
160[g]	111.3	10.0	–	121.3	0.88	5.8	780
Total households							3800

Married + 3[k]							
50	103.3	7.35	− 14.8	95.9	0.10	8.4	4
66	103.2	12.15	− 15.6	99.8	0.13	4.8	11
80	102.9	12.15	− 12.7	102.4	0.15	− 2.0	22
110	93.0	12.15	0.2	107.2	0.24	13.4	30
130	103.0	12.15	–	115.2	0.77	8.9	n.a.
190[h]	135.5	12.15	–	147.7	0.86	7.9	500
Total households							1300

Notes: [a] Assuming non-working wife where applicable, unless otherwise specified. Figures from Appendix B, interpolated for incomes between £10 points.

[b] Assuming (i) fall in gross real wages of *all* workers = 4 per cent, and applying elasticities of net to gross income,

$$\left(= \frac{1 - MRT}{1 - ART} \right); \text{ ART is average tax rate}$$

from Table B.1 in Appendix B; (ii) a rise in general expenditure tax of 1 per cent, lowering net post-tax real wages by 1 per cent also.

[c] Elasticities of net to gross income, see [b].

[d] Source FES, 1980; incomes uprated by rise in average earnings index (whole economy) to November 1982 basis, i.e. by 28 per cent.

[e] FES 1980 gives as average people working per household, 0.89 for incomes < £100 and 1.15 for incomes £100–30 (November 1982 basis), hence assumption of non-working wife reasonable here.

[f] Average persons working 1.236 per household (FES 1980) for those with income under £130, 1.525 for £130–60. In the latter case, allowance is made for working wife; man assumed to earn £105, wife £55.

[g] 1.42 persons working under £130, 1.58 working £130–60. Calculations assume man earns £80, wife £50, in the first case; in second case that man earns £105, wife £55.

[h] 1.46 persons working. Assumed that man earns £130, wife £60.

[i] Calculations for FIS incomes based on social security statistics 1980, Table 32.36. Earnings there relating to October 1979 uprated to November 1982 by whole economy earnings index rise of 47.4 per cent. It is assumed that distribution of children per family follows distribution in Table 32.30 and is the same for each income group. Only one earner is assumed per family; tax is computed as for married man with non-working wife. Take-up rate of 50 per cent in 1978–9 assumed for FIS in calculating true population within FIS range; based on DHSS note *The Take-Up of FIS: Note on The Estimate Derived from the Family Finances Survey*, July 6, 1981.

[j] Number of households from census breakdown based on FES 1980, and social security statistics for FIS take-up (see [i]). Multi-adult households included with single. There are estimated to be 500,000 households with two adults and four or more children.

[k] FIS poverty levels assumed: m + 1: 86; m + 2: 97; m + 3: 108. FIS is paid in package as 0.66X (Poverty level minus net income after *all* deductions including work expenses and other transfers).

THE DISTRIBUTIONAL IMPACT OF THE 'PACKAGE' OF UNEMPLOYMENT AND POVERTY TRAP PROPOSALS

Table II.1.6 shows the position of households before and after the package, based on the FES 1980, and our simulated effects on real wages (– 2½ per cent overall).

For those in work on low incomes (but not exceptionally low ones), real disposable income improves by up to 14 per cent with a typical range of 3–7 per cent.

For those on very low incomes, the abolition of the poverty trap does imply some worsening. However, there are very few of these households, approximately 80,000 on our estimates based on FES 1980. Of course it would be possible to retain the passported benefits, so protecting this group, but at the cost of partially restoring the poverty trap; alternatively one may raise the FIS 'poverty levels', so as to reduce the numbers of those affected, but at the cost of higher marginal tax rates for those further up the low-income scale and the administrative cost of increasing coverage of the FIS scheme substantially.

We have already estimated the distribution of replacement ratios for those out of work, using the FES and DHSS study. About 15 per cent had replacement ratios of unity or more; another 8.5 per cent of 0.9 or more; 9 per cent of 0.8 or more; and 12.5 per cent 0.7 or more. Thus we could say that real disposable income (RDI) would fall among the unemployed as shown in Table II.1.7.

The percentage fall in RDI is the direct effect of the cap minus the rise induced by tax cuts etc, the indirect effect of the whole package as shown earlier.

TABLE II.1.7

% fall in RDI	*% of unemployed*
21	15
18.5	8.5
10	9
1	12.5
0	55

This is an inevitable feature of any scheme to get people back to work via market incentives, unless one is prepared to impose much higher tax burdens on the rest of the population in order to raise much further the incomes of those employed at the lower wages which compete with these benefit levels. It remains the case that the opportunity for work at lower gross real wages, but higher net real wages than before, remains for the overwhelming majority of the unemployed.

Furthermore, it must be remembered that a ratio system is widely accepted in Continental Europe as explained earlier and set out in a later section.

THE EXCHEQUER COSTS OF THE PACKAGE

The direct costs, output and wages constant, are estimated as:

	£ billion, 1982–3 prices
Child benefits up by £2.15 per child	1.6
Tax thresholds raised by 40 per cent	4.2
Reduction in benefits paid to unemployed (cap of 0.7)	−1.2
Changes to FIS and passported benefits to FIS employees	–
Total	4.6

Against this, the rise in output by 3.0 per cent and of employment is estimated to bring in an additional £3.0 billion in the long term, leaving £1.6 billion to find.

In evaluating the effects of this package, we assume that it is PSBR-neutral, in order to abstract from all 'macroeconomic' or 'demand' effects, and concentrate solely on the *tax structure* effects. In other words we assume that some view has already been taken about the appropriate PSBR and the demand-cum-inflation effects have already occurred.

It follows that conceptually we need some 'general revenue' measure with which to compare our package. For this purpose we assume a general consumer expenditure tax (on *all* such expenditure), which falls neutrally on home and foreign goods and employment and unemployment income.

In *practice* we suggest the package will be carried out, not by raising expenditure taxes, but by using resources freed by falls in the PSBR below its target path. Hence expenditure taxes would not rise; rather they would simply not fall as they would otherwise in the absence of the package.

The £1.6 billion net cost estimated above would require an offsetting rise in such an expenditure tax by about 1 per cent, implying a 1 per cent rise in the RPI relative to factor costs. We assume this in computing the effects below, and we also assume that unemployment benefits are not indexed to this change in the RPI (so that as noted it is neutral on *all* incomes).

The Phasing of the Package and its Effects on the PSBR

The package involves a substantial shift of purchasing power from the unemployed to the employed on low incomes; this is how it is proposed that unemployment be reduced via market forces. However, because the Exchequer costs are likely to occur rather earlier than the revenue benefits of increased supply, the package needs to be phased so that the net current cost to the Exchequer can be met from available budgetary savings elsewhere within the PSBR targets. Clearly, we can only indicate a plausible phasing given the present state of information about PSBR out-turns. We take the current PSBR targets as a guide in this. We may allow for anticipatory effects if the programme is announced with a 'second stage', but people may be unwilling to accept the second stage as sufficiently likely until the first stage is well under way. We therefore make no allowance for such effects.

An optimal phasing of the package elements needs:

(a) to maximize the response of unemployment;
(b) to be socially acceptable;
(c) to avoid the need to *raise* any tax rates in order to meet the existing PSBR targets.

By bringing in the cap immediately, the effects on unemployment would begin at once. The justice of the cap idea should, we feel, be readily apparent to the population, though naturally there will be an outcry from those directly affected and their representatives. Such an idea is widely accepted on the Continent and has a long history in this country (going back at least to the Poor Law Amendment Act 1834).

The change in FIS and the abolition of passported benefits can be brought into operation with some delay (perhaps 12–18 months) in order to cushion the impact on the very poorest families in employment. The incentive effects would begin to operate at once, so there would be no loss in effectiveness.

In order to maximize the impact of the package, all of it should be announced at the same time, together with details of the phasing.

The major elements using Exchequer resources are the 40 per cent rise in thresholds and the £2.15 on child benefit. Because families with children are most highly represented in the unemployment trap and so likely to suffer most from the cap, the child benefit element should come in at once, since it will alleviate most the impact on their standard of living from the cap. This leaves the rise in thresholds as the element to be phased to fit the PSBR profile. If we assume arbitrarily that resources available for tax cuts (the 'fiscal adjustment' built into PSBR targeting) will be £2.5 billion in 1983–4, and a further 0.5 billion in 1984–5, then a possible phasing is a 25 per cent rise in thresholds in 1983–4 followed by a further 15 per cent rise in 1984–5. Table II.1.8 (*overleaf*) shows the summary effects.

This illustrative programme implies that the package would more or less absorb available resources in 1983–4 and 1984–5 but leave room for further tax cuts – of a form to be decided – subsequently. It is of course *only* illustrative.

TABLE II.1.8 *Phasing of Programme: Effects on Exchequer Resources*

Fiscal years	*1983–4*	*1984–5*	*1985–6*	*1986–7*	*1987–8*
Child benefits	1.6	1.6	1.6	1.6	1.6
Tax thresholds	2.6	4.3	4.4	4.4	4.5
Cap reduction in benefits	– 1.2	– 1.2	– 1.2	– 1.2	– 1.2
Gain in revenue from higher supply	– 0.6	– 1.5	– 2.1	– 2.6	– 3.2
Cumulative effects on PSBR net	2.4	3.2	2.7	2.2	1.7
Available resources within PSBR target	2.5	3.0	3.0	3.0	3.0
Adjustment in other taxes (– is tax cuts)	– 0.1	+ 0.2	– 0.3	– 0.8	– 1.3

Note: + is loss of net revenue, 1982–3 prices, £ billion

CHAPTER 2

The Problem of Union Power

THE ARGUMENT RECAPITULATED

It is not original to suggest that unions create unemployment. It has been a widespread claim by those economists who have urged more freedom for market forces. What they have generally had in mind was that unions raise wages for *unionized* workers, some of whom as a consequence will lose their jobs (or equivalently other non-unionized workers will fail to get jobs in unionized industries). The workers displaced will find it hard to gain employment in the non-union sectors because of the limited opportunities there, and will for the most part be unemployed.

Two elements have been lacking in this argument. First, there has been some vagueness about why workers would not find jobs in the non-union sector, since they would drive non-union wages down there until there was full employment. Second, the order of magnitude of the unemployment which could result from union power has not been indicated; this is obviously very important because if the magnitudes are trivial, the ordeal by fire required to reduce union power would not be politically attractive.

The findings of this book are two-fold. First the operation of the tax and benefit system prevents wages in the non-union sector from dropping much, because benefits are 'flat rate' (other than ERS, now abolished, for six months) and for low-income jobs they may be so close to net earnings that the jobs would become unviable and unattractive for workers if wages fell very far. Hence the non-union sector has only a small ability to absorb workers displaced by the union sector. Secondly upon estimating relationships which incorporate the role of the tax and benefits system, we have found that the substantial rise in union power since the early 1960s has raised unemployment by about one million. This is a round number probably at the upper end of what politicians and practical men may have suspected, but, if correct, it must weigh heavily in the political scales against the fuss involved in reducing union power.

This work is bound to be controversial at this stage because it challenges much wishful thinking. But it will be a long time before all the additional evidence has been sifted – particularly the immense amount of potential information in the Family Expenditure Survey – which may settle all the interlocking issues involved. But by the time such research has been done, it may be too late to take the necessary action. Already the tide of union power has swept in irresistibly. Some recent events have suggested it may be receding. But who can tell what access of strength it may gain in the next economic upturn and beyond? Now may be the last major opportunity available to politicians to push the tide out once and for all. To lose such an opportunity on the chance that our estimate of the effect of union power may be much too high would be a dangerous gamble. Compared with it, the risk that the highly unpopular union movement will be able to resist successfully and damagingly the necessary legislation to cut its powers seems a risk substantially less to be feared.

The basic ideas related to the effect of union power have been described above. But it seems worthwhile briefly to recap on this point.

A union exists to raise the wages of its members to an 'optimal' amount, given, first, that higher union wages mean fewer union jobs, and, second, the wages that their members could get in the non-union sector. The union typically determines an optimal union wage which is some way above the non-union wage. A monopolist raises his price to the point at which his profits are maximized; this point will be above that which would have been set by free competition and will reduce the size of the market – so with a union monopoly.

Workers who lose their jobs as a result of their monopoly power will then seek jobs in the non-union sector. These additional supplies of labour force wages down there, until supply is equal to demand. But at this point we note that the social security system guarantees a minimum income regardless of work and that taxes apply to workers with very low incomes. As wages in the non-union sector fall, they become progressively less attractive (after tax) to workers forced out of the union sector. Some, perhaps many, will not be prepared to take the jobs on offer for such rewards. They will go on the dole. The major way in which supply is equated to demand in the non-union sector by falling wages is through the contraction of supply. Demand rises as wages fall, but the tax and social security system imparts a 'floor' to wages, which causes major withdrawals from the labour market as wages get too close to this critical level. Consequently wages cannot fall enough to create much additional demand.

This analysis is sometimes criticized on the grounds that the resulting unemployment is labelled 'voluntary'. Many people feel, rightly, that unemployment is a tragic misfortune and cannot be regarded in any meaningful sense as voluntary. Consequently they fell inclined to dismiss the analysis. But such a feeling is inspired by a complete misconception. There is nothing in the analysis to suggest otherwise than that unemployment is unpleasant and degrading. The point of the analysis is that the alternatives to unemployment, non-union jobs at non-union wages, are even less attractive. What is more, workers who take jobs in the non-union sector would, of course, prefer to work in the better paid union sector. It is a technical convention in economics to call the decisions of these people 'voluntary', because they are doing their best even in poor circumstances, but they could just as well be described as involuntarily forced out of the union sector.

No amount of re-labelling, however, will avoid the basic problem society faces: how to create permanent jobs for pay that people will accept. The analysis clearly indicates that one major way to do this is to reduce the power of unions to raise union wages. As union wages fall, the demand for union labour rises, people are withdrawn from the non-union sector, non-union wages rise and more people are prepared to work in it.

A POLICY FRAMEWORK

Monopoly power in the labour market from the union side now rates as a major allocational issue. Monopoly power in goods markets was the major allocational issue in the post-war period, resulting in important legislation such as the Restrictive Trade

Practices Act of 1956, new institutions such as the Monopolies Commission and tax changes like the successive tariff-cutting 'rounds'.

In British history the trades unions have been the instigator of major social reforms. Once they were a 'countervailing force' in an economy where major employers held the whip hand in negotiations. But their historical role as social reformer is no longer relevant. The need for a countervailing force has disappeared in an economy where employers' monopoly power has been heavily curtailed by the stronger competition in goods markets and the emergence of industrial relations institutions such as the industrial courts. It is hard to escape the conclusion that the public interest requires measures to deal with labour market monopoly power in an analogous way to goods market monopoly power. A corollary is that, since the power is vested in the unions by exceptionally favourable laws, it is no use hoping that non-legal measures, such as incomes policies, 'confrontations' or exhortations, will have any effect on the problem. Only changes in laws and institutions which take away union power will remove its effects on unemployment, output and the interests of non-unionized workers.

THE PRESENT SITUATION

A fairly full account of the history and present state of union legislation is attached as Appendix D. The following points emerge from this account as the 'present state of play'.

(1) Ministers have been unwilling to *abolish* civil immunities or the closed shop, preferring rather to restrict them and to ensure that they are used in a 'responsible' way. This attitude may, however, be changing.

(2) Powers *now exist* to take legal action against uses of pickets and secondary action, which are *not being used*, either by the private sector or, most surprisingly, by government departments.

(3) Powers now conferred by the 1982 Act, which further restrict the scope of industrial action and make the closed shop inoperative when it has not been sanctioned by an 80 per cent majority of the workforce, may also – if (b) is a guide – not be

used. In fact, some employers have already said they will not do so. Some unions (e.g. the National Union of Mineworkers) have said they will openly defy this and previous legislation.

There may be a number of factors impeding progress. First, the emotive power of 'union rights' is less than it was 10 or 50 years ago, but some people fear that it might flare up, if bold and tactless moves were made – martyrs could be created, etc. Second, the law is now immensely complicated, and at this stage quite untested in a large number of respects. Setting legal precedents now could be very costly, whether to a private employer or to a government department (subject to cash limits and so properly conscious at last of budgetary control).

Third and perhaps most important of all, there is what one might call the 'protection racket syndrome'. A union, which has strength in the workplace, can wreak financial havoc, even though it could ultimately lose a legal action and pay large damages. The employer is likely to be unwilling to risk this, much as a club owner will fear to take the local Mafia to court.

It is clear that independently of the adoption of the proposals we detail below, there is an immediate need to catch up in the enforcement of existing laws. (There is also scope for detailed extensions, clarification and tightening up, such as compulsory secret ballots for union elections and strike calls; these details will become apparent as experience of enforcement accumulates.)

Turning to the enforcement issue in respect of criminal law, there is in principle no problem. The police, under the direction of the Home Secretary, in conjunction with the local police authorities, can be ordered and given the necessary support to implement the law. We have in fact seen this happen with the much tighter regulation of pickets since 1979 and the effective disappearance, as a result, of the strictly criminal mass picket.

In the civil law as it affects the public sector employers, there is also in principle no problem of enforcement. All government departments can take civil action to enforce their rights. The budgetary implications of this should be recognized in framing their cash allocations. But clearly they can be ordered to take the necessary action.

However, in the civil law as it affects the private sector, there is a serious problem of enforcement in principle. This is that it may well be in nobody's individual interest to take legal action that is in the public interest.

This has been recognized in the law governing monopolies and restrictive practices – i.e. by firms in the goods market. In civil law, it is not possible for consumers of a product to take the supplier(s) to court for damages from monopoly practice. We therefore do not rely on such private actions to curb monopolies and restrictive practices. Instead we have a Monopolies Commission, whose job it is to report on practices that are referred to it by the Secretary of State for Trade as being potentially damaging to the public interest. In the light of that report, the Minister may bring an order in Parliament regulating or forbidding these practices and ordering whatever other action is necessary. From this point disobedience becomes a criminal matter, for the Attorney-General.

It is natural to think of extending this mode of action to monopolies and restrictive practices in the labour market. (Incidentally by extending it in this way it embraces actions and situations *not* involving unions.) The Monopolies Commission is at present empowered to investigate labour markets; but no labour market situations have ever been referred to it by the Secretary of State for Trade. We take up this point below as part of our innovative proposals for strengthening and simplifying the legal framework regulating labour market competition.

PROPOSALS FOR REFORM

The immense power wielded by unions in the British economy is plain for all to see. As a result of that power, the thinking of policy makers has been conditioned to accept labour market monopoly; such acceptance has led most people involved in policy discussion not to question the basis of such things as union immunities under the common law. This acceptance is highly dangerous to constructive reform, and has bedevilled all earlier proposals.

We begin from the basic conception that the labour market should be free of all restraints on competition, except those for which a positive case based on the public interest can be sustained. Any action which causes workers to act in combination in order to fix the terms of their employment is a restraint of competition. Such actions include the calling of strikes, the denial of work to non-union workers (the pre-entry closed shop), and the enforcement of union membership on all workers in an industry (the post-entry closed shop). Similarly, any action which causes employers to act in combination for the same purpose is a restraint of competition. This includes most conspicuously concerted bargaining by employers' associations.

It may be said that such a conception is Utopian and has no hope of implementation. It would certainly be opposed by a variety of groups with vested interests; the unions of course, and some employers who would fear transitional disruption. We would certainly accept that full implementation of free competition in the labour market could not occur rapidly and might never come. Our point is, however, that it should be the ultimate aim of all actions taken in this area. The rate of progress will depend on a variety of pressures, but the aim must be clear for any progress to occur. With that aim we do not believe rational men can disagree, in the light of the damage to the British economy inflicted by labour market imperfection.

With this aim in mind, we make three sets of proposals, for implementation at the earliest possible moment in whatever order is most expedient.

(1) The actions of unions should be subject to the common law *without exception*, that is, all union immunities under common law be repealed. The common law upholds contracts between employer and employee and recognizes the 'tort' of inducement to breach of contract. Union immunities from such tort cases allow them to call strikes without fear of action for damages. Strike calls are a *prima facie* restraint of trade and should not therefore be given immunity by society, since society's interest lies in competition. If unions and employers wish to sign contracts with clauses explicitly permitting strike calls under specified circumstances, then this could freely be done. The lack of immunities would not prevent it and would in fact stimulate the bringing of industrial action within the framework of the contracts. Any such contracts, however, would be potentially subject to investigation by the Labour Monopolies Commission proposed as (3) below.

(2) A 'status provision' should be legislated which would invalidate any contract between employer and worker contingent on the union status of the worker. Such a provision – analogous to a variety of similar provisions already in existence under common law – would render null and void any closed-shop agreements, explicit or implicit.

(3) A Labour Monopolies Commission should be set up under an extension of existing competition legislation, which would enunciate the 'public interest' in labour market competition. This Commission would be an independent body with power to investigate any apparent breach of the public interest, to publish a report about it, and to bring a case, based on its report, to the common law courts requesting that remedies to uphold the public interest as suggested by the report be mandated by the courts. The Commission's independence would ensure, as with anti-trust actions in the USA, that no *political* intervention is necessary, or for that matter possible, on the part of any future government hostile to competition. Its power would cover breaches by both sides of the labour market, so that the proposals overall are seen to be completely even handed between employers and workers. The powers are sweeping and would institute over a decade a body of case law with substantial impact on labour practices.

The combination of these three proposals would require modest legislation which would, incidentally, simplify in a major way the present tangle of labour law, returning it to the framework of the original common law. The proposals combine the withdrawal of legal protection currently given explicitly or implicitly – a negative act which alone might not be sufficient to curb union power because of custom, practice and intimidation – with the invention of a weapon for positively changing labour practices regardless of employers', employees', and unions' own narrow interests, which may alone be insufficient to prosecute the public interest and may even interfere with it. This combination of negative and positive changes should be sufficient to introduce a very substantial degree of competition into the UK labour market over the next decade.

Legal details of these proposals with drafting suggestions etc. are now appended in some depth.

AN ALTERNATIVE SYSTEM OF INDUSTRIAL RELATIONS

Since the beginning of this century, trades unions have held unique privileges in law, and occupied an unrivalled position in the courts with the sole exception of the Crown itself. The immunities from legal process are considered in Appendix D and need not be reiterated here; the general impression is that these immunities are unnecessarily wide, and have been used by unions to acquire and secure inequitably powerful advantages over others with whom they deal. We therefore call for the restitution of the rule of law and equality of treatment before the courts, so as to provide a more balanced position for those who are parties to collective agreements, and to permit unions to represent their membership interests in a more efficient and responsible way. It is our opinion that the only way in which the necessary changes can be effected, is by the abolition of all legal privileges conferred upon trades unions and by the restoration of the common law to situations in which unions are a party. By abrogating the unique privileges presently conferred by statute, such bodies would still be powerful enough to represent their members' interest effectively, but not irresponsibly. The acceptance of common law principles represents the acceptance of common sense in an area which seems so sadly neglected by such considerations. Given this constitutional claim, we shall now consider the likely impact of such a change upon the face of industrial relations and then detail its likely effects.

The Common Law Basis

It should be made clear at the outset that our proposed adoption of a common law basis in no way affects the existing legal provisions as between employer and employee as detailed in Appendix D; its only effect is upon the position of trades unions, their officials and related persons. In particular it is worth emphasizing that cases of unfair or wrongful dismissal would not, *per se*, be affected by the proposed change, nor would the rights of employers to sue individual employees for strikes or other breaches of their contract of employment.

The main effect of adopting the common law basis would be to make the union and its officials liable to common law actions such as attempted or actual inducement to breach of contract of employment. Clearly the proposals would expose unions to an extensive range of legal liabilities, and it is our view that one way in which the union may seek to restrict this exposure is by entering into legally binding collective agreements with employers and their associations. The idea of collective contracts is not particularly radical, since it has been widely adopted in a number of overseas countries (for example, France, West Germany and the United States) and indeed it was an assumed situation under the Industrial Relations Act 1971.

The coupling of a contractual basis with the abrogation of immunities, which is our preferred framework, can be seen as conferring a number of advantages over the existing scheme of industrial relations. First, it provides a fairer and more responsible basis for industrial bargaining, by removing the rights of unions unilaterally to break agreements with impunity. It would be more equitable also for employers who formerly encountered difficulties in bringing actions against individual workers, rather than the more powerful and wealthy unions who frequently inspired or induced such breaches. Second, whilst some would argue that the alternative basis of industrial relations would be met by the same vituperative actions and malignant reactions as those encountered by the former Conservative administration, we would point out that our proposals are in no way coercive or paternalistic. For if unions do not wish to enter into a contract, they are in no way required to do so, they are simply open to the common law remedies if, for example, they attempt to induce a breach in the contract of employment between the employer and the employees. Viewed in this light, unions may recognize the advantages of a contractual basis, since it affords rights as well as responsibilities.

Assuming such a basis were adopted, the significance of the proposals can best be seen by considering their likely effect upon strikes and other forms of industrial conflict. Clearly unions would be liable for any breach of the collective contract and could be sued by the employer, or any other third party not too remote from damage. Strikes, including political strikes and other forms of industrial action, would be taken, subject to *de minimis* rule, to represent a fundamental breach of the contract giving the employer the normal common law remedies. It may be argued that this adds little to existing, proposed and contemplated legislation, but this misses the point that, whereas successive governments have adhered to the central theme of immunity, attempts have been made to whittle away a number of specific immunities. By adopting such a course, there have been a succession of harmful confrontations between the protagonists, which we feel is best resolved by a once and for all change in the legal environment pervading the industrial relations scene. Moreover by adopting the new comprehensive legal regime, all union nominated officers, as well as unofficial or even disruptive representatives, are put on the same liability basis, since legal actions may now be instituted against these 'third parties'. By contrast, the existing and contemplated legislation fails adequately to get to grips with these fundamentals and will produce piecemeal and partial legislative solutions as confusing as they are confused.

However, by far the most important advantage of our proposals over any form of legislative provision (whether providing extended or restricted immunities) is that, by removing externally imposed restraints and privileges, the parties to collective bargaining are more able freely to negotiate their own terms as to the price and conditions of labour supply, without the distortionary impact of one party having a statutorily indemnified unilateral right of repudiation. Lest it be argued that the ending of legal protectionism will result in all trades union and other industrial action becoming unlawful, it is to be noted that the ending of legislative immunities does not necessarily preclude the possibility of collusive *de facto* immunities being established between employers and trades unions. Nor does it prevent the negotiation of contracted immunities, which we would regard as providing flexibility in the new scheme, as well as forming central issues in the negotiations as to the price and conditions of labour supply.

The negotiation of contractual immunities can be viewed in both positive and negative terms – indeed, at the present time, it is possible for employers to negotiate 'non strike' clauses, and for this employers invariably make compensatory finance available; however, under the new scheme, strikes and other forms of industrial action will *prima facie* give rise to contractual and/or tortious liability, unless the contracting parties permit such actions as part of the collective contract. A period of more active negotiation and contract drafting is therefore envisaged, in which such issues as defining the permitted rights, for exercise in the defined circumstances, after exhausting prescribed procedures (e.g. 30 days' notice of strike, or cooling-off period, or balloting of plant membership, arbitration etc.) become part of the price determination process itself. The central difference between the proposed legal framework and the existing one is that, by removing the unfair privileges currently enjoyed by unions, and making them responsible for their agreements, the commitments which are made will be more likely to reflect the true economic value of labour services, undistorted by legislative regulation.

On a more practical level, we envisage the provision of such a framework as reducing the need for industrial conflict rather than permitting it. As indicated earlier, not every employer will bring an action for every breach. Forbearances on the right to bring actions will lead to *de facto* immunities being established, and the development of these and similar understandings will lubricate the workings of the new system as they do at present in relation to most breaches of contract by individual employees. Indeed we expect most employers to be at least as reluctant to bring legal actions against the unions under the new scheme, as they have been in the past to bring actions against individual employees in breach of their contract of employment. The main reason for this reticence is that good employers want good industrial relations, and this cannot be brought about by suing unions for every single breach, indeed to attempt to do so would be prohibitively expensive. However by adopting the alternative legal framework, unions would be bound so that actions *could* be brought for breach, thereby providing employers with a back-up position which is not available to them under the existing scheme. Moreover, such agreements will provide an agreed objective guideline having a restraining influence upon trades unions in exercising their *de facto* power, and at the same time providing them with a shield against irresponsible and unrepresentative elements within the union who may otherwise have sought to break the undertakings with employers.

The contractual unprivileged basis would also require reasonableness by the latter, as well as the former, for if contracts were enforced with undue rigidity then either employers or unions would be forced into financial difficulties. Taking the extreme example of a firm which, after a number of breach actions against the union, was able to bankrupt it, the union would have little to lose by subsequent actions and may reciprocate by encouraging disruptive action eventually leading to the firm's liquidation. By this somewhat extreme example we can clearly see how our framework actually deters legal involvement, yet provides a useful shield behind which both the parties can extract compliance with the terms of their agreement. The removal of immunities and restoration of a fairer basis to collective bargaining will ensure the necessary background for the development of good industrial relations with the minimum reliance on the law and its current immunities.

To ensure the successful implementation of our proposals, a number of potentially difficult areas must be isolated and dealt with. Clearly, if employees do not wish to accept the terms of employment offered them by a specific employer, they may leave that firm and seek employment elsewhere. However, in the case of a monopoly employer, attempts may be made to force workers to accept 'unfair' wages. In such a situation we see the union and employees bringing this matter to the attention of the Labour Monopolies Commission (LMC) which will investigate and report on the contract and determine whether or not its terms are such that only a monopolist employer could have imposed them. An affirmative declaration by the Commission would then require the parties to renegotiate the relevant terms by reference to comparable market conditions. Conversely, if a collusive agreement were entered into by the parties, one or both of whom had monopolistic powers, then the terms of the agreement could also be examined by the Commission, to determine whether that agreement was contrary to the public interest. Similarly, if the terms of any collective agreement were to attempt to override the rights granted by employers in individual contracts of employment with their workers, the LMC would have powers to intervene. Before considering the role of the Commission in detail, let us consider the likely impact of the substantive reforms on actions pursuant to strikes, such as picketing.

The new legal framework would not permit such action during the currency of any existing contract. Even under the existing law this may constitute breach of contract and this, as we have noted, would not be affected by our proposals. As for trades unions or other persons engaged in picketing, this would now give rise in all cases to actions for inducing a breach or conspiracy or intimidation.

Picketing or other forms of industrial pressure could be brought after the expiration of the current contract, and before renegotiation of the new contract. Such picketing would be subject to such common law actions as intimidation, breach of the peace, obstruction, etc. Moreover if individual workers, whether or not members of the union, were to accept management's offer by being prepared to work, the pickets would be liable for inducement to breach of contract, or collectively for conspiracy, if they attempted to prevent those persons from working. In the case of a union concerting such action, it too would be liable. It is remarkable that, whilst our proposals appear radical, many of the law reforms in this and other countries are simply retractions of earlier immunities which are now realized as unnecessary incumbrances upon the freedom of collective bargaining.

The Closed Shop and Status Provisions

In addition to the effects upon strikes and other industrial disputes, the proposed framework may also have significant implications for the closed shop. Under the new framework, employees and trades unions would contract with employers, and although unions could impose closed-shop conditions on employers, and they in turn impose it as a pre- or post-entry qualification for workers, it should be legislatively provided that the personal contract between employer and employee is not subject to any 'status' qualifications, (other than that required by statute, e.g. race or sex legislation). As such, the employer will not be empowered to ask any questions which directly or indirectly touch upon trades union status (this works for the benefit of unionists as well as non-unionists) and any terms in a collective agreement which provide otherwise shall be null and void. In the case of breach of this provision, the prospective employee may bring an action for loss of prospective earnings which he may otherwise have enjoyed had the contract been offered to him. Such a person would apply for a declaration of prevention of free entry in the common law courts. In the case where an existing employee has been dismissed as a result of non-union membership, where such a person can show that the employing firm has (either of its own accord or as a result of union pressure) dismissed him as a result of a *de facto* status provision, then he may obtain a declaration of enforced dismissal.

THE LABOUR MONOPOLIES COMMISSION

The second major reform which we see as complementing our first proposal involves the establishment of a Labour Monopolies Commission which would be an independent statutory body with administrative functions and quasi-legal powers to investigate, report and direct upon monopoly powers which appear to exist within labour markets. Its primary administrative function would be similar to that exercised by the Monopolies and Mergers Commission (MMC) under the various competition legislations, but confined solely to matters relating to labour monopolies. The position, powers and effects of trades unions on labour markets would certainly be one of the main areas of concern, but as indicated in our earlier reform proposals, monopolistic employer and union forms of 'unfair labour practices' (e.g. pre-entry closed shops and enforced dismissals) would also be within its purview. Indeed the Commission would be actively engaged in investigating and reporting on any situation or practice which could be considered as uncompetitive or restricting market responsiveness. Whilst the general tenor of the proposal is to carry over the product monopolies legislation into labour market situations, there are a number of important differences between the two markets and this leads us to advocate the need for an independent commission separate from the MMC with quite different procedures and enforcement powers.

The first difference concerns what criteria should be used in determining whether or not a labour monopoly exists. Clearly the definition of monopoly for product markets (e.g. the 25 per cent rate) would be too restrictive: indeed it is our opinion that any per cent rate will be similarly unsatisfactory, although such a basis may be a useful back-up if expressed in terms of occupation and/or industry. Our own preference is for an activity definition of the labour market expressed in terms of the 'public interest', where the latter term is defined so as to embrace all potential situations. A consolidating definition embracing the Fair Trading Act 1973 s.84 and the Restrictive Trade Practices Act 1976 ss.10 and 19 as suitably amended, could be employed as an 'initial' basis for jurisdiction, although drafting along the lines of the Competition Act 1980 s.2 and Fair Trading Act 1973 s.79 (5), would be more appropriate for giving the Commission powers to investigate the unfair labour practices discussed earlier. In any event, these are drafting details which need not detain us here; what is important to note is that the scope of the Restrictive Trade Practices legislation and the anti-monopolies and competition legislation (under s.62) are too narrow and isolated to have any real impact on labour market monopolies.

Whilst we feel that this central economic objective in itself establishes the need for an independent Commission, there are a number of procedural difficulties which would be encountered if the MMC were given extended jurisdiction to carry out the terms of our second reform proposal. For example, under existing provisions the method of referrals to the Monopolies and Mergers Commission seems particularly passive and ineffective, and its procedure for enforcement appears singularly inappropriate. Thus, in the first place, the investigative function is initiated not by the body itself but by the Director of Fair Trading (a government appointment) or the Secretary of State for Trade, and this basis of referrals seems unsatisfactory for the purposes we have in mind. It is essential for the Labour Commission to be able to initiate investigations of its own accord without referrals or reference to third parties, especially those persons who may be seen as 'political' reference sources. Similarly, it has been seen that the MMC has no effective enforcing powers itself. If a monopoly is found to exist, the report will be enforced by the Secretary of State, after Parliamentary scrutiny in the courts.

We would once again seek to avoid any apparent political involvement in the more sensitive area of trades union and other labour monopoly practices, and at the same time prefer to see the Labour Commission's report and recommendation in effect operating on the plaintiff's case for consideration before the common law courts. If this procedure were adopted, it would then be incumbent upon the monopolist defendant to consider whether or not to challenge the evidence, and whilst this may lead to a certain degree of duplication of the earlier investigation, it does afford a certain 'safeguard' to defendants, whilst the sanction of heavy legal costs will at least inhibit spurious and 'political' defences becoming the established practice. Alternative enforcement procedures are of course available, such as the LMC having its own powers of enforcement; indeed this may very well be the best method of dealing with at least some of the unfair industrial practices referred to earlier. After an extensive examination of those alternatives we feel that the above procedure is not only the most acceptable, but also the least controversial, and if the first proposal considered earlier were adopted, an integrated scheme of competitive industrial relations would be established, and collectively they would be enforced by the ordinary courts of the land.

Although our preference is for an independent Labour Monopolies Commission, quite distinct in function, procedure and enforcement from the MMC, we do see it as having similar powers of information and requirement of witnesses, as well as means of enforcing those procedures by way of contempt, just as currently enjoyed by the latter. Moreoever, transfers of information and possibly joint enquiries are envisaged, so as to remove the monopoly powers and practices which have plagued our industrial and commercial competitiveness and caused significant and unnecessary increases in unemployment. The programme of reducing monopolies and increasing flexibility and competitiveness, which has expanded during the present administration, should now be put into full effect.

CHAPTER 3

Related Issues

A NOTE ON MINIMUM WAGES AND WAGES COUNCILS

Effective minimum wages – that is those that succeed, by inspection and enforcement, in raising wages above market-clearing levels – have an effect like that of union power. They reduce jobs where wages have been raised and displace workers into other sectors not so regulated, where wages fall until supply equals demand. In essence, the government is acting as a union for the workers whose wages are then raised; in some cases, the government actually does this in response to requests from unions unable to exert enough power themselves.

It follows clearly enough that a government which wishes to create jobs by curbing union power should also act in its own 'backyard' by putting an end to minimum wages. This is the least it can do.

The present minimum wage and related regulations in force are documented in what follows.

In 1909 Wages Councils were established with the intention of protecting workers from sweat-shop conditions and low rates of pay, particularly in fragmented industries in which it was hard to organize collective bargaining; as such they were a substitute for trades unions in these areas. The number of Wages Councils grew rapidly after World War 1, but since World War 2 there has been a moderate decline. There are now 26 Wages Councils (see Table II.3.1) covering about 2.5 million industrial workers and about 400,000 establishments in the UK. Parallel to Wages Councils is the Agricultural Wages Board which is separate, but has a similar role and powers covering only agriculture.

At present under the Wages Councils Act 1979, supported by the Employment Protection Act 1975, Councils, independent of Govern-

TABLE II. 3.1 *List of Wages Councils* (Wages Councils Act 1979)*

Aerated Waters Wages Council (England and Wales)
Aerated Waters Wages Council (Scotland)
Boot and Shoe Repairing Wages Council
Button Manufacturing Wages Council
Clothing Manufacturing Wages Council
Coffin Furniture and Cerement Making Wages Council
Cotton Waste Reclamation Wages Council
Flax and Hemp Wages Council
Fur Wages Council
General Waste Material Reclamation Wages Council
Hairdressing Undertakings Wages Council
Hat, Cap and Millinery Wages Council
Lace Finishing Wages Council
Laundry Wages Council
Licensed Non-residential Establishment Wages Council
Licensed Residential Establishment and Licensed Restaurant Wages Council
Linen and Cotton Handkerchief and Household Goods and Linen Piece Goods Wages Council
Made-up Textiles Wages Council
Ostrich and Fancy Feather and Artificial Flower Wages Council
Perambulator and Invalid Carriage Wages Council
Retail Bespoke Tailoring Wages Council
Retail Food and Allied Trades Wages Council
Retail Trades (Non-Food) Wages Council
Rope, Twine and Net Wages Council
Sack and Bag Wages Council
Toy Manufacturing Wages Council
Unlicensed Place of Refreshment Wages Council

Notes: *Unless their title indicates otherwise, all Councils cover the whole of Great Britain
Address of Secretary of all the Councils:
Office of Wages Councils
12 St James's Square
London SW1Y 4LL

ment have the legal power to fix minimum wage rates and other conditions of employment such as holiday entitlement, hours of work, etc. in certain specified industries. These awards have the power of law and employers can be subject to substantial fines for failure to comply with such awards. The Councils' members are appointed by the Employment Secretary, though independent of Government; usually they consist of nominees of employers' associations and trades unions, with some form of independent chairman. They are backed up by the Wages Inspectorate, an arm of the Department of Employment.

The British system of minimum wage legislation has enabled the UK to ratify the International Labour Office (ILO) Convention No. 26 of 1928; it will be possible to renew or renounce such ratification again in 1985. Other industrial countries, e.g. USA, France, West Germany, etc, have similar minimum wage laws. In the USA, the Fair Labour Standards Acts in 1945 and 1960 have established the principle there, but there are now moves afoot to dismantle certain aspects of these Acts.

The two largest Councils in the UK, the Retail Food and Retail Non-Food, cover around 1.75 million of the total 2.5 million workers, and over 230,000 establishments (58 per cent of total) whilst, at the other end of the scale, the Flax and Hemp Council covers some 2,300 workers in 12 factories and the Ostrich Feather Council embraces 28 individual plants and 1500 workers. The coverage is generally the older types of industry and trade with a large component of small firms.

Once established, however, it has proved historically somewhat difficult to abolish any Wages Council. For instance 19 years occurred between the last meeting of both the Drift Net and Fustian Cutting Councils before they were finally formally abolished. Eleven Councils were abolished in the period 1974–8 and only one – the Pin, Hook and Eye Council – has been abolished since 1979. Others, however, have been merged, but continue to function as before in their new clothing. The abolition of a Council in reality entails a reference under the two relevant Acts (Employment Protection Act 1975 and Wages Councils Act 1979) to the independent Advisory, Conciliation and Arbitration Service (ACAS) with no scope for a time limit for reporting, thus making it very difficult indeed to achieve any early or prompt abolition despite any economic damage a Wages Council may be causing. There have consequently been no references to ACAS since 1979 for any abolition. This compares somewhat unfavourably with an equally important area of employment policy, namely industrial training, where a joint Departmental/Manpower Services Commission (MSC) review of Industrial Training Boards (ITBs) led to a rationalization of ITBs so as to align with other employment policy initiatives. No such similar action has been possible over Wages Councils, although their retention is inconsistent with present employment policy.

In terms of direct public expenditure cost, Wages Councils and their associate Inspectorate cost around £3 million annually. The staff numbers involved have recently been reduced as part of the policy to reduce civil service numbers, but around 25,000 units are still visited annually by wages inspectors.

Indirectly, as a result of jobs destroyed by Council awards, there will be a further revenue cost; but we have no estimate of this. Qualitative evidence, however, suggests that many Council awards have not reflected the individual financial or geographic aspects of the firms and industry in question. There have been cases where firms, especially small ones, have been forced to close or abandon an extension as a result. There has been little concern over the ability to pay. Often awards have been retrospective and difficult to interpret, making budgeting and future development planning extremely difficult, particularly for the small businessman. Some recent awards, particularly the latest by the Retail Food Council of about 9 per cent plus a shorter working week and increased London weighting were clearly unwarranted by market pressures.

The contribution of Wages Councils to the relief of poverty and to assisting the socially disadvantaged has been generally adjudged negative both in the UK and USA. The record shows that Councils have not improved the relative position of the low-paid, nor alleviated poverty. Consequently the only argument here for retaining the Councils is that the relative position of the low-paid would be worse if the Councils were to be abolished, but no evidence can be found to support this. Similar arguments can be applied to youths, women and ethnic minorities – many awards have resulted in pricing these people out of jobs. The disadvantaged groups in a normal labour market situation naturally warrant a lower rate of pay and any attempt to increase it by a Council over the market rate only serves to limit their employment opportunities; this has been particularly true for young workers. Recent American research backs up British experience on this aspect. (See for example Peter Linneman (1982), 'The economic impact of minimum wage laws: a new look at an old question' *Journal of Political Economy*, Vol. 90, pp. 443–69.)

In any case, financial aid to those in work on low earnings is now met nationally through FIS and various associated social security schemes and locally via rebate schemes, e.g. rent and rates. Proposals in this book will maintain this system, but in a manner that avoids the poverty trap. Council awards are therefore unnecessary in this aspect, besides causing unemployment among the very groups where help is aimed.

Wages Council awards are also inconsistent with other aspects of current employment policy, e.g. the Young Workers Scheme (YWS), whereby lower wages for youth are encouraged and subsidized so as to stimulate employment, or the New Training Initiative (NTI) where some low allowances are paid for those participating in it.

Abolition of the Wages Council system would, it can be confidently postulated, serve to expand employment, offer competitive wages for the socially disadvantaged, create an incentive for youth training, remove inconsistencies with other parts of present employment policy and alleviate rather than promote poverty. In short, if a Wages Council comes to be regarded as effective, it is therefore harmful; if it is looked upon as ineffective, it is therefore otiose and useless. Both counts add up to a positive case for steps towards the removal of minimum wage legislation, namely through the eventual abolition of Wages Councils. The declaratory effects, as well as the economic ones, would be a firm signal to all concerned.

MOBILITY AND THE REGIONAL DIMENSION

Unemployment in the UK varies widely across regions. Earlier, we examined some of the regional facts, and found a high correlation between relative unionization and unemployment across regions. This was what one would expect, for under the present UK tax and benefit system, tax and benefit rates are identical between regions; this is likely to put a *national* floor beneath non-union wages, so that regional variations in demand and in union power will not be accommodated by falls in non-union wages in the regions worst affected. These regions will therefore react with differentially increased unemployment.

The relief of high unemployment is surely to be regarded as a primary objective of regional policy, taking priority over the objective of preserving regional population. Success in relieving regional unemployment will also reduce national unemployment (because rising real wages in the poor regions will bring more people back into work than falling real wages in the rich regions will induce people not to work, owing to much larger gaps between wages and benefits in the rich regions). There are two main mechanisms that could provide relief, if we suppose that we must indeed preserve a national system of tax and benefit rates – a supposition we maintain.

Labour Mobility

The first mechanism is labour mobility from poor to rich regions. Unfortunately, the mechanism is severely clogged for those people most afflicted by unemployment, unskilled and semi-skilled workers on low incomes who live in rented council houses. For they cannot move without losing their rights to subsidized accommodation. The right is not transferable to another area, at least without a long waiting period in the queue for council houses there, during which period the family will have to pay substantially higher private sector rents, themselves artificially raised by rent control restrictions. Hence a man unemployed on Merseyside is the less likely to be attracted to moving to a job in the South East, in view of the additional expenses. The wage he would require in that job would price him well out of that market.

Steps have been taken by the Conservative Government to improve this mechanism. Council house rents have been raised, and the council house sale programme has been pushed ahead. These policies should be continued. In particular, the aim should be to bring council house rents up to economic levels as soon as possible.

However, no action has been taken on private sector rent decontrol. We have been unable in the time available to examine in detail what detailed action could be taken to improve incentives to rent privately. But we do strongly urge that decontrol be undertaken as soon as possible, after the appropriate study of the best legal means to this end.

Regional Employment Incentives

The second mechanism is to depress wage costs to employers and increase work incentives for employees in the poor regions. This mechanism too has been clogged by the operation of the tax and benefit system, which effectively sets a floor below regional wage costs. Regional grants and loans subsidise *capital costs* for a discrete period. While they will for that period make some impact on regional unemployment, their impact is limited both in time, since once the period is over the firm involved may not replace the capital stock (a frequent occurrence) and in size, since the wrong input is being subsidized, labour and jobs being the objective.

We have two policy proposals to boost this mechanism. First, we have suggested above a 'cap' (or ceiling) for benefit income ratios. This has the very important implication for regions, that in a poor region benefits will be *de facto* lower than in a rich region. There would now be no effective floor below wages in this poor region since, as wages there fell, so benefits would fall in line. This is likely over a reasonable period to help substantially in reducing regional disparities in unemployment.

Second, we suggest that a regional labour subsidy be introduced, with a rate per man employed to be related to the unemployment rate in the region – somewhat along the lines of the previous Regional Employment Premium. Our investigations have revealed that the EEC regional fund might be in a position to finance a modest scheme of this sort, and we have made no explicit cost allowance for it therefore. The role of such a scheme would be to reduce the impact, on real worker incomes in the regions, of the market-induced reduction in real wages and the fall in benefits implied by the cap scheme, even after the general rise in tax thresholds that should accompany its introduction.

PART III

Comparative Analysis of Four Major European Countries

THE NATURE OF TAX/BENEFIT SYSTEMS ON THE CONTINENT

We studied four Continental systems, those of Belgium, France, West Germany and Italy. Before we get down to detailed analysis of each country, we can make a number of general points which are highly relevant to the UK.

There is effectively no 'poverty trap' in these countries. The major reason is that 'family assistance' is not means tested. There is no equivalent of the means-tested FIS and passported benefits. Instead, family benefits are paid, on the same basis as child benefits here, on the basis of number of dependents, regardless of income.

This is subject to qualification for the very lowest income groups who may receive social assistance. It has proved impossible to obtain absolutely precise information about this, which is discretionary ('according to need') in all four countries. The impression given by our contacts is that this assistance is not important, except for a very small minority of workers – i.e. it is a safety net from the most extreme poverty. We have assumed in what follows that this impression is correct.

A second reason for the absence of the poverty trap is the 'tapered' tax rates on low incomes employed in all four countries. Instead of the standard rate applying to these low incomes, each country has a set of 'tax tables' which embodies MRTs rising slowly towards the standard rate.

This means that, just as there is no poverty trap, so net incomes in work are permitted to fall quite steeply as gross income falls. MRTs do not appear to exceed 40 per cent on low incomes (above the social assistance level).

As is well known, VAT is used to raise a higher proportion of taxes in these countries. Especially with higher rates on luxuries, this does not alter the picture of relatively low MRTs on low incomes. Even including VAT, MRTs do not exceed 50 per cent on low incomes, and are generally quite a lot lower than this.

Turning to unemployment compensation, the countries can be divided into two that have benefit/income *ratio* systems, where there is no 'unemployment trap' (France and Italy); one that has a system very like the UK with flat rate minimum entitlements where the unemployment trap is as serious as here (Belgium); and finally one that has a 'mixed' system intermediate between these (Germany) where there is evidence of a trap though only at the very lowest income levels. This difference has proved interesting, enabling us to compare experiences. It is certainly no coincidence that Belgium shares with the UK unemployment rates substantially higher than the other three.

We now briefly describe each country's system, our primary concern being with its impact on unemployment. Appendix E contains fuller details.

BELGIUM

There is no standard rate of income tax in Belgium. Tax is levied on the basis of graduated tax tables up to 80 per cent above average earnings; tax allowances are given for dependents. Marginal tax rates start at around 30 per cent at one half of average earnings, and rise continuously up to 47.5 per cent at this point. From here, the MRT rises to 72 per cent at 10 times average earnings. These figures include social security contributions by employees at 10.1 per cent (average and marginal at all incomes). Table III.1 illustrates this.

VAT is levied at 17 per cent in Belgium (but exceptionally 6 per cent on basic necessities; a further tax of 8 per cent is added making 25 per cent for 'luxuries'). Hence total MRTs for employees rise from around 42 per cent at one half of average earnings, reaching a top rate of around 80 per cent at 10 times average. These rates are much lower than in the UK at low incomes, similar at average earnings and about 10 percentage points higher for higher incomes.

Social security contributions by employers are at the rate of 38.85

per cent of gross wages. This is very high compared with the UK's 12 per cent, and turns out to be an important element in Belgian performance.

'Family welfare' is dealt with via child benefits only. These are, however, somewhat higher than rates in the UK. For example, for two children aged 7 and 11, child benefit in 1980 was around £13.50 per week (against £11.70 currently in the UK); for four children (aged 7, 11, 14, 16) it was around £40 per week (against £23.40 here currently). These benefits do not vary with income.

TABLE III.1 *Marginal and Average Rates of (Direct) Tax* in Belgium (1981) (average earnings = 100)*

	Single		*m + 2 – wife not working*	
Earnings	*MRT*	*ART*	*MRT*	*ART*
150	47	32.8	47	29.7
100	44.5	26.7	39.4	22.8
70	36	20.8	36	15.2
50	30	17.4	30	11.8

Note: * Employee social security contributions included: the rate is 10.1 per cent (average and marginal) at all income levels.

There is no Family Income Supplement otherwise, apart from 'public assistance', administered by local authorities on a rigorous and discretionary basis. There are no benefits (such as housing cost subsidies, free school meals), related to income levels. (This statement does not apply to benefits for the old or invalids or other special groups which are excluded from our analysis.) Public assistance is reported as being used sparingly for cases of real hardship and descends from the medieval poor laws. It appears therefore that this is of minor significance.

Unemployment compensation which is not taxable is at the rate of 60 per cent of gross earnings for all employees in their first year of unemployment. Thereafter heads of households only (with minor exceptions) receive this rate indefinitely, while others drop to a rate of 40 per cent of gross earnings indefinitely. However, these ratios to gross earnings are qualified by minimum and maximum flat rate payments (which in 1980 were BF 4910 (about £60) per week maximum for all employees and BF 3740 (£47) minimum for heads of households, BF 2900 (£36) for others).

It is these qualifications which give the system its close similarity to that of the UK's now completely flat rate system.

The effect is illustrated in Table III.2. Replacement ratios for heads of household rise from around 90 per cent of *net* income (after work expenses) at average earnings levels, up to 124 per cent at one half of average earnings if they have a typical family, and 143 per cent if they are single (worse because tax hits them harder at work). These are indefinite in duration. For others, after a year, at these levels the ratios drop respectively to around 60 per cent rising to 110 per cent. This 'unemployment trap' is in fact more vicious than that in the UK. For the lowest income groups, income in work is not

TABLE III.2 *Belgian Replacement Ratios* (1981)*
(average earnings = 100)

Earnings	*m + 2, wife not working*	*Single*
For heads of households (ratios are for Year 1 and all successive years)		
150	65	(66)
100	89	92
70	96	101
50	124	143
For others (assume have taxable status as single)	*Year 1*	*All subsequent years*
150	(66)	(66)
100	92	61
70	101	78
50	143	110

* Assumes work expenses of BF 660 per week.

subsidized and therefore replacement ratios rise well over 100 per cent, whereas in the UK they hover just above 100 per cent for these families. For single persons, ratios are much higher in Belgium than in the UK at all income levels because Belgian compensation as a fraction of gross earnings does not vary with family size.

According to estimates from Eurostat, trades union membership in Belgium has risen from 62 per cent of registered workers in 1960 to 76 per cent in 1978. The great majority of unions are organized into three large confederations. The degree of power exercised by unions is likely to be considerable. The unionization rate is 20 percentage points higher than that in the UK, and centralization appears to be greater. The rise in unionization over the last two decades is of the same order as in the UK. Nevertheless, it has been commented that these estimates are unreliable, with conflicting estimates from other sources.

This brief description suggests that the appropriate labour market model for Belgium is the one used for the UK. The total labour supply curve (i.e. that responding to non-union real wages) will resemble the truncated curve for the UK. Unions will fix a mark-up over non-union real wages heavily influenced by real benefits grossed up for direct taxes on workers. Taxes on employers will shift the demand curve to the left for labour in both union and non-union sectors.

Estimates of this model are shown in Table III.3. In the real wage equation the coefficients on benefits and unemployment are very well determined. That for *UNR* is just significant at the 5 per cent level, while the significance of T_L just falls short of this. Data problems may account for these less robust estimates. *UNR* was noted earlier as being somewhat unreliable. The T_L series is accurate only from 1970; the data prior to this was constructed from the social security contribution rate, assuming the income tax rates were constant at 1970 levels. There is no evidence of autocorrelation in the equation. The unemployment equation is estimated by non-linear least squares because of evidence of autocorrelation. The key coefficients in the equation are well determined; in particular real labour costs have a strong positive effect on unemployment.

With the necessary *caveats* at this stage, it is quite striking how similar the coefficients are to those for the UK. The long-run values compare as is shown in Table III.4.

TABLE III.3 *Estimates for Belgium on UK-style Model of Real Wages and Unemployment (Quarterly data: 1962.1–1980.1,* t-*values bracketed)*

Dependent variable	$\log w_t$	U_t *(millions)* *(Non-linear least squares)*	
Constant	− 5.36 (1.91)	Constant	− 2.1 (2.9)
*D*1	− 0.019 (4.0)	*D*1	− 0.008 (3.9)
*D*2	− 0.006 (1.4)	*D*2	− 0.023 (9.3)
*D*3	− 0.024 (5.2)	*D*3	− 0.025 (9.5)
T_{Lt}	0.83 (1.6)	$\log \hat{O}_t$	− 0.116 (7.0)
$\log (b_t)$	0.19 (3.8)	$(\log \hat{w}_t) + T_{Ft}$	− 0.08 (7.6)
$\log N_t$	0.3 (1.0)	t	− 0.0002 (0.9)
UNR_t	0.51 (2.1)	$\log U_{t-1}$	− 0.92 (53.8)
$\hat{U}_t$ (millions)	− 0.28 (3.7)	$\log N_t$	0.26 (2.9)
t	0.004 (4.8)		
$\log w_{t-1}$	0.34 (3.5)		
$\bar{R}^2$	0.998		
DW	2.25	ϱ_2	− 0.36 (2.9)
χ^2_4 *	8.4	χ^2_4	2.1
		DW	1.72

Notes: Mnemonics as for UK model (pp. 121–2).
* Godfrey, 1978, test for autocorrelation. See also fn. to Table A.2, p. 124.

TABLE III.4

L/R *Coefficient on*	*Real wage equation*				*Unemployment equation*	
	Real benefits	*Tax rates*	*Unemployment*	*Unionization*	*Real labour costs*	*Output*
Belgium	0.29	1.2	0.055*	0.77	7.7	− 11.2
UK	0.48	0.48	0.10	1.96	4.1	− 8.5

Note: * Belgian effect converted to UK basis by calculating at mean unemployment in sample period, 0.13 million.

The implicit long-run elasticity of labour supply response to the (non-union) replacement ratio is also therefore similar, at 5.25 against 4.75 in the UK.

Though we have not been able to research Belgium to the same depth as the UK, we must regard the Belgian model as striking corroboration of our UK thesis, even to the extent of orders of magnitude. This is, however, not surprising in view of the close parallels in their unemployment compensation systems. The parallelism is mirrored in the unemployment trends of the two countries. Unemployment rates stand at over 16 per cent now in Belgium, against 12.5 per cent in the UK; in 1964 they stood at 1–2 per cent in both countries.

Though we have not yet completed work on a full model of Belgium, we would guess that simulated total effects from introducing benefit ratio ceilings in Belgium would be of similar order to those simulated earlier for the UK.

FRANCE

As in Belgium, there is no standard rate and tax is levied in a graduated way. Allowances for family size are given by a quotient system see (see Appendix E for details). Marginal tax rates rise continuously from about 10 per cent on the lowest incomes to a maximum of 75 per cent. These rates include social security contribution rates of 11.9 per cent on gross wages up to FF6590 per month (1.5 times average earnings) with 5.5 per cent as the *marginal* rate above this (see Table III.5).

TABLE III.5 *Marginal and Average Tax Rates In France (1981) (average earnings = 100)*

Earnings	*Single*		*m + 2*	
	MRT	*ART*	*MRT*	*ART*
140	39	26.1	22	15.1
100	33	21.9	18	12.7
70	28	18.3	12	12
60	33	15.8	12	12

VAT is generally levied at 17.6 per cent, with exceptions of 33.33 per cent on 'luxuries' and 7 per cent on food, transport, books, and other 'necessities'. Total MRTs for employees hence rise from about 25 per cent to 80 per cent; these rates are lower than in the UK for low incomes.

Social security contributions by employers are 30.75 per cent of gross wages up to FF6590 per month, with a marginal rate of 8 per cent above this.

Family welfare is again dealt with solely by child benefits. There is no benefit on the first child, but benefit rises sharply with family size. For the second, the benefit in 1980 was FF70 per week (about £7), the total amount therefore for a typical family (against £11.70 in the UK currently). For a family with four children (aged 7, 11, 14 and 16) total benefits were FF296 per week (about £30), against £23.40 currently in the UK. As compared with the UK larger families get more benefit, small families get somewhat less.

The system of emergency poor relief ('social aid') resembles that of Belgium as far as can be ascertained. There are here too no tied subsidies related to income levels. Social aid is dispensed at the local level on a discretionary basis, and appears to be of negligible importance.

The tax and family welfare system therefore implies reasonable incentives and low MRTs for those in work, while setting an income 'safety net' at very low 'subsistence' levels.

The similarity with Belgium however ends, as we turn to the unemployment compensation system. Virtually all employees are eligible for benefit ('special benefit') averaging about 68 per cent of gross earnings in their first year of unemployment. The exact formula is a small flat amount plus 65 per cent in the first quarter of unemployment, falling to 50 per cent in the fourth quarter. For the second year of unemployment, the percentage drops to around 50 per cent ('basic benefit', consisting of the same flat amount plus 42 per cent of gross earnings). For older workers only does this rate of benefit continue for up to the fourth year of unemployment, but for workers under 50 it ceases at the end of the second year. Once this basic benefit has ceased, the worker receives 'end of entitlement benefit' which in 1980 was a very small flat rate amount of FF154 per week (around £15).

Though the percentages given relate to gross earnings, they are less distorted than in Belgium as a guide to true replacement ratios, because in France alone of these four Continental countries are benefits taxable.

Furthermore, there are no minimum flat rate benefits in France. There is only a maximum flat rate which occurs at incomes 4.5 times average earnings or above. The result is that replacement ratios do not rise substantially as income levels fall, except the very lowest covered by social aid; at the same time they only start to drop significantly at very high income levels. Table III.6 illustrates this. Hence the French employment system is close to a pure ratio system, that is, one where the ratio is constant across the income scale. The ratio itself is high for the first year but then drops steeply over time. For most employees after two years, the system becomes flat rate but at such a low level that for only the very poorest would it afford a replacement ratio of any interest.

Because of the difference in system, our model could not be applied to France in the same form as to the UK. Figure III.1 illustrates the nature of the French labour market. The supply curve is shifted leftwards, but without any significant change in slope, as the replacement ratio is raised and then held invariant across all

TABLE III.6 *French Replacement Ratios (1981) (average earnings = 100)*

	Unemployed for				
Earnings	*3 Months*	*6 Months*	*1 Year*	*2 Years*	*After 2 Years*
m + 2 – wife not working*					
50	n.a.	n.a.	127.8	108.8	57.2
66	100	101.4	108.9	90.3	39.9
100	98.9	96.6	96.2	77.8	27.8
200	96.6	91.7	n.a.	n.a.	n.a.
*Single**					
50	n.a.	n.a.	132.4	110.2	50.2
66	100.7	101.4	120	97.5	36.5
100	98.9	96.6	108.5	86.1	25.4
200	96.6	92.1	n.a.	n.a.	n.a.

Source: for 3 months and 6 months figures only: OECD (1982) *Unemployment Compensation Replacement Rates*. These ratios do not allow for work expenses; for other ratios: Appendix E, estimates including work expenses.

* Aged less than 50, dismissed for 'economic reasons'.

relevant income ranges. We may reasonably suppose that this supply curve is rather inelastic. Unemployment is measured by the distance between $\bar{L}$ and $S'S'$, provided that $\bar{L}$ corresponds to those eligible for benefits.

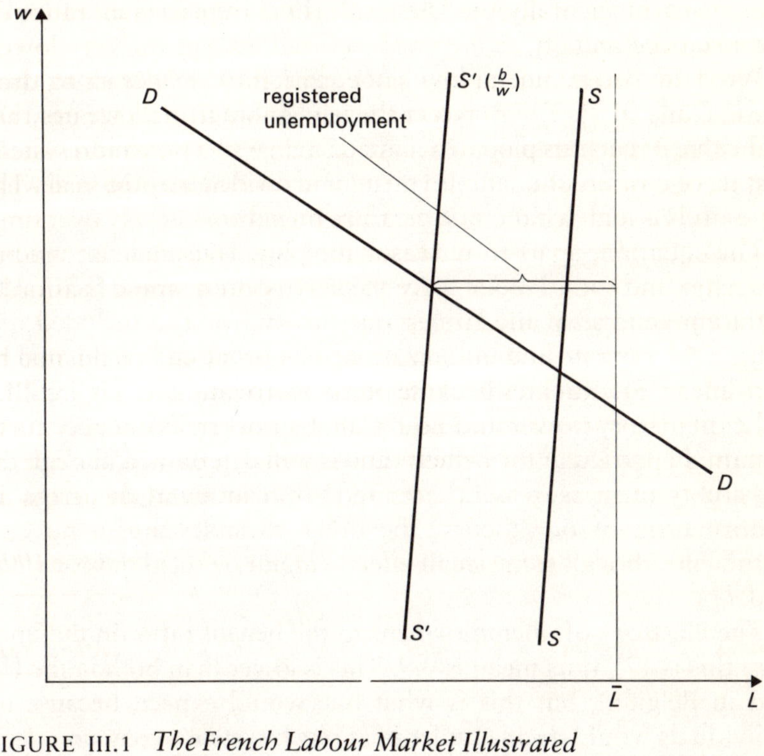

FIGURE III.1 *The French Labour Market Illustrated*

Now our model determines unemployment as a function of the (exogenous) benefit ratio and (exogenous) demographic factors, with little if any impact from real wages. Real wages are then mainly determined by the interaction of the total supply of labour (i.e. $\bar{L}$ minus unemployment, already determined) with the demand for labour. From our point of view, the real wage equation is of little interest, since real wages do not affect unemployment. The result of this set-up is that variables which affected unemployment in the UK and Belgium – such as employer taxes, union power, personal direct taxes, and world trade – barely do so here, rather they affect essentially the level and/or structure of real wages. For example, increased union power will raise real wages in the union sector, but because the total labour supply is unchanged, it will lower real wages in the non-union sector in such a way that the total demand for labour is unchanged. Its effect is to raise the union/non-union wage differential, but to leave average real wages broadly unchanged (this being incidentally the 'classical' effect of unions in an undistorted labour market).

We estimated an unemployment equation for France along these lines (Table III.7). To construct the benefit/wage ratio we used the real value of benefits paid to a married man with two children in the first three months of unemployment, and divided it by our real wage series. It is a somewhat crude measure however.

The equation, apart from seasonality, has as its main arguments this ratio and total labour force to proxy demographic factors; to maintain generality and to test our theory, we also included real wages, the tax rate and unionization. The equation is estimated by non-linear least squares because of autocorrelation. It has substantial explanatory power and no residual autocorrelation appears to remain. In particular the benefit ratio is well determined, though the possibility of measurement error requires caution at this stage. In confirmation of our theory, the other variables are in no case significant, though some small effects cannot be ruled out for *UNR* and T_L.

The elasticity of unemployment to the benefit ratio (in the units here this is 17) at its mean is 0.9. This is lower than both in the UK and in Belgium, but this is what one would expect, because no individuals would decide under the French system to remain unemployed for long periods, let alone indefinitely. The effect of this system will be to encourage workers to take higher duration spells but to continue to participate in employment on a regular basis.

WEST GERMANY

The tax and welfare system is similar to that of France and Belgium. Graduated tax tables produce MRTs which rise from about 35 per cent to a top rate of 65 per cent inclusive of 11 per cent social security contributions by employees (see Table III.8). VAT at 13 per cent (with a reduced rate of 6.5 per cent on 'necessities') raises these

TABLE III.7 *Unemployment Equation in France (Quarterly Data: 1963.1–1980.4, Non-linear least squares,* t*-ratio bracketed)*

Dependent variable	U_t *(millions)*
Constant	− 0.35
	(0.04)
$D1$	− 0.08
	(2.1)
$D2$	− 0.15
	(3.1)
$D3$	− 0.08
	(2.3)
$(b)/(w)t$	0.007
	(2.8)
$\log N_t$	− 0.044
	(0.05)
$\log \hat{w}_t$	0.12
	(0.5)
T_{Lt}	0.64
	(1.4)
UNR_t	3.3
	(1.3)
U_{t-1}	0.74
	(4.6)
ϱ_1	0.65
	(2.9)
ϱ_2	− 0.82
	(8.4)
ϱ_3	0.55
	(2.6)
DW	1.93
Box Pierce χ^2_8 (5 per cent critical value = 15.5)	10.4

Note: Mnemonics as for UK model (pp. 121–2).

TABLE III.8 *Marginal and Average Tax Rates in Germany, 1981 (average earnings = 100)*

	Single		*m + 2*			
Earnings	*MRT*	*ART*	*MRT*		*ART*	
133	53.9	32.5	35.4		24.3	
100	45.8*	26.7	35.4*		20.7	
60	37.7	23.3	35.4	(100)	13.5	(11.1)

* Interpolated

MRTs to a range from 43 per cent to 70 per cent. Employers' social security contributions are at a rate of 20.9 per cent of gross wages.

Family welfare again consists only of child benefits which are not means tested. The rates in 1980 were 11.5 DM per week (first child), 23 DM (second child), 46 DM for each subsequent child – respectively about £2.75, £5.50 and £10.75. These are lower than UK rates for average family size, but higher for the largest families.

There is also 'social aid'. As in France and Belgium it is administered by the local authorities. Income has to be supplemented up to 'levels of need', but there seems to be substantial discretion. Also '*Wohngeld*' is provided on a means-tested basis, i.e. housing costs are paid in full for those who fall below the statutory poverty levels. It has been possible to extract 'illustrative' details of these levels from German officials. These are of considerable interest since they are the closest approximation to the British supplementary benefit system to be found on the Continent.

The illustrative figures are 78 DM per week for a man, 62 DM for his wife, 59 DM for children over 11, 51 DM for children aged 8–11, 35 DM for younger children, 115 DM for rent (*Wohngeld*).

Replacement ratios and MRTs using these figures are placed in brackets in Tables III.8 and III.9. It can be seen that, if local government officials were to stick to them closely, and the criteria became widely known, there would be both a poverty trap and an unemployment trap in Germany as in the UK. At this stage it is probably wrong to make this assumption; it appears that local discretion is considerable, that some secrecy surrounds possible practices in each locality, and that quite possibly there are in many localities stringent tests of 'willingness to work' etc. Nevertheless, social aid payments have become significant since the mid-70s: in 1978, they were DM 10.45 billion, and in addition DM 2.1 billion was paid in *Wohngeld.*

Unemployment compensation in principle follows a ratio system. For the first year, the worker receives 68 per cent of his net income, thereafter 58 per cent indefinitely. While there are no explicit minimum rates, social aid may have introduced them implicitly; a maximum rate also occurs at 1.7 times average earnings. Table III.9 shows the resulting replacement ratios net of 33 DM per week assumed work expenses.

TABLE III.9 *Replacement Ratios – Germany (1981)** *(average earnings = 100)*

	Unemployment duration			
Earnings	*3 months*	*6 months*	*1 year*	*Thereafter*
m + 2 – wife not working				
66	94.2	88.8	79 (114)	69 (114)
100	94.0	88.3	75	65 (75)
200	92.2	81.2	n.a.	n.a.
Single				
66	93.0	86.7	77	65 (74)
100	96.3	88.5	74	63
200	92.7	84.0	n.a.	n.a.

Source: 3 months and 6 months (1978) OECD, 1982. These ratios do not allow for work expenses. Other ratios: Appendix E, include work expenses.
Note: * Figures in brackets assume 'social aid' illustrative levels set out in text.

The German labour market is therefore rather closer to the UK flat rate benefit regime than to a pure regime such as Italy or France. Unlike France, too, benefiit support is indefinite in duration. It can be pictured as in Figure III.1, showing a regime with a benefit ratio, only there will also be some tendency towards truncation at the lower end of the supply curve owing to social aid. The implication is that unemployment will depend not only on the statutory benefit ratio but also on real wages (negatively) and on union power (positively). Such an equation is shown in Table III.10 (without tax rate, since no time-series for this was available).

Non-linear least squares was used because of autocorrelation in the residuals; no significant autocorrelation beyond that allowed for here appears to remain. The statutory benefit ratio (now 68 per cent) in the first year was used for the replacement ratio series, *B*. This in fact only changed once in the period, in 1975 first quarter, when it rose from 62 per cent where it had been since 1960, to the current 68 per cent level. Hence B_t moves like a dummy variable. The coefficient on it is nevertheless well determined, in spite of its limited variation. The long-run elasticity of unemployment to the benefit ratio at the mean is 4.2, very similar to the UK estimate. This is consistent with a sizeable impact on German unemployment (around 0.3 million) arising from the rise in rates enacted in 1975. A further large increase appears to have arisen from the rise in unionization by about 4 percentage points since the mid-70s (the long-run impact of one percentage point change in *UNR* is 0.23 million, about the same as in the UK at current unemployment). Since then in fact German unemployment has risen by one million.

A contributory factor may also have been the increasing use of social aid, which we have not incorporated in this analysis. It should also be stressed that, unlike French benefit ratios, German ratios stay indefinitely at over 60 per cent.

Given the 'mixed' nature of the German model, we also estimated an equation for real wages (regarded as a 'demand price'). This equation is also shown in Table III.10 and is of some interest. Rises in output (rise in demand) and unemployment (fall in supply) raise real wages as expected, also rises in employer taxes (leftward shift of demand) lower them, though the coefficient falls just below the 5 per cent significance level.

ITALY

The Italian tax and welfare system follows the lines of the previous three. MRTs (Table III.11) rise from 8 per cent to a top rate of 82 per cent reached at 60 times average earnings. These rates include employee social security contributions of 7.8 per cent. Standard

TABLE III.10 *Unemployment and Real Wage Equation for Germany (Quarterly data, non-linear least squares, t-values bracketed)*

Dependent variable	U_t *(millions)* *1961.4–1980.1*		*log* w_t *1962.1–1980.4*
Constant	29.7 (1.0)	Constant	– 0.01 (0.8)
$D1$	0.15 (11.6)	$D1$	0.0014 (0.3)
$D2$	– 0.04 (1.0)	$D2$	0.011 (2.1)
$D3$	– 0.05 (3.7)	$D3$	0.036 (6.5)
		t	– 0.0003 (1.1)
$B^*{}_t$	2.5 (2.3)	T_{ft}	– 0.11 (1.6)
$\log N_t$	– 3.7 (1.2)	$\log \hat{O}_t$	0.24 (7.9)
UNR_t	17.9 (2.4)		
$\log \hat{w}_t$	– 0.18 (0.5)		
		$\hat{U}_t$	3.3 (5.2)
U_{t-1}	0.23 (1.1)	$\log w_{t-1}$	0.77 (22.9)
ϱ_1	0.92 (6.6)	ϱ_1	– 0.32 (2.6)
		ϱ_2	– 0.58 (4.6)
ϱ_3	– 0.09 (1.1)	ϱ_3	– 0.28 (2.2)
		ϱ_4	– 0.24 (2.0)
DW	2.08	DW	1.93
Box Pierce statistic (χ^2_8)	7.1	χ^2_8	13.7

* Statutory replacement ratio for 1st year: (i.e. 68 per cent currently)

VAT at 15 per cent (with four other rates, 2 per cent, 8 per cent, 18 per cent and 35 per cent), implies that VAT-inclusive MRTs rise from 22 per cent to a top rate of 84 per cent. Employers' social security contributions are at the rate of 40.25 per cent, one of the highest in Europe.

TABLE III.11 *Marginal and Average Tax Rates – Italy (1981) (average earnings = 100)*

Earnings	*Single*		*m + 2*	
	MRT	*ART*	*MRT*	*ART**
150	26	16.3	26	16.3
100	23	12.6	23	12.6
70	16	8.4	16	8.4
50	8	8	8	8

* excluding child benefit

Italy has a history of massive tax evasion, culminating in the tax reforms of 1974, which brought about the current system. This has reduced evasion; nevertheless, employers are believed still to evade the very high rates of social security contribution and there is certainly general evasion. Total tax evaded was recently estimated by a former Italian Finance Minister at 30,000 billion lire (about 7 per cent of GDP and 25 per cent of current tax revenue). The black economy in Italy has been variously estimated at 15–40 per cent of GDP. Hence the tax rates must be used carefully – and largely discounted – in any analysis.

Family welfare is dealt with by family allowances. These are flat benefits paid to each dependent provided their independent income does not exceed certain thresholds, but they do not vary with income otherwise. They are also extremely small. In 1980, a married man with two children and non-working wife would have received 6840 lire per week (under £4).

Social aid operates in Italy at the local authority level as in the other three Continental countries; it is discretionary payment of the poor law type. Little information could be obtained about the level of these payments, but the impression gained is that they are of little importance.

Unemployment compensation is on a pure ratio basis. There is a short-time scheme where workers laid off for a part of the week receive 80 per cent of their lost pay (net); this is in practice renewable indefinitely. Such workers are not of course recorded as unemployed but as on short time, though the distinction with such indefinite support is a fine one. For those wholly unemployed, compensation is paid at the rate of 2/3 of previous net pay; it is renewable in practice indefinitely.

TABLE III.12 *Replacement Ratios – Italy (1981) (average earnings = 100)*

Earnings	*3 months**	*6 months**	*1 year and all subsequent years*
m + 2 – wife not working			
50	n.a.	n.a.	90
66	77.2	59.4	83
100	85.0	61.8	79
200	79.2	57.1	76
Single			
50	n.a.	n.a.	88
66	77.8	55.2	81
100	77.9	54.7	76
200	78.4	55.4	73

Source: * OECD (1982) for 3 months and 6 months 1978; these ratios do not allow for work expenses. Others, Appendix E, include work expenses.

This 'special' benefit was started in 1968 and restricted to those made redundant. For those ineligible, 'normal' compensation is an exiguous 800 lire per day (less than 40p). This is paid indefinitely but can be ignored. There are no maximum or minimum rates set in respect of special benefit; hence it is a pure ratio system (apart from the 'normal' compensation).

We treated the Italian case as the French one, estimating an unemployment equation with the benefit ratio (the 'special' one) and labour force as arguments – Table III.13. Though the coefficient on the benefit ratio is significant, significant autocorrelation of 4th order is present, indicating that our seasonal adjustment procedure is deficient; allowance for the 4th order process reduces the benefit ratio effect to insignificance.

It would appear that in Italy the problems of data, perhaps more importantly of the rival lay-off subsidy scheme, and of the informal economy, make it hard to identify any clear effect of the formal benefit system; deeper research into Italian data and institutions is necessary.

TABLE III.13 *Unemployment Equation – Italy (Quarterly data: 1962.1–1980.4, t-values bracketed)*

Dependent Variable	U_t *(millions)*
Constant	− 11.1
	(1.5)
*D*1	0.083
	(1.8)
*D*2	− 0.173
	(3.8)
*D*3	0.088
	(1.9)
B_t^*	0.13
	(2.0)
log N_t	1.15
	(1.6)
U_{t-1}	0.75
	(8.6)
$\bar{R}^2$	0.78
DW	2.00
χ_4^2†	25.4

Notes: * the special benefit/income ratio: 0 to 1968; 0.68 thereafter.

† Godfrey, 1978, test – see also fn. Table III.3.

CONCLUSIONS

While our work on these four Continental countries is far from complete, there are a number of interim conclusions that emerge with relevance to UK unemployment.

First, the nature of the benefit system is crucial. Specifically, it matters much whether it is a *ratio* system, preventing the ratio of benefits to earnings from rising to high levels, or a flat rate system where the unemployment trap is likely to become progressively serious as incomes fall. Flat rate systems, as in the UK, are likely to induce high unemployment. This is illustrated by Belgium which alone of the four countries studied had such a system, very similar to that of the UK. Belgium has a very high unemployment level, rather higher than that of the UK and substantially higher than in the other three countries.

Second, the formal statistical tests have shown that the ratio of benefits to wages plays an important role in the determination of unemployment in at least three out of the four countries as in the UK.

Third, union power has a statistically important effect on unemployment. Both in the one country with a flat rate benefit system (Belgium) and in a second country (Germany) with a system intermediate between ratio and flat rate, union power has a powerful effect on unemployment. In the other two as expected, union power does not affect unemployment significantly; rather – though this was not investigated – it is likely to affect only the relative wages of union and non-union workers.

Fourth, there is no poverty trap of real importance in these countries (with the possible exception at very low incomes of Germany), because income assistance is given at the local level under stringent conditions descended from poor laws, while family allowances and child benefits are not in general means tested.

Finally, the evidence of these countries confirms that a *ratio* system of unemployment benefit (such as is implied by the cap proposal discussed earlier in the book) can be socially acceptable, as it is indeed accepted in France, Italy and (with some modification) Germany. In similar vein, less generous and more discretionary income assistance to the poor in work is socially accepted in all four countries. The proposals made earlier for improving the poverty trap rank as substantially more generous relative to average income levels than these Continental systems, and should accordingly be easily capable of social acceptability.

In all, we regard this examination of Continental experience as yielding substantial corroborative evidence and support for our policy proposals.

DATA SOURCES

Belgium

1.	Consumer price index – all items	1960:1–1981:4
2.	Industrial production index – total	1960:1–1981:3
3.	Unemployment – insured unemployed	1960:1–1981:4
4.	Index of hourly wage rates – mining, manufacturing, transport	1960:1–1981:4
5.	Money supply – MI	1960:1–1981:3

1–5 From OECD main economic indicators and DRI data bank

6. Trade unionization rate (linearly interpolated) — Annual, 1960–1980

From *Chiffres Significatifs de l'Évolution Sociale dans la Communaté Européenne de 1960 a 1980 (1981) Brussels, September*

7. Civilian labour force (linearly interpolated) — Annual, 1960–1980

From Eurostat 'Chronos' Computer, SOEC Luxembourg

8. Benefits (linearly interpolated) — Annual, 1971–1980

From *Office National de l'Emploi Rapport Annuel 1980* 1971 figure benefits = 0.6 gross wages used as a base to determine benefits from 1960 to 1970 from a wage index

9. Employer social security contributions — 1960–1980

From *Office National de Securité Sociale* (ONSS)

10. Employee social security contributions and average tax loss by married man plus two children constructed from series from ONSS; additional data from P. De Grauwe.

France

1.	Consumer price index – total	1960 : 1–1981 : 4
2.	Industrial production index – total	1960 : 1–1981 : 3
3.	Unemployment – total	1960 : 1–1981 : 4
4.	Index of hourly earnings – manufacturing	1960 : 1–1981 : 4
5.	Money supply – MI	1960 : 1–1981 : 3

1–5 From OECD main economic indicators and DRI Data Bank

6.	Trade unionization rate (linearly interpolated) same source as Belgium	Annual, 1960–1980
7.	Civilian labour force (linearly interpolated) same source as Belgium	Annual, 1960–1980
8.	Benefits (used to construct ratio) From INSEE	1960–1982
9.	Employers' social security contributions	1960–1981

From *Conseil National du Patronat Français*

10. Employee's social security contributions and average tax loss by married man plus two children constructed from series from *Ministère du Travail*

Germany

1.	Consumer price index – total	1960 : 1–1981 : 4
2.	Industrial production index – total	1960 : 1–1981 : 4
3.	Unemployment – total	1960 : 1–1981 : 4
4.	Index of hourly earnings – manufacturing	1960 : 1–1981 : 4
5.	Money supply – MI	1960 : 1–1981 : 4

1–5 From OECD – same source as Belgium

6.	Trade unionization rate (linearly interpolated) same source as Belgium	Annual, 1960–1980
7.	Civilian labour force (linearly interpolated) same source as Belgium	Annual, 1960–1980
8.	Benefits – ratio used as in main text	
9.	Employer social security contributions	1960–1980

From German Economic Institute

Italy

1.	Consumer price index – all items	1960 : 1–1981 : 4
2.	Industrial production index – total	1960 : 1–1981 : 4
3.	Unemployment – total	1960 : 1–1981 : 4
4.	Index of hourly wage rates – manufacturing	1960 : 1–1981 : 4
5.	Money supply – MI	1960 : 1–1981 : 4

1–5 From OECD – same source as Belgium

6.	Trade unionization rate (linearly interpolated) same source as Belgium	Annual, 1960–1980
7.	Civilian labour force (linearly interpolated)	Annual, 1960–1980
8.	Benefits – ratio used as in main text	
9.	Employer social security contribution	1960–1980

From *Instituto Nationale Della Previdenza Sociale, Roma* (INPS)

10. Employee social security contributions and average tax loss by married man and two children
    From *Ministro per le Finanze* and INPS, Rome.

APPENDICES

APPENDIX A

The Liverpool Model

A BRIEF ACCOUNT OF THE OVERALL LIVERPOOL MACROECONOMIC MODEL

The UK model has the structure set out in Minford (1980). (For detailed support of the following account, the reader is referred there; a listing of the model equations is available from the authors on request.) The model consists of the following.

(a) An interrelated set of private sector demands for stocks of money, government bonds (and net foreign assets), and durable goods, and for a flow of non-durable consumption goods; these demands depend on wealth and real returns.

(b) A government supply function of (narrow M1) money which together with the government and foreign sector budget constraints determines also the supply of bonds plus foreign assets.

(c) Efficient financial markets in the operational sense that expected returns are equated across domestic and international financial assets.

(d) Rational expectations (Muth, 1961) which is implemented operationally by using the model's forecasts as the expectations.

(e) The supply of output is modelled via a price equation, derived from an aggregate production function as a mark-up over costs which varies with the level of output.

(f) The labour market has a significantly large union sector, the non-union sector clears continuously (at levels heavily influenced by social security benefits). But the union's real wage target is seen as the outcome of intertemporal maximization of potential members' incomes, and given adjustment costs in firms' demand for labour, this gives rise to a union real wage which is a mark-up over expected non-union real wages and also dependent on lagged union real wages and firms' other cost factors. This real wage target is translated into a one-year nominal wage contract on the basis of expected inflation. Aggregating together union and non-union wages and substituting out firms' demand for labour, we obtain a reduced form real wage equation related positively to output, lagged real wages and employer taxes on labour, and negatively to unexpected inflation, benefits and employee taxes. Hence if there is unanticipated inflation, real wages fall, and so do output costs; the supply curve of output therefore shifts outwards temporarily. In subsequent periods, real wages gradually return to equilibrium, and output with it. This Lucas-type supply function is, however, derived by a rather different route from that chosen by Lucas and Rapping (1969), as explained in Part I.

(g) The current account external balance depends on the real exchange rate (defined as domestic relative to foreign consumer prices adjusted for the exchange rate) and domestic and foreign absorption (total final expenditure). As real wages, and so the real exchange rate rise, the demand for UK output and so labour falls, given balance on current account.

THE LABOUR MARKET IN DETAIL

Labour Market Structure

We distinguish a non-union and union sector for a given industry. The non-union sector we suppose to be competitive, with atomistic suppliers of labour facing atomistic firms. In Britain, this sector consists primarily of the small business sector of private industry. Examples are the numerous small road haulage firms in the highly unionized (approximately 95 per cent) Transport and Communication sector dominated by British Rail, British Road Services and the National Bus Company, and the large numbers of family engineering firms in the Metal Goods sector (approximately 69 per cent unionized). Additionally the major parts of certain sectors are non-unionized, this applies notably to agriculture (only 22 per cent unionized), construction (27 per cent), and timber and furniture (35 per cent).

The extent of formal unionization is not necessarily a good guide to the extent of union dominance over wages, because wage agreements for non-union employees are frequently linked automatically to union agreements (under 'agency shop' arrangements), and on the other hand wage agreements nationally negotiated by unions in highly unionized sectors (such as vehicles or engineering) are merely reference points for shop floor negotiation in individual firms in which the union may be powerless. Mulvey (1976) for example suggests in a study of 77 MLH manufacturing industries in 1976 that the union/non-union wage differential was 0 for industries covered only by national agreements, against 46–48 per cent for industries covered by company, district or local agreements, and 41–46 per cent for those covered by national with supplementary agreements. Unfortunately coverage data is only available from the early 70s; and even this is not free of interpretational problems. Unionization is the only reasonably long time-series, and it seems likely to be reasonably well correlated with the extent of union dominance in wage agreements. As a measure of the absolute extent of the non-union sector at a point of time it is unreliable; but the coverage data confirm the view that there is a significant part of the British economy where unions have no direct influence on wages. For example, in April 1973, as against an average unionization rate of 49 per cent, the extent of coverage by national-with-supplementary, or by company, district and local agreements was 43 per cent for manual men, 35 per cent for manual women and much less for non-manual workers. Given that the public sector has very high unionization rates, and effective coverage is probably close to 100 per cent, the extent of the non-union sector in Britain's private sector should not be underestimated.

Empirical Work on the UK Labour Market

Our labour demand (unemployment) and supply (wage) equations discussed in the text (for full details see Minford, 1982b) have been deliberately kept to the simplest form in order to economize on degrees of freedom. Possibly intensive searching would yield some insights into nuances of dynamic structure; but we doubt if much could be gained, because the major exogenous variables in the labour subsector are benefit and tax variables, for which the best predictor turns out to be close to the current value. The first differences of all these exogenous variables except T_L appear to show no significant autocorrelation up to the 8th order other than purely seasonal. T_F exhibits some negative 1st and 8th order autocorrelation which could form the basis for a better predictor. Planned/expected output creates more of a problem. Nickell (1981) reports encouraging results for a labour demand function in which quite complicated patterns of coefficients on future expected values are generated. At this stage, we have merely looked at expected values up to a year ahead using instrumental variables for the quarterly version and the model predictions for the annual.

Our study relates to most of the post-war time-series data conveniently available from the CSO's data bank; namely quarterly data for the whole economy, for manufacturing and for individual industries and for annual data for the whole economy only. The Liverpool model is annual and so only the latter equation is used in it; but the other work serves as a further check and is possibly more informative because it is quarterly.

Whole Economy Time-series

The results that follow are based on benefits and average net direct taxes paid by a married man with two children whose wife is not working. Clearly this is not properly representative of those on the margin of employment and unemployment. We have also therefore checked the sensitivity of our results for a variety of weighting procedures. A full set of results for benefits and tax series weighted according to unemployment shares for six household-types (single, married + 0, up to + 4 children) is available on request, but is not different in important aspects from those shown here.

A benefit-denial variable turned out to be generally insignificant in the quarterly analysis. An annual series was also not available for our full annual sample. We therefore dropped this variable altogether from the reported results.

In the tradition of most previous work, we began with unrestricted reduced form equations for wages and unemployment. While seriously affected by collinearity, arising from the lack of restrictions, they indicated clearly that the basic theory could provide powerful explanation. Benefits, tax and unionization variables were generally of correct sign and significant in both equations. We therefore proceeded to restricted structural estimation of our wage and unemployment equations.

With virtually no experimentation we arrived at the TSLS results shown in Table A.2. All variables have the correct sign and are significant. In the 'supply' or 'wage' equation we tested the following restrictions: that the coefficients on benefits b and tax rates T_L were (a) equal to each other and (b) also both equal to unity in the long run. (a) would come about if the benefit/net non-union wage *ratio* affected the supply of labour, an assumption that is widely made in the literature. (b) would occur under certain additional conditions, that in general seem unlikely to be met. In general we find that (a) is met, but (b) is not and report the results for (a) accordingly.

The fact that benefits and direct taxes have an equal coefficient in the supply or wage equation, but one that is significantly less than unity in the long run, suggests that versions of this equation with unemployment as the dependent variable and the benefit/income *ratio* as a regressor are mis-specified (unless the level of real wages is also included). The reason lies in the way w_c the non-union real wage, enters the supply equation which is as a complex dynamic term.

Unionization enters the supply equation strongly. The long-run elasticity of real wages to *UNR* (at its mean value of 0.48) is about unity.

It is tempting to attempt to derive an estimate of the union mark-up from this coefficient. However, it is clear that the coefficient is a convolution of factors which cannot be disentangled without further restrictions. What we can say is that there is *prima facie* evidence of a rise in the union mark-up during our sample period; and this is consistent with a number of studies (as indicated in the survey by Parsley, 1980), and most recently by Layard *et al*, 1978.

Another issue on which these results throw some light is the prevalence of one-year non-contingent contracts. The term $(\Delta \log P - PEXP_{-1})/4$ will have a coefficient of minus unity if such contracts are universal in the sector under investigation; its absolute size below unity indicates the proportion of workers governed by such contracts. It is normally regarded as a 'stylized fact' about the UK that most wages are governed by such contracts. Indeed this is confirmed by evidence from wage *rates*. Yet in Italy where inflation rates have been similar over the past decade, indexation is virtually universal, and this of course is equivalent to a shortening of contract length. Belgium and the Netherlands also have widespread indexation in spite of a lower inflation experience. It is also the case that recorded labour contract lengths (on wage rates) declined in the UK from about two years in the early 1950s to around one year by the mid-1970s (Minford and Hilliard, 1978). There is therefore some evidence that UK contract behaviour is sensitive to the inflation rate and yet that it is out of line with some Continental behaviour.

Our results which relate to earnings suggest that one-year contracts are far from universal. In fact the coefficient on P^{ue} was ultimately dropped because it had the wrong sign, besides being insignificant.

It is possible to reconcile this finding with the prevalence of one-year contracts for wage *rates* by appealing to wage drift. Presumably matters are arranged on the shop floor so that earnings are indexed to some degree to the inflation rate. Variation in overtime and piece rates or clocking on/off conventions, could well be used to achieve this effect. On this basis the UK contract behaviour is seen to be roughly in line with the Continental practices cited. At the same time there seems no reason to believe that the *change* in contract lengths evidenced by wage rate data would be seriously misleading. (Indeed, Minford and Hilliard found it to reflect the predictions obtained from a transactions-cost minimization approach.)

Other features of the real wage equation are the significant role of unemployment, the fairly speedy adjustment rate (90 per cent in two years), and the modest negative effect on real wages of the rising workforce. The unemployment term implies that the supply curve of labour is not infinitely elastic ('real wage rigidity') but has a pronounced upward slope; the (partial) long-run elasticity of unemployment to real wages is around −8, implying at current rates an elasticity of *labour supply* to real wages of just over unity and to real benefits of about −0.5.

The negative effect of the rise in workforce presumably reflects its bias towards married women and juveniles, who have, it would seem, in spite of strong opposition from male-dominated unions, succeeded in somewhat lowering the real supply price of labour.

The speed of adjustment should reflect approximately that of unionized firms in their labour demand decisions, (i.e. in the *U* equation). No cross-equation constraint was applied but the free estimates are encouragingly close (0.69 versus 0.75).

The demand for labour (here the unemployment) equation shows strong effects of output, real wages grossed up for employee taxes paid by employers, and productivity. The restriction that real wages and taxes have the same coefficient is rejected. This odd result does, however, not occur for manufacturing (results not reported) and suggests that it may be due to unusual behaviour in the non-manufacturing sector (especially perhaps the public sector). The unrestricted equation gives a much higher coefficient on taxes than on wages, which is hard to rationalize. We therefore prefer and have reported the restricted estimate.

Various issues can be raised with these equations. As far as specification tests are concerned, the equations are reasonably invariant both to changes in time period and to relatively obvious specification changes. Tables A.3 and A.4 illustrate. Stability over time periods is fairly impressive, both equations pass the Chow test and an *F*-test for equality of coefficients. (The Chow tests give *F*-values for the wage equation of 1.1 (truncated at 76.4), 0.6 (truncated at 67.1), for the unemployment equation of 1.04 and 1.0 respectively. The *F*-tests for constancy of coefficients (with the sample split in 1973) were 0.68 for real wages and 0.11 for unemployment.) The key parameter values do not move much; the only exception is the real wage cost coefficient in the unemployment equation, which drops away if experience from the mid-60s is not included.

The unemployment equation is free of autocorrelation, as indicated by the χ^2_4 test. The wage equation suffers from 3rd order autocorrelation; the χ^2_4 test is just significant at the 5 per cent level, and it turns out that the residual at the 3rd lag is also just significant in the regression for that test. However, the autocorrelation is modest and, while we have not corrected formally for it, correction does not affect our estimates.

Inclusion of a time trend in the wage equation and the labour force in the unemployment equation leaves parameter values unchanged, and both additional variables are insignificant.

Various other variables have been suggested as potential candidates for inclusion in the wage equation, within its overall specification. These include: the age structure of the population (those less than 20, A20, those more than 55, A55), the degree of toughness in denying benefit (*TOUGH*), inflows (*INF*) and outflows (*OUT*) from the unemployment register. Table A.4 shows results with a variety of these. They are uniformly disappointing, however. Table A.4 also shows that, if benefits and direct tax are split up, the coefficients are not significantly different, though that on tax is less well determined and the higher of the two. If employers' tax and real wages are split up in the unemployment equation, there is a significantly higher coefficient on tax which is strongly positive, while the coefficient on real wages drops to nothing. Nevertheless, it does seem reasonable to treat all real wage costs inclusive of tax as the relevant entity. What this result and the sensitivity of this coefficient to inclusion of mid-60s data suggest is that the specification of 'real wage costs' probably requires more research (notably on the expectational aspects).

Is there reverse causation from real wages to real benefits, and if so is it such as to bias our results? The vast proportion of benefits paid out (i.e. excluding the earnings related supplement which applied to under 20 per cent of the unemployed) have been determined by reference to flat rate entitlements and not by a ratio to earnings, and these entitlements are fixed about six months in advance of the year to which they apply. Furthermore, the entitlements have been mainly governed by political considerations (e.g. the Wilson Government's decision to raise benefits substantially in the late 60s) and the ratio to real wages has been permitted to vary considerably, as real wages have varied. This suggests that politicians have had in their minds varying 'poverty base lines' which have borne little systematic relationship since the mid-60s to real wages. It is, however, possible that current price changes affect both real wages and real benefits jointly. We used a version of the Wu test of exogeneity (see Smith, 1982) to check this; this regresses real wages on an instrumental variables (IV) estimate of real benefits, the other variables, and the residual of benefits from this IV estimate. Exogeneity is tested by the significance of this residual. As Table A.6 shows, there is some evidence of endogeneity, but it does not bias the coefficients seriously as the equation with the IV estimate of benefits above reveals.

We also found (Table A.5) no significant relationship from *lagged* real wages to real benefits, which suggests that whatever is determining benefits, it is probably not real wages. In fact, real benefits follow a random walk according to this work; that is, its change is random with no evidence of other determinants. This is not too surprising a result with such a highly politicized variable.

Unionization itself may respond to real wages and unemployment, and hence may bias the coefficients. We also carried out the Smith/Wu test for this, with a clearly negative result (Table A.5).

A word is necessary about the annual results for 1955–79, Table A.1. These were first estimated using *expected* output and inflation from the Liverpool model; however actual output outperformed the expected. As in the quarterly equations, the contract (unanticipated inflation) term is either zero or the wrong sign; nevertheless, this is surprising because the data are for wage *rates* where contracts are unambiguously important. This may be the result of aggregation over the calendar year. However, the long-run coefficients are similar to the quarterly ones for 1964–79. Such differences as there are (i.e. rather higher coefficients on *UNR* and *POP*) are presumably the result of the rather longer time period covered.

Empirically, therefore the whole economy equations give a reasonably robust performance. Nevertheless, they are based on a limited number of observations and one would wish to corroborate the coefficient estimates from other evidence. We now turn to our other work, before finally putting this in the context of previous work.

The Evidence from 17 Industries

The model we described earlier can be used at the industry level as a micro model. In our unemployment registration system, people register for particular jobs so that they can be classified by industry; we interpret the unemployment figures by industry as mirroring the original activities of the unemployed and so as closely reflecting changes in employment in that industry. Besides unemployment, we have real wages and output by industry, and – kindly provided from his unpublished research by Professor George Bain of Warwick University – we have unionization rates in 13 of the industries; where we do not have them, we have used some closely matching rates and failing that the aggregate unionization rate. The other variables do not vary across industries and remain our aggregate figures.

Tables A.6 and A.7 show our results industry by industry. It is striking how in all industries bar one, the benefit variable has a highly significant effect on real wages, while unionization in the industry is significant in eight of the industries and has *t*-values over 1.5 in another two. Agriculture has a perverse sign, possibly because the farm workers' union, though strong on paper, has been traditionally moderate. In the unemployment equations, in 15 of the industries real wage costs are significant, often highly so, and in the other two they have the appropriate sign and are merely not so well determined.

Hence for our key coefficients, for benefits, union power, and wage costs, there is widespread evidence in the industry level data. This represents strong and striking confirmation of our model of wages and unemployment at the most detailed level. There are over 1000 observations in these industry samples.

The Cross-Sectional Evidence from Regional Data in the UK

We do not have extensive time-series data on UK regions. However, we have annual data from 1971 to 1980, on wages, unemployment, working days lost in industrial disputes, working days lost through sickness, much of this is broken down by sex and manual/non-manual. We have, for 1978 alone, New Earnings Survey data on coverage by union agreements broken down in the same way. While this is insufficient data to estimate the full model across regions, it is sufficient to estimate for 1978 only the total (or 'reduced form') relationships between wages, unemployment etc, and the major exogenous variables, unionization (in this case union coverage) and some measure of regional resource endowments, to account for regional variation in demand for labour. This is likely to shed additional light on the controversial effects of union power. We looked at the effects on working days lost for good measure, since these can be an additional way of taking out benefits from additional union power.

Two measures were tried for regional endowments; one was public sector investment as a proxy for public capital and another was a single zero – one dummy for the South East. (Other measures are unfortunately not available at this stage.) It can be seen that these measures are in fact highly correlated, because of the South East's very high resource endowment.

The results for 1978 are shown in Table A.8.

There are limited numbers of observations covering 10 regions in all (SE, E. Anglia, SW, W. Midlands, E. Midlands, Yorks and Humberside, NW, NE, Wales and Scotland). Nevertheless, the results are of some corroborative interest, since they offer almost a controlled experiment in the effect of a single influence – unionization (contaminated only by the relative endowment factor).

For both men and women, union power has a highly significant effect on unemployment. For manual men the effect on real wages is significantly positive; for non-manual men and for women, the effect on real wages is positive, though not highly significant. There are strong positive effects on working days lost through both disputes and sickness. There is further confirmation here of our model, in particular, here in its unionization aspect.

NOTES TO TABLES A.1–A.8

Data = Quarterly 1964 (2) to 1979 (2), by SIC Industry Categories

		SOURCES
U (U_i)	Unemployment (of industry i)	Department of Employment (DE) *Gazette*
O (O_i)	Total output of all industries (of industry i)	Central Statistical Office
w (w_i)	Real average earnings (of industry i)	Central Statistical Office
T_F	Employers NI contributions as percentage of gross (national) average earnings, male manual workers, national figures.	*Annual Abstract of Statistics* DE *Gazette*
UNR (UNR_i)	National unionization rate (rate for industry i)	DE *Gazette* and Prof. George Bain, Warwick University
POP	National working population	*Economic Trends*
p^{ue}	$\Delta \log P - (PEXP_{-1}/4)$	

$PEXP_{-1}$	Expected average change of price level in coming year, i.e. expectation of: $\log [E_{-1} (P_0 + P_1 + P_2 + P_3)/4 - \log (P_{-1} + P_{-2} + P_{-3} + P_{-4})/4]$ The expected value in this expression $E_{-1}(\ \ )$ was derived by an instrumental regression on lagged values and on rates of change of output and money supply.	
b	A weighted average of real benefits (national figures) $\left[\frac{(B + \text{ERS}) \times 0.3 + (B + R + M) \times 0.7}{P}\right]$	
B	Flat rate benefits, man with wife and second child	Department of Health and Social Security
ERS	Earnings related supplement based on gross average earnings	K. Holden, University of Liverpool
R	Local authority rents	Department of the Environment
M	School meals	Department of Education and Science
T_L	Percentage of national gross average earnings lost in taxes and national insurance contributions (national figures) (man with wife and second child)	K. Holden, University of Liverpool
P	Retail price index (all items)	*Economic Trends*
$\hat{}$	denotes use of instrumental variable estimate	
$D1/2/3$	Seasonal dummies	

TABLE A.1 *3SLS Estimates of Supply and Demand Equations on Annual Data (t-values)**

1955–79	$\bar{R}^2$	*DW*	*BP*(6)	See
$\log U_t = 49.11 + 1.82 (\log \hat{w} + T_F)_t - 3.44 \log \hat{O}_t + .079\,t + 0.53 \log U_{t-1}$ (2.43) (1.09) (1.70) (1.16) (2.93)	0.87	1.52	11.2	0.185
$\log w_t = 3.95 - 0.034 \log \hat{U}_t + 0.12 (\log b + T_L)_t + 0.95\, \mathrm{UNR}_t - 0.61 \log \mathrm{POP}_t + 0.72 \log w_{t-1}$ (0.80) (0.93) (2.96) (2.78) (1.35) (4.5)	0.97	2.47	2.3	0.024

* *Notes*: Unexpected inflation failed to enter with the right sign.
For other notes, see notes above on pp. 121–2; the only exception is that b, T_L here refer to benefits and taxes weighted according to household shares in unemployment.

TABLE A.2 *Real Wage and Unemployment Equations for Whole Economy, (quarterly 1964.2–1979.2, t-values bracketed)*

$$\underset{}{\log w_t} = \underset{(1.5)}{0.34} - \underset{(2.75)}{0.00162D1} + \underset{(.41)}{0.0024D2} + \underset{(.77)}{0.0044D3} - \underset{(2.1)}{0.024} \log \hat{U}_t + \underset{(3.1)}{0.11} [(\log b) + T_L]_t$$

$$+ \underset{(2.4)}{0.45\, UNR_t} - \underset{(0.1)}{0.016 \log N_t} + \underset{(12.0)}{0.77 \log w_{t-1}}$$

$$\bar{R}^2 = 0.47;\ \text{S.e.e.} = 0.0125;\ \chi^2_4 = 10.3^*;\ DW = 1.719$$

$$\log U_t = \underset{(5.2)}{13.3} + \underset{(0.01)}{0.000419D1} - \underset{(3.52)}{0.125D2} + \underset{(0.13)}{0.0044D3} - \underset{(4.5)}{2.17} \log \hat{O}_t + \underset{(2.7)}{1.04} [(\log \hat{w}_t) + T_{Ft}]$$

$$+ \underset{(2.6)}{0.008\, t} + \underset{(11.3)}{0.744 \log U_{t-1}}$$

$$\bar{R}^2 = 0.96;\ \text{S.e.e.} = 0.4986;\ \chi^2_4 = 2.9^*;\ DW = 2.008$$

Source: Godfrey, 1978.

Notes: Instrumental estimates shown by ˆ

Instruments used: (Lagged) inflation, output, real wages, real benefits, unemployment; (current) change in log $M1$, T_F, UNR, T_L, $D1$, $D2$, $D3$.

* This is the Lagrange Multiplier test for residual independence (the regression residuals are regressed on the right-hand side variables and their lagged values, up to 4 in this case ; $T \times R^2$ where T is the sample size is distributed as χ^2). The critical value of χ^2_4 is 9.5 at the 5 per cent level (11.1 at the 2.5 per cent level).

TABLE A.3 *Real Wage and Unemployment Equations for Different Samples (whole economy, constant and seasonal dummies included but not reported)*

Dependent variable = *log* w_t						*log* U_t					
Sample =	64.2–79.2	64.2–73.1	73.2–79.2	64.2–76.4	67.1–79.2	Sample =	64.2–79.2	64.2–73.1	73.2–79.2	64.2–76.4	67.1–79.2
log $\hat{U}_t$	−0.024	0.010	−0.033	−0.022	−0.027	log $\hat{O}_t$	−2.17	−3.36	−2.2	−2.48	−2.2
	(2.1)	(0.5)	(1.6)	(1.8)	(1.7)		(4.5)	(3.4)	(3.3)	(4.7)	(4.6)
$(\log b_t) + T_{Lt}$	0.12	0.06	0.126	0.13	0.11	$(\log \hat{w}_t) + T_{Ft}$	1.04	1.69	0.07	1.7	0.18
	(3.2)	(0.7)	(1.4)	(2.9)	(2.0)		(2.7)	(1.3)	(0.1)	(3.2)	(0.3)
UNR_t	0.45	0.63	0.48	0.65	0.47	t	0.008	0.010	0.013	0.005	0.013
	(2.4)	(1.8)	(0.9)	(2.3)	(1.8)		(2.6)	(.7)	(2.2)	(1.3)	(3.4)
log N_t	−0.02	0.21	0.09	0.2	0.006	log U_{t-1}	0.74	0.78	0.71	0.70	0.68
	(0.07)	(0.4)	(0.1)	(0.7)	(0.02)		(11.3)	(8.7)	(7.0)	(9.5)	(9.0)
log w_{t-1}	0.77	0.72	0.77	0.68	0.78						
	(12.2)	(3.7)	(7.4)	(6.3)	(11.0)						
$\bar{R}^2$	0.98	0.95	0.86	0.98	0.97		0.96	0.94	0.90	0.94	0.94
S.e.e.	0.0155	0.0103	0.0183	0.0152	0.0161		0.097	0.062	0.116	0.096	0.097
RSS	0.01242	0.00181	0.00875	0.00975	0.010912		0.4987	0.0693	0.3624	0.3985	0.4035
DW	1.72	1.95	1.62	1.74	1.67		2.0	1.56	2.16	2.12	2.05

TABLE A.4 *Some Alternative Specifications (quarterly 1964.2–1979.2)*

Dependent variable = log w_t								*log* U_t		
			1964.2 – 1978.4				64.2 – 77.4			
$\hat{P}_t^{ue}$	0.3 (0.4)	0.4 (0.7)	–	–	–	–	–	$\log \hat{O}_t$	– 2.43 (5.6)	−2.13 (4.3)
$\log \hat{U}_t$	−0.023 (1.7)	−0.023 (1.8)	−0.029 (1.7)	−0.02 (1.6)	−0.02 (1.3)	−0.02 (2.0)	−0.02 (1.7)	$\log \hat{w}_t$	−0.04 (0.1)	–
$\log b_t$	0.11 (1.9)	–	–	–	–	–	–	$(\log \hat{w}_t) + T_{Ft}$	–	1.23 (2.5)
$(\log b_t) + T_{Lt})$	–	0.11 (1.9)	0.12 (3.1)	0.13 (3.3)	0.14 (2.6)	0.12 (3.2)	0.13 (2.7)	T_{Ft}	2.0 (4.7)	–
T_{Lt}	0.16 (1.0)	–	–	–	–	–	–	t	0.019 (4.6)	0.006 (1.3)
UNR_t	0.44 (2.3)	0.40 (1.5)	0.47 (2.2)	0.43 (2.2)	0.37 (1.5)	0.44 (2.2)	0.35 (1.6)	$\log U_{t-1}$	0.59 (8.1)	0.75 (11.2)
t	–	0.0003 (0.2)	–	–	–	–	–			
$\log N_t$	−0.002 (0.01)	−0.05 (0.2)	0.04 (0.2)	−0.08 (0.3)	−0.07 (0.3)	−0.02 (0.1)	−0.2 (0.6)	$\log N_t$	–	0.78 (0.5)
$\log w_{t-1}$	0.76 (11.1)	0.74 (8.6)	0.78 (12.1)	0.76 (11.3)	0.76 (11.6)	0.77 (11.8)	0.76 (8.2)			
log (*INF*)	–	–	−0.01 (0.5)	–	–	–	–			
log (*OUT*)	–	–	–	−0.02 (0.8)	–	–	–			
TOUGH	–	–	–	–	–	–	−0.007 (0.6)			
A55	–	–	–	–	–	0.0001 (0.5)	–			
A20	–	–	–	–	−0.04 (0.5)	–	–			

TABLE A.5 *Tests of Exogeneity for* b *and* UNR *(quarterly 1964.2–1979.2, constants and seasonal dummies included but not reported)*

Dependent variable	$\log w_t$				$\log b_t$	
$\hat{p}^{ue}$	0.42 (0.7)	−0.04 (0.1)	0.14 (0.3)	–	$\log b_{t-1}$	0.96 (18.4)
$\log \hat{U}_t$	−0.022 (1.8)	−0.023 (1.8)	−0.023 (2.0)	−0.020 (1.8)	$\log U_{t-1}$	0.009 (0.5)
$(\log \hat{b}_t) + T_{Lt}$	0.12 (3.0)	0.09 (2.2)	–	–	$\hat{p}^{ue}_t$	−0.15 (0.3)
$(\log b_t) + T_{Lt}$	–	–	0.12 (3.1)	0.11 (2.8)	$\log w_{t-1}$	−0.06 (0.5)
UNR_t	0.45 (2.2)	0.49 (2.4)	–	–	T_{Ft}	0.05 (0.4)
$\log N_t$	0.005 (0.02)	−0.16 (0.7)	0.03 (0.1)	−0.03 (0.1)	t	−0.0001 (0.1)
$\log w_{t-1}$	0.76 (11.1)	0.84 (14.2)	0.77 (11.4)	0.79 (12.4)	$\bar{R}^2$	0.93
$\log b_t - \log \hat{b}_t$	0.13 (1.85)	–	–	–	DW	1.76
$\hat{UNR}_t$	–	–	0.42 (2.0)	0.40 (1.9)	Box Pierce (χ^2_{16})	11.0
$UNR_t - \hat{UNR}_t$	–	–	0.63 (1.4)	–		

NOTES TO TABLE A.6

Industry Mnemonics

CAI	Chemical and Allied Industries
PPP	Paper, Printing and Publishing
TEX	Textiles
LLF	Leather
CF	Clothing and Footwear
TF	Timber and Furniture
AG	Agriculture
CON	Construction
MG	Metal Goods
GEW	Gas, Electricity and Water
TC	Transport and Communications
MM	Metal Manufacture
SME	Shipbuilding and Marine Engineering
V	Vehicles
BPG	Bricks, Pottery and Glass
FDT	Food, Drink and Tobacco
EEG	Electrical Engineering

TABLE A.6 *Real Wage Equations for Individual Industries (quarterly: 1964.2–1979.2, constants, seasonal dummies included but not shown)*

Dependent variable $\log w_{it}$	*CAI*	*TEX*	*LLF*	*CF*	*TF*	*PPP*	*AG*	*CON*	*MG*+	*GEW*	*TC*	*MM*+	*SME**	*V**	*BPG*	*FDT*	*EEG**	*Average*
$\dot{p}^{ue}$	–	–	–	– 0.64	– 0.10	– 0.46	–	–	– 0.45	–	– 0.31	– 0.92	–	– 0.48	–	–	–	–
t				(0.09)	(0.15)	(0.7)			(1.2)		(0.43)	(2.1)		(0.5)				
$\log \hat{U}_{it}$	– 0.008	– 0.007	– 0.005	– 0.013	– 0.008	– 0.006	– 0.076	– 0.02	– 0.009	– 0.038	– 0.029	– 0.015	– 0.028	– 0.007	– 0.011	– 0.015	– 0.009	– 0.02
	(0.4)	(0.8)	(0.5)	(1.2)	(0.8)	(0.6)	(1.6)	(1.4)	(1.0)	(1.6)	(1.5)	(1.5)	(1.3)	(0.7)	(1.0)	(1.1)	(1.1)	
$(\log b_t) + T_{Lt}$	0.125	0.24	0.135	0.13	0.18	0.15	0.34	0.2	0.11	0.11	0.13	0.14	0.17	0.15	0.102	0.10	0.12	0.15
	(1.9)	(4.1)	(2.9)	(2.8)	(2.9)	(3.0)	(3.1)	(3.2)	(2.5)	(1.3)	(2.6)	(2.6)	(2.7)	(2.4)	(2.3)	(2.0)	(2.9)	
$U\hat{N}R_{it}$	0.49	0.44	0.54	0.49	0.63	0.27	– 0.33	0.13	0.34	0.54	0.19	0.24	0.56	0.40	0.19	0.32	0.39	0.34
	(2.1)	(2.7)	(1.1)	(1.5)	(2.0)	(1.4)	(0.24)	(0.47)	(2.0)	(3.1)	(1.2)	(1.6)	(1.8)	(1.4)	(1.4)	(2.3)	(1.8)	
$\log N_t$	– 0.78	– 0.48	– 0.18	0.15	0.005	– 0.38	1.9	0.25	0.0004	– 0.01	– 0.4	– 0.001	– 0.17	– 0.81	– 0.36	– 0.62	– 0.29	
	(1.4)	(1.3)	(0.7)	(0.5)	(0.02)	(1.2)	(1.9)	(0.7)	(0.3)	(0.03)	(1.2)	(0.6)	(0.4)	(1.8)	(1.0)	(1.63)	(1.1)	
$\log w_{it-1}$	0.64	0.37	0.88	0.63	0.82	0.71	0.62	0.75	0.65	0.59	0.84	0.68	0.65	0.70	0.72	0.67	0.78	0.69
	(6.8)	(2.5)	(12.5)	(6.2)	(12.4)	(7.72)	(6.3)	(9.6)	(5.7)	(5.7)	(14.1)	(6.4)	(6.6)	(7.3)	(7.3)	(7.3)	(11.9)	
R^2	0.95	0.96	0.94	0.94	0.96	0.96	0.82	0.93	0.97	0.94	0.97	0.96	0.95	0.93	0.97	0.97	0.98	
DW	1.77	2.18	2.42	2.23	1.9	1.79	1.78	2.14	1.96	2.26	1.77	1.95	2.0	1.75	1.73	1.94	1.71	
Box-Pierce* (16)	11.09	4.12	21.69	5.30	3.66	9.23	5.56	7.49	6.60	9.74	9.60	11.63	17.41	14.98	5.62	8.04	10.83	

* *National UNR* (not instrumented) in place of UNR_i which is not available.

+ UNR_i for Metal Engineering Industry used for both MG and MM, whose UNR_i not available.

* Approx χ^2_{16} (5 per cent critical value = 26.3).

TABLE A.7 *Unemployment Equation Results for Individual Industries (quarterly 1964.2–1979.2, constant and seasonal dummies included but not tabulated,* t-*values bracketed)*

Dependent variable = *log* U_{it}

	CAI	TEX	LLF	CF	TF	PPP	AG	CON	MG	GEW	TC	MM	SME	V	BPG	FDT	EEG	Average (unweighted)
$\log \hat{O}_t$	−1.6	−3.7	−3.6	−4.8	−2.4	−2.3	−1.3	−2.7	−2.9	−1.2	−1.6	−1.9	−1.0	−3.7	−2.8	−2.5	−2.3	−2.5
	(5.3)	(3.0)	(3.5)	(3.4)	(3.5)	(3.5)	(3.1)	(5.2)	(3.4)	(4.1)	(6.2)	(2.0)	(1.6)	(1.8)	(3.6)	(4.9)	(3.7)	
$\left(\frac{\hat{O}_{it}}{O_t}\right)$	−2.8	−2.9	−6.6	−19.7	−50.3	−21.9	–	0.1	−46.8	−22.5	–	−18.5	33.8	46.8	−18.7	−5.2	–	–
	(0.5)	(0.3)	(0.6)	(0.9)	(3.1)	(2.0)		(0.3)	(2.4)	(3.8)		(1.1)	(1.4)	(1.7)	(1.1)	(8.5)		
$(\log \hat{w}_{it}) + T_{Ft}$	1.3	3.3	1.5	1.3	1.9	1.8	0.37	2.1	2.8	2.0	0.84	2.1	1.1	2.8	2.5	1.6	2.4	1.9
	(5.8)	(3.2)	(2.4)	(1.0)	(3.1)	(4.0)	(1.2)	(5.0)	(3.3)	(5.8)	(5.7)	(2.3)	(2.6)	(2.4)	(4.0)	(5.3)	(4.2)	
t	0.002	−0.0007	0.013	0.022	0.005	0.006	0.004	0.006	−0.005	−0.0	0.0034	−0.011	−0.0	0.017	0.0007	0.006	−0.002	
	(0.8)	(0.1)	(2.9)	(2.5)	(1.6)	(2.3)	(1.1)	(1.4)	(1.0)	(0.01)	(2.7)	(1.2)	(0.03)	(2.0)	(0.2)	(2.4)	(0.7)	0.004
$\log U_{it-1}$	0.79	0.63	0.68	0.6	0.68	0.71	0.83	0.75	0.62	0.90	0.81	0.79	0.84	0.62	0.69	0.73	0.77	0.73
	(16.7)	(7.0)	(8.4)	(6.4)	(9.1)	(10.7)	(10.7)	(12.5)	(7.0)	(25.5)	(17.3)	(9.8)	(15.5)	(5.6)	(9.4)	(13.8)	(12.9)	
$\bar{R}^2$	0.98	0.84	0.92	0.88	0.94	0.97	0.93	0.97	0.94	0.98	0.97	0.88	0.83	0.62	0.91	0.98	0.95	
DW	1.89	2.25	2.0	2.3	1.77	1.42	1.72	1.79	1.75	1.4	1.82	1.68	2.0	1.64	2.1	2.0	1.6	
Box-Pierce* (16)	13.5	10.1	7.9	8.4	17.1	20.7	21.1	13.3	12.8	17.4	12.3	15.6	14.9	14.6	9.3	13.9	13.2	

*Approx χ^2_{16} (5 per cent critical value = 26.3)

TABLE A.8 *Real Wages, Unemployment, Working Days Lost Equations for Regional Data in 10 Regions – 1978, (constants included but not reported,* t*-ratios bracketed)*

Dependent variable	*Union agreement coverage*	*SE dummy*	*Public sector* investment (£ bn)*	$\bar{R}^2$
A: log *w*				
Manual men	0.5	0.09	–	0.31
	(2.3)	(2.0)		
	(0.8)	–	0.07	0.38
	(2.5)		(2.2)	
Non-manual men	0.23	0.06	–	– 0.07
	(1.0)	(1.1)		
	0.24	–	0.06	0.03
	(1.2)		(1.4)	
All men	0.47	0.10	–	0.31
	(2.3)	(2.1)		
	0.45	–	0.08	0.4
	(2.5)		(2.5)	
Manual women	0.22	0.12	–	0.34
	(1.3)	(2.5)		
	0.21	–	0.10	0.54
	(1.7)		(3.5)	
Non-manual women	0.09	0.14	–	0.92
	(1.4)	(8.9)		
	0.07	–	0.1	0.9
	(0.8)		(7.0)	
All women	0.13	0.13	–	0.83
	(1.4)	(5.8)		
	0.1	–	0.1	0.88
	(1.3)		(7.0)	
B: *U*				
All men	2.86	0.09	–	0.63
	(3.4)	(0.4)		
	3.0	–	0.13	0.66
	(4.0)		(0.9)	
All women	3.75	0.07	–	0.53
	(2.67)	(0.2)		
	4.2	–	0.2	0.56
	(5.3)		(0.8)	

Dependent variable	*Union agreement coverage*	*SE dummy*	*Public sector* investment (£ bn)*	$\bar{R}^2$
C: *Working days lost by all men and women*				
(i) through sickness	6.33	0.51	–	0.79
	(5.5)	(1.8)		
	6.2	–	0.4	0.80
	(6.0)		(2.0)	
(ii) through disputes	6.8	0.36	–	0.68
	(3.9)	(0.8)		
	6.4	–	0.3	0.68
	(4.2)		(1.0)	

**Source*: *Cambridge Economic Policy Review*, July 1980, Vol. 6, No. 2, 'Urban and regional policy with provisional regional accounts, 1966–78'.

The Natural Rate: Estimates and Policy Effects

Our evaluation of the properties of the equations for the whole economy are based on the annual data because of compatibility with the rest of the model, the fact that they were estimated using rational expectations predictors from the model, and the longer period covered (1955–79). The long-run structural coefficients of these equations are:

$$\log U^* = -7.3 \log O^* + 3.87 (\log w^* + T_F) + 0.168t \text{ (years)}$$
$$\log w^* = -0.12 \log U^* + 0.43 (\log b + T_L)$$
$$- 2.18 \log POP + 3.39\ UNR$$

(* denotes equilibrium value of variable)

For comparison, those of the quarterly equations are:

$$\log U^* = -8.48 \log O^* + 4.06 (\log w^* + T_F) + 0.031t \text{ (quarters)}$$
$$\log w^* = -0.10 \log U^* + 0.48 (\log b + T_L)$$
$$- 0.07 \log POP + 1.96\ UNR$$

These, as can be seen, are not too different, with the possible exceptions of *POP* and *UNR*, but the annual are based on a longer sample which must be the major reason for this difference.

It turns out that in the rest of the model the long-run relationship between real wages and output, when absorption is constrained by the condition that the current account is in balance, is:

$$\log O^* = -0.65\, e^* + 0.46 \log WT$$

and that the long-run relationship between the real exchange rate and real wages (given by the price equation from the production function) is:

$$e^* = 1.86\,(\log w^* + T_F) - 0.033t \text{ (years)}$$

where WT = index of world trade volume, e = real exchange rate.

These equations were used for the evaluation of natural rates carried out in the main text.

APPENDIX B

A Detailed Account of the Tax and Benefit System of the UK in November 1982

INTRODUCTION

In analysing the causes of distortions in labour markets, it will be useful to begin by outlining the structure of the present systems of taxation and social security and then consider the type of figures generated under the existing systems and by their interaction.

THE PRESENT TAX STRUCTURE

Under current tax legislation, it is necessary to aggregate all chargeable incomes from the various recognized schedular sources (after allowing for permitted source deductions) so as to arrive at gross statutory income. From this we deduct certain types of financial obligation known as charges on income, the most important in the present context being relief for interest paid on owner-occupied houses. The resultant figure is known as the net statutory income from which is deducted the various personal allowances. Insofar as the concern is with persons in work or capable of work, the only relevant allowances are single person's (or wife's earned income) allowances and married man's allowance – the other personal allowances may be taken as having little effect on the work–leisure decision. Once taxable income has been computed in this way, the relevant amount is subjected to tax at the appropriate rate(s). The relevant rate for low income earners and those with taxable incomes up to £12,800 is 30 per cent, which is the basic rate of income tax. Leaving aside some obvious simplifications which may be considered desirable, the major difficulties stemming from the tax system centre on the level of tax thresholds and starting rate of income tax. For reasons already stated, we have preferred to concentrate our attentions on the former, whilst recognizing that the full dovetailing of FIS into the tax system cannot occur until computerization of the pay-as-you-earn system is achieved.

THE SOCIAL SECURITY SYSTEM

In the main body of the text a distinction was made between the 'unemployment' and 'poverty' traps. The former refers to the situation where an unemployed person receives benefits larger in amount than the earnings he may reasonably expect from employment. The poverty trap, by contrast, applies only to persons who are currently in work, but are dissuaded from further work effort because of the loss of means-tested benefits as their earnings increase. This distinction leads us to consider the social security system; first as regards those currently out of work who are entitled to unemployment and related benefits, and second as it concerns those who are in work but by virtue of their low earnings are entitled to some form of Family Income Supplement.

Benefits Payable to the Unemployed

At the outset it is necessary to distinguish between those persons who are unemployed for a short period of time (up to 12 months) and those who are unemployed over the longer period of time. For short-term claimants, the primary system of income support is provided by unemployment benefits which can be obtained as of right, provided the claimant had paid a certain number of national insurance contributions. The contribution conditions will not be detailed; it will suffice to note that, provided they are met, unemployment benefit (UB) will be given, whether or not the claimant has any other income. As this is not a means-tested benefit, the amount of the benefit will not be reduced if, for example, the claimant's spouse is working or if the household has investment income or capital resources by which it could otherwise maintain itself. By contrast, supplementary benefit, which is a complementary system of income support for short-term claimants, is a means-tested benefit, so that if the unemployed person's circumstances are such that he would receive more on this scale than on unemployment benefit, the latter will be 'topped up' to the supplementary benefit level of entitlement. Before considering the exact relationship between these two systems of income support for persons temporarily unemployed, it will be useful to consider how the level of primary support is calculated.

Until recently, unemployment benefit was seen to comprise two major elements. First, there was a scale rate element which was a flat rate benefit dependent upon age and domestic status, and second there was an earnings related supplement (ERS) which was paid in addition to the scale rate, and which, subject to certain conditions, represented a certain percentage of previous earnings. The ERS was seen as a means of temporarily cushioning the immediate impact of becoming unemployed, and so was only paid for the first six months of unemployment; thereafter, only the flat rate benefit was payable. After twelve months of unemployment even the flat rate benefit stops and thereafter the supplementary benefit applies.

As a result of the abolition of ERS during 1982, we expect that most short-term benefit claimants will in future be entitled to a level of state income commensurate with the SB scale, since the flat rate benefit is less than that provided by the supplementary scheme. In general terms, the only instances in which the UB rates will exceed the means-tested SB entitlement is where the latter has been reduced because of other household income (e.g. husband unemployed, but wife working) or where the household has capital resources in excess of the prescribed level. The only other major factor which may affect the decision of short-term beneficiaries as to whether or not to claim SB 'top up' is that rent and rate rebates which can be claimed from local authorities are available only to those on UB not those on SB.

We may summarize the present position by saying that the supplementary benefits level of income support is of relevance not only to the longer term unemployed, but also to many claimants who have been registered unemployed for twelve months or less. Let us therefore consider this scheme in some detail.

The level of supplementary benefit entitlement is determined by reference to several recognized categories of need. Firstly there are prescribed scale rate benefits which are intended to provide for day-to-day living expenses. These are determined by the domestic status of the claimant at the rates shown in Table B.2. As already indicated, these rates are higher than those provided by the UB scale rates. The second category of financial need which is recognized in calculating supplementary entitlement refers to housing costs. Tenants may claim for rent (provided reasonable) and rates; owner-occupiers can claim mortgage interest (not capital) payments, rates and £78 for nominal repairs. The third category of need relates to special circumstances, for example 'extra' payments may be incurred for heating or laundry or diet. The most relevant special circumstance allowance is the extra heating allowance available to households with one or more dependent children under five years old, since this is given automatically, regardless of whether or not there is any incapacity in the family. And in addition to these statutorily recognized needs categories, it is possible to claim Exceptional Needs Payments (ENP) which are discretionary lump-sum grants. Moreover, in an attempt to reduce the administrative costs of social security, a 'passport' system has been evolved, whereby entitlement to SB automatically entitles the claimant to free prescriptions, dental/optical treatment and school meals. However it should be borne in mind that SB is a means-tested benefit, so that the total value of all these benefits will be reduced by the amount of child benefit or earnings from part-time work (the first £4 is disregarded) or any other income.

Benefits Available to those in Work

It must not be thought that social security benefits can be claimed only by the unemployed, for there are a number of benefits which may be claimed by low-income earning families. By far the most important welfare benefit is Family Income Supplement (FIS) which may be claimed by those in full-time work with dependent children, provided the family 'income' does not exceed the prescribed amount. The details of how to compute family income and the limits of prescribed income, as well as the maximum amounts of supplement payable, will not be considered here, though they have of course been fully taken into account in Tables B.1–B.9 (pp. 147–91). What is important, indeed vital so far as a proper understanding of the poverty trap is concerned, is the formula for determining the amount of FIS payable, for this leads us to observe that for every extra £1 earned, 50 pence may be lost in benefit.

The general rule for determining the amount of FIS payable is that it represents one half the difference between the prescribed income level and the actual income received. Thus, if the legislation provided that the prescribed income level for a married couple with two children was £82, and the family income received was £72, then FIS payable is £5. The problem is that for every extra £1 earned, 50 per cent will be lost in FIS entitlement. Taking the previous example, earnings have now increased to £73, so FIS payable is £4.50, i.e. one half of (£82–73). We can see that this means-tested benefit is detrimental to those who seek to achieve earnings by increased work effort, for the rate of withdrawal of income subsidy represents an implicit tax of 50 per cent on earnings, and this is in addition to the explicit rate of income and national insurance taxation which adds another 38.75 per cent. As such, those in receipt of FIS may face an overall marginal tax rate of nearly 90 per cent for every extra £1 (gross) earnings. Indeed the marginal tax rates can be much higher, since those who claim FIS are automatically entitled to the same passported benefits as previously referred to under SB; they may also be entitled to rent and rate rebates, free school meals and a number of discretionary local authority benefits. If the total value of these benefits is taken into account, then as earnings increase, the rate of withdrawal of these means-tested benefits can be very high indeed. Detailed computations of marginal tax rates for low-income earners and the assumptions upon which they are based may be found in Table B.1.

INTERACTION OF TAX–TRANSFER SYSTEMS

Although it is widely recognized that both the tax and social security systems have failings in their own right, it should now be apparent that from a work-incentive viewpoint, the essential problem lies in the interaction of the two systems. Indeed let us be more specific about the interactive difficulty, for as we have seen the poverty trap is the *additive* tax burden imposed by the tax (38.75 per cent) and the implicit tax on subsidy withdrawals (at least 50 per cent); whereas the unemployment trap, where persons can receive more on the dole than in work, arises as a result of high benefit levels relative to low tax thresholds and high starting rates of tax. Although both traps may be alleviated by increasing tax thresholds and reducing initial tax rates, as we have already seen, such actions cannot in themselves remedy the poverty and unemployment anomalies. It is not necessary for us to reiterate our earlier theoretical analysis, instead we shall consider what in fact happens and how the present tax–transfer systems happen to be so damaging to those who seek to improve their economic well-being by hard work and increased responsibilities.

MARGINAL TAX RATES FOR DIFFERENT FAMILY TYPES (TABLE B.1)

Table B.1 (pp. 147–52) seeks to show how the marginal rate of tax is calculated for five types of family grouping (ranging from single persons to married couples with four children), given various gross earnings levels (ranging from £50 to £160 per week). In the Table B.1 series we have considered the position of an adult male taxpayer claimant, and in the case of married couples we have assumed the wife does not work; as regards the position of female persons this is considered in Table B.5.

The format of the tables shows the status of the earner for each income level less the tax and national insurance payments, so that the post-tax earnings may be readily computed. To this is added any social security payments to which the person may be entitled so as to arrive at gross disposable income. Bear in mind that some welfare benefits (e.g. FIS and CB) are given only if there are dependent children, whilst other benefits are given solely on income criteria (e.g. rent and rate rebates). We can now calculate the gross disposable income, from which work expenses assumed arbitrary at £8.25 per week, are deductible in arriving at net disposal income. The other assumptions underlying the figures are that tax rates and allowances, including national insurance payments as well as national welfare benefits rates, are those in force as at 1 December 1982. Housing costs assumed are £15 per week, representing £12 in rent and £3 in rates and whilst this is based on local authority estimates it does seem to be on the low side. (If other assumptions are made then the appropriate rebate tables may be consulted.) The main reason is that as rebate tables for December 1982 are not yet available, we have based our calculations on 1981 tables and local authority tenanted housing cost figures (source DHSS, *Social Security Statistics 1981*, Table 34.60). Work expenses assumed are £8.25 per week and this once again probably underestimates the cost of average travelling expenses to work (etc.) A similar figure has been used by Ralph Howell in his pioneering work *Why Work*? and so provides some means of comparing his results as at 1 January 1981 with our estimate at 1 December 1982. Where FIS is granted, there is an automatic entitlement to passported benefits, and in quantifying the value of these benefits we have taken the figures supplied by the DHSS (FIS1 1982), namely £1.50 per adult per week for medical and dental services, £3.00 for each child in respect of free meals and £1.50 for free milk and vitamins for each child that is under five years old.

Having dealt with all underlying assumptions we can now discuss the tables in detail.

In Table B.1(i) the position of single persons is considered and it can be seen that the tax system is progressive for those only earning up to about £110 per week. Thereafter it becomes proportional at the basic rate of income tax (38.75 per cent). The reason for this is that, whilst the basic rate of income tax is always present, rent and rate rebates are being lost as incomes rise up to about £100 and this is reflected in the marginal rates for one income level further up the scale. In Table B.1(ii), which represents the position of married couples, we have a similar tax profile with the marginal tax rate settling at the basic rate at income levels of about £120 per week.

However, when married couples with children are viewed we can see some very high marginal rates occurring. In Table B.1(iii) we consider a couple with one child, so for the first time we have FIS and passported benefits being withdrawn as the income of those on lowest earnings increases. And whilst marginal tax rates of more than 100 per cent are encountered at the lowest income levels, this shoots up to nearly 150 per cent for those in the £80.90 per week income range, for there FIS, rebates and passported benefits are all being withdrawn; only when gross income exceeds £120 per week is the underlying (proportional) basic rate of income tax likely to be encountered.

Tables B.1(iv) to (vi) describe the position of families with 2, 3 and 4 dependent children respectively, and much the same pattern is followed: namely, that those on the lowest incomes are met by marginal rates in excess of 100 per cent and as the qualifying level of FIS, passported benefits and rebates is exceeded, the marginal tax rates shoot up dramatically; thereafter followed by a falling marginal rate until the (proportional) basic rate is achieved at income levels of between £130 and £140 per week.

Table B.1 therefore informs us of the circumstances where excessively high marginal rates of tax are encountered and why they arise. In short it depicts the poverty trap and its essential characteristics.

TOTAL BENEFITS FOR DIFFERENT FAMILY TYPES (TABLE B.2)

Table B.2 (p. 153) shows how Supplementary Benefit entitlement is calculated for each of the five family groups, given our stated assumptions. In calculating the benefit entitlement of those claimants with dependent children, it is important to note that the amount of SB child allowance (not to be confused with child benefit which is payable to all persons with children) depends on the age of the child. As such we have tried to provide a family profile where the first child is aged under 5 years, thereby entitling the claimant to £8.75 child allowance and £1.90 extra heating allowance. Where there is a second child, the age assumed is between 11 and 15 years, resulting in a further £13.15 per week entitlement. Where there are three children, the third child is assumed to be between the ages of 5 and 11, giving rise to a further £8.75 per week. And finally in a four-child family we have assumed one child under 5 years, one under 11 years and two children aged between 11 and 15 years. Clearly if the age assumptions are changed, then the benefit entitlement may also change, but having stated our assumptions explicitly and noted that the type of family structure here envisaged is not particularly unrealistic, our results appear reasonable and representative of actual entitlements.

REPLACEMENT RATIOS FROM TABLES B.1 AND B.2 (TABLE B.3)

Table B.3 (p. 154) shows how the 'longer term' replacement ratio is calculated for each of the five family groups. It will be remembered that this ratio represents the benefit entitlement available if unemployed, as compared with the net earnings which such a person may reasonably expect in employment. The former figure is taken from Table B.2; and the latter figure shows net income entitlement as determined by Table B.1, on the assumption that the claimant's previous earnings (and hence potential present earnings) are the same gross amounts as shown in Table B.1. The vital observations to look for in the replacement ratio table are when, and under what circumstances, it exceeds or approximates unity, for in this event benefit entitlement exceeds net earnings potential so that an individual who seeks to optimize his position financially will remain unemployed – here we are in the unemployment trap. For single persons and married couples it will be seen that the ratios fall from amounts in excess of unity (those who fomerly worked at the lowest gross income levels) to relatively low levels for those who formerly enjoyed higher earnings. In general terms the lower the former earnings, the more worthwhile (or less costly) will be unemployment, both in absolute terms and relative to those who formerly enjoyed higher earnings. As for families with children, the general observation is that as the number increases the replacement ratio remains close to unity for increasingly higher levels of gross income.

SHORT-RUN REPLACEMENT RATIOS (TABLE B.4)

Table B.4 (pp. 154–65) compares the position of those who are initially working for six months and then become unemployed for the remaining six months with those who are working for the whole of the year. As unemployment benefit now represents taxable income, we have considered the work incentive profile on the assumption that the tax allowances are set off against the first six months of the financial year, so that only the excess allowances may be set off against income arising in the latter half of the year.

This enables us to understand more clearly the effects of the taxation of unemployment benefit upon the incentive to supply labour services.

In Table B.4(i) we depict the position of a single person in receipt of various levels of pre-unemployment income and our general conclusion is that the lower these earnings, the higher the replacement ratio, so that persons with higher income levels are less liable to benefit as a result of unemployment.

In Table B.4(ii) we look at the position of married couples and much the same profile is exhibited, but replacement ratios are significantly higher at the same pre-employment earnings as those illustrated in Table B.4(i).

Similarly, Tables B.4(iii) to B.4(vi), where we have considered families with one to four children, say that once again the replacement ratios tend to be correspondingly higher as the number of dependent children increases.

MARGINAL TAX RATES FOR MARRIED WOMEN (1)
(TABLE B.5)

In Table B.5 (pp. 166–75) the position of working wives is considered. The marginal rates of tax (as in Tables B.1(i) to B.1(vi) are calculated for two situations: first wife working, husband working (earning £130 p.w.) and second wife working, husband unemployed (earning unemployment benefit). For the latter calculation it is assumed the husband transfers his residual (unconsumed) tax allowance to his wife. In the first instance the marginal tax rate for all levels and categories of income earners is constant at the basic rate of income tax, normally 38.75 per cent. As such there is no disincentive effect for those persons who seek higher earnings. By contrast, where the husband receives unemployment and related benefits, a high marginal rate of tax is encountered at the lowest level of earnings and only gradually is the basic rate of income tax encountered. The reason for this has already been considered in relation to Table B.1, namely it is the withdrawal of means-tested benefits which exacerbates the position of the lowest income earners.

MARGINAL TAX RATES FOR MARRIED WOMEN (2) (TABLE B.6)

This table (pp. 176–80) represents an extension of Table B.5 in that the husband is now unemployed for more than 12 months, so that his entitlement to unemployment benefit is exhausted. Given our assumptions as to the wife's earnings and the full transference of his tax allowance to her, together with the welfare benefit entitlements available (e.g. FIS, child benefit and rebates), the husband will not be entitled to any supplementary benefit. Moreover, although the wife's post-tax earnings are enhanced as a result of the tax allowance transference, because the means-tested benefits are calculated on a gross income basis, high marginal rates of tax are still encountered. The tables, as may be expected, therefore, exhibit the highest marginal rates of tax at the lowest levels of wife's earnings and only reach the basic marginal tax rate at income levels of about £130 p.w., so that once again the greatest disincentive to work supply exists at the lower levels of income.

MARRIED COUPLE, BOTH INITIALLY WORKING (1) (TABLE B.7)

In Table B.7 (pp. 181–5) we are considering the position of a married couple with both parties working throughout the tax year, and comparing this with the situation where (a) the husband becomes unemployed at the beginning of the tax year, but the wife remains employed; and (b) the man remains working throughout the year but the wife becomes unemployed at the beginning; and (c) where both parties are unemployed from the beginning of the tax year.

One important difference between the circumstances depicted in (a) and (b) is that if the husband becomes unemployed, he can transfer his residual tax allowances to his wife, but if the wife becomes unemployed she cannot transfer her unconsumed tax allowances to her husband. This arises from the fact that whereas the lower personal allowance may be set off against total income generally, the wife's earned income relief is available only against her own earnings. So that if those earnings exceed this relief there can be no transference of the unconsumed allowance.

The top part of the table depicts the situation where the wife receives average female manual earnings (£85 p.w.) and the husband average male manual earnings (£140 p.w.). The bottom part of the table depicts the position where both parties are in receipt of 75 per cent of their respective average earnings. It will be observed that in all cases the couple will be financially better off if the husband remains working and the wife becomes unemployed, than if the converse situation were to occur and that the worse situation will be where both parties remain unemployed throughout the financial year.

MARRIED COUPLE, BOTH INITIALLY WORKING (2) (TABLE B.8)

Table B.8 (pp. 186–90) is analogous to Table B.7 in that the same employment situations are considered, save that we have considered Table B.7(a) (b) and (c) in the context of longer term unemployment benefits – Unemployment Benefit having been exhausted after one year, the relevant basis of entitlement being Supplementary Benefit. Once again the husband who is unemployed may transfer his tax allowance to his wife, but not *vice versa*, so that the same conclusions hold as for Table B.7 above.

REPLACEMENT RATIOS FROM TABLES B.7 AND B.8 (TABLE B.9)

This table (p. 191) presents the replacement ratios derived from Tables B.7 and B.8.

Column 1 gives the short-run replacement ratios calculated by dividing row 3 by row 1 in Tables B.7(i) to B.7(v) for the different family types initially earning both average and 75 per cent of average earnings. This shows the percentage of total income lost as a result of the wife becoming unemployed with the husband still working. Similarly, the column 2 ratios are calculated in the same way except here from Tables B.8(i) to B.8(v). Hence the long-run situation is depicted – that is, comparing total net income where both husband and wife were working, to where the husband is employed but the wife is in her second year of unemployment, her Unemployment Benefit having been exhausted.

Column 3 ratios are calculated by dividing row 4 by row 2 in Tables B.7(i) to B.7(v) hence comparing total net income for the family types where the wife is employed and husband unemployed, to total net income where both are unemployed. This shows the percentage of total income lost as a result of the wife becoming unemployed. The same method has been employed for column 4. Here the ratios are derived from Table B.8(i) to B.8(v) illustrating the long-term situation – that is comparing husband unemployed for longer than one year and wife employed, with both parties unemployed for longer than one year.

The above table illustrates the incentives for a wife to participate in employment. Even when her husband is working, short term unemployment spells (column 1) are relatively attractive for her particularly if she is low-paid; total withdrawal from the labour market (column 2) is, however, less attractive. If her husband is unemployed, incentives to participate are generally very low (columns 3 and 4).

TABLES B.1 (i)–B.1 (vi) *Marginal Tax Rates for Different Family Types*

TABLE B.1 (i)

Status	*Earnings per week*	*Tax due*	*NI*	*Child benefit*	*FIS*	*Rent rebate*	*Rate rebate*	*Others*	*Work expenses*	*Net income*	*Difference*	*MRT*
Single	50	5.97	4.40	–	–	7.65	2.03	–	8.25	41.06	–	–
Single	60	8.97	5.27	–	–	5.93	1.36	–	8.25	44.80	3.74	62.6%
Single	70	11.97	6.15	–	–	4.23	0.75	–	8.25	48.61	3.81	61.9%
Single	80	14.97	7.02	–	–	2.53	0.23	–	8.25	52.52	3.91	60.9%
Single	90	17.97	7.90	–	–	0.83	–	–	8.25	56.71	4.19	58.1%
Single	100	20.97	8.77	–	–	–	–	–	8.25	62.01	5.30	47.0%
Single	110	23.97	9.65	–	–	–	–	–	8.25	68.13	6.12	38.8%
Single	120	26.97	10.52	–	–	–	–	–	8.25	74.26	6.13	38.7%
Single	130	29.97	11.40	–	–	–	–	–	8.25	80.38	6.12	38.8%
Single	140	32.97	12.27	–	–	–	–	–	8.25	86.51	6.13	38.7%
Single	150	35.97	13.15	–	–	–	–	–	8.25	92.63	6.12	38.8%
Single	160	38.97	14.02	–	–	–	–	–	8.25	98.76	6.13	38.7%

TABLE B.1 (ii)

Status	*Earnings per week*	*Tax due*	*NI*	*Child benefit*	*FIS*	*Rent rebate*	*Rate rebate*	*Others*	*Work expenses*	*Net income*	*Difference*	*MRT*
Married	50	0.89	4.40	–	–	11.88	3.00	–	8.25	51.34	–	–
Married	60	3.89	5.27	–	–	9.73	2.66	–	8.25	54.98	3.64	63.6%
Married	70	6.89	6.15	–	–	7.58	1.91	–	8.25	58.20	3.22	67.8%
Married	80	9.89	7.02	–	–	5.64	1.25	–	8.25	61.73	3.53	64.7%
Married	90	12.89	7.90	–	–	3.94	0.65	–	8.25	65.55	3.82	61.8%
Married	100	15.89	8.77	–	–	2.24	0.18	–	8.25	69.51	3.96	60.4%
Married	110	18.89	9.65	–	–	0.71	–	–	8.25	73.92	4.41	55.9%
Married	120	21.89	10.52	–	–	–	–	–	8.25	79.34	5.42	45.8%
Married	130	24.89	11.40	–	–	–	–	–	8.25	85.46	6.12	38.8%
Married	140	27.89	12.27	–	–	–	–	–	8.25	91.59	6.13	38.7%
Married	150	30.89	13.15	–	–	–	–	–	8.25	97.71	6.12	38.8%
Married	160	33.89	14.02	–	–	–	–	–	8.25	103.84	6.13	38.7%

TABLE B.1 (iii)

Status	Earnings per week	Tax due	NI	Child benefit	FIS	Rent rebate	Rate rebate	Others	Work expenses	Net income	Difference	MRT
Married + 1 child	50	0.89	4.40	5.85	16.30	9.46	2.50	7.50 (passported)	8.25	78.07	–	–
Married + 1 child	60	3.89	5.27	5.85	11.30	8.21	2.14	7.50	8.25	77.59	– 0.48	104.8%
Married + 1 child	70	6.89	6.15	5.85	6.30	7.11	1.78	7.50	8.25	77.25	– 0.34	103.4%
Married + 1 child	80	9.89	7.02	5.85	1.30	6.23	1.45	7.50	8.25	77.17	– 0.08	100.8%
Married + 1 child	90	12.89	7.90	5.85	–	4.71	0.92	–	8.25	72.44	– 4.73	147.3%
Married + 1 child	100	15.89	8.77	5.85	–	3.01	0.34	–	8.25	76.29	3.85	61.5%
Married + 1 child	110	18.89	9.65	5.85	–	1.42	–	–	8.25	80.48	4.19	58.1%
Married + 1 child	120	21.89	10.52	5.85	–	–	–	–	8.25	85.19	4.71	52.9%
Married + 1 child	130	24.89	11.40	5.85	–	–	–	–	8.25	91.31	6.12	38.8%
Married + 1 child	140	27.89	12.27	5.85	–	–	–	–	8.25	97.44	6.13	38.7%
Married + 1 child	150	30.89	13.15	5.85	–	–	–	–	8.25	103.56	6.12	38.8%
Married + 1 child	160	33.89	14.02	5.85	–	–	–	–	8.25	109.69	6.13	38.7%

TABLE B.1 (iv)

Status	Earnings per week	Tax due	NI	Child benefit	FIS	Rent rebate	Rate rebate	Others	Work expenses	Net income	Difference	MRT
Married + 2 children	50	0.89	4.40	11.70	20.80	9.46	2.49	10.50 (passported)	8.25	91.41	–	–
Married + 2 children	60	3.89	5.27	11.70	15.80	8.31	2.14	10.50	8.25	91.04	– 0.37	103.7%
Married + 2 children	70	6.89	6.15	11.70	10.80	7.30	1.78	10.50	8.25	90.79	– 0.25	102.5%
Married + 2 children	80	9.89	7.02	11.70	5.80	6.28	1.44	10.50	8.25	90.56	– 0.23	102.3%
Married + 2 children	90	12.89	7.90	11.70	0.80	5.34	1.14	10.50	8.25	90.44	– 0.12	101.2%
Married + 2 children	100	15.89	8.77	11.70	–	3.77	0.59	–	8.25	83.15	– 7.29	172.9%
Married + 2 children	110	18.89	9.65	11.70	–	2.07	0.13	–	8.25	87.11	3.96	60.4%
Married + 2 children	120	21.89	10.52	11.70	–	–	–	–	8.25	91.04	3.93	60.7%
Married + 2 children	130	24.89	11.40	11.70	–	–	–	–	8.25	97.16	6.12	38.8%
Married + 2 children	140	27.89	12.27	11.70	–	–	–	–	8.25	103.29	6.13	38.7%
Married + 2 children	150	30.89	13.15	11.70	–	–	–	–	8.25	109.41	6.12	38.8%
Married + 2 children	160	33.89	14.02	11.70	–	–	–	–	8.25	115.54	6.13	38.7%

TABLE B.1 (v)

Status	Earnings per week	Tax due	NI	Child benefit	FIS	Rent rebate	Rate rebate	Others	Work expenses	Net income	Difference	MRT
Married + 3 children	50	0.89	4.40	17.55	25.00	8.31	2.51	13.50 (passported)	8.25	103.33	–	–
Married + 3 children	60	3.89	5.27	17.55	20.30	7.25	2.14	13.50	8.25	103.33	0.00	100.0%
Married + 3 children	70	6.89	6.15	17.55	15.30	6.25	1.78	13.50	8.25	103.09	– 0.24	102.4%
Married + 3 children	80	9.89	7.02	17.55	10.30	5.28	1.44	13.50	8.25	102.91	– 0.18	101.8%
Married + 3 children	90	12.89	7.90	17.55	5.30	4.42	1.14	13.50	8.25	102.87	– 0.04	100.4%
Married + 3 children	100	15.89	8.77	17.55	0.30	3.58	0.84	13.50	8.25	102.86	– 0.01	100.1%
Married + 3 children	110	18.89	9.65	17.55	–	1.93	0.31	–	8.25	93.00	– 9.86	198.6%
Married + 3 children	120	21.89	10.52	17.55	–	0.48	–	–	8.25	97.37	4.37	56.3%
Married + 3 children	130	24.89	11.40	17.55	–	–	–	–	8.25	103.01	5.64	43.6%
Married + 3 children	140	27.89	12.27	17.55	–	–	–	–	8.25	109.14	6.13	38.7%
Married + 3 children	150	30.89	13.15	17.55	–	–	–	–	8.25	115.26	6.12	38.8%
Married + 3 children	160	33.89	14.02	17.55	–	–	–	–	8.25	121.39	6.13	38.7%

TABLE B.1 (vi)

Status	*Earnings per week*	*Tax due*	*NI*	*Child benefit*	*FIS*	*Rent rebate*	*Rate rebate*	*Others*	*Work expenses*	*Net income*	*Difference*	*MRT*
Married + 4 children	50	0.89	4.40	23.40	27.00	7.74	2.65	16.50 (passported)	8.25	113.75	–	–
Married + 4 children	60	3.89	5.27	23.40	24.80	6.18	2.11	16.50	8.25	115.58	1.83	81.7%
Married + 4 children	70	6.89	6.15	23.40	19.80	5.22	1.75	16.50	8.25	115.38	– 0.2	102.0%
Married + 4 children	80	9.89	7.02	23.40	14.80	4.37	1.42	16.50	8.25	115.33	– 0.05	100.5%
Married + 4 children	90	12.89	7.90	23.40	9.80	3.52	1.12	16.50	8.25	115.30	– 0.03	100.3%
Married + 4 children	100	15.89	8.77	23.40	4.80	2.65	0.82	16.50	8.25	115.26	– 0.04	100.4%
Married + 4 children	110	18.89	9.65	23.40	–	1.78	0.51	–	8.25	98.90	– 16.36	263.6%
Married + 4 children	120	21.89	10.52	23.40	–	0.49	0.07	–	8.25	103.30	4.4	56.0%
Married + 4 children	130	24.89	11.40	23.40	–	–	–	–	8.25	108.86	5.56	44.4%
Married + 4 children	140	27.89	12.27	23.40	–	–	–	–	8.25	114.99	6.13	38.7%
Married + 4 children	150	30.89	13.15	23.40	–	–	–	–	8.25	121.11	6.12	38.8%
Married + 4 children	160	33.89	14.02	23.40	–	–	–	–	8.25	127.24	6.13	38.7%

TABLE B.2 *Total Long-term Benefits for Different Family Types*

Status	Supplementary benefit scale rate	Child allowance	Housing costs (local authority based)	Heating allowance (for child under 5 years old)	Free milk and vitamins (for child under 5 years old)	Free school meals	Free dental optical and prescriptions per adult	Total benefits
Single	25.70	–	15.00	–	–	–	1.50	42.20
Married	41.70	–	15.00	–	–	–	1.50 + 1.50	59.70
Married + 1 child under 5 years old	41.70	8.75	15.00	1.90	1.50	3.00	1.50 + 1.50	74.85
Married + 1 child under 5 1 child 11–15	41.70	8.75 + 13.15	15.00	1.90	1.50	6.00	1.50 + 1.50	91.00
Married + 1 child under 5 1 child under 11 1 child 11–15	41.70	17.50 + 13.15	15.00	1.90	1.50	9.00	1.50 + 1.50	102.75
Married + 1 child under 5 1 child under 11 2 children 11–15	41.70	17.50 + 26.30	15.00	1.90	1.50	12.00	1.50 + 1.50	118.90

TABLE B.3 *Replacement Ratios for Different Family Types, Net Income From Table B.1, Benefits from Table B.2.*

Gross income	*Single person*	*Married man**	*Married man* + 1 child*	*Married man* +2 children*	*Married man* + 3 children*	*Married man* + 4 children*
50	102.7%	116.3%	95.9%	99.6%	99.4%	104.5%
60	94.2%	108.6%	96.5%	99.9%	99.4%	102.9%
70	86.8%	102.6%	96.8%	100.2%	99.7%	103.0%
80	80.4%	96.7%	96.9%	100.4%	99.8%	103.1%
90	74.4%	91.1%	103.3%	100.6%	99.9%	103.1%
100	68.1%	85.8%	98.1%	109.4%	99.9%	103.2%
110	61.9%	80.8%	93.0%	104.4%	110.5%	120.2%
120	56.8%	75.2%	87.8%	99.9%	105.5%	115.1%
130	52.5%	69.9%	81.9%	93.7%	99.7%	109.2%
140	48.8%	65.2%	76.8%	88.1%	94.1%	103.4%
150	45.5%	61.1%	72.3%	83.2%	89.1%	98.2%
160	42.7%	57.5%	68.2%	78.8%	84.6%	93.4%

* wife not working

TABLES B.4(i)–B.4(vi) *Short-run Replacement Ratios*

TABLE B.4(i)

Status	*Earnings per week*	*Earnings after 6 months*	*Tax allowance*	*Residual allowance*	*UB/ Earnings*	*Tax on UB/ Tax, N.I.*	*Net income Unemployed/ In work*	*Child allowance*	*Child benefit*	*Rent rebate*	*Rate rebate*	*Other benefits S.B. Sup Ben P.B. Passports*	*Total (less work expenses)*	*Replacement ratio*
Single	50	1300	1565	265	25.00	4.44	20.56			9.30	2.77	3.63 1.50	37.76	
				10.20 pw	50.00	11.94 4.40	33.66	–	–	7.65	2.03	S.B. P.B. –	35.09	107.6

Single	60	1560	1565	5	25.00		7.44	17.56	–	–	9.30	2.77	3.63 S.B.	1.50 P.B.	34.76	97.0
				20 pw	60.00	17.94	5.27	36.79			5.93	1.36	–		35.83	
Single	70	1820	1565	–	25.00		7.50	17.50	–	–	9.30	2.77	3.63 S.B.	1.50 P.B.	34.70	87.8
					70.00	21	6.15	42.85			4.23	0.75	–		39.58	
Single	80	2080	1565	–	25.00		7.50	17.50	–	–	9.30	2.77	3.63 S.B.	1.50 P.B.	34.70	79.8
					80.00	24	7.02	48.98			2.53	0.23	–		43.49	
Single	90	2340	1565	–	25.00		7.50	17.50	–	–	9.30	2.77	3.63 S.B.	1.50 P.B.	34.70	72.8
					90.00	27	7.90	55.10			0.83	–	–		47.68	
Single	100	2600	1565	–	25.00		7.50	17.50	–	–	9.30	2.77	3.63 S.B.	1.50 P.B.	34.70	65.5
					100.00	30	8.77	61.23			–	–	–		52.98	
Single	110	2860	1565	–	25.00		7.50	17.50	–	–	9.30	2.77	3.63 S.B.	1.50 P.B.	34.70	58.7
					110.00	33	9.65	67.35			–	–	–		59.10	
Single	120	3120	1565	–	25.00		7.50	17.50	–	–	9.30	2.77	3.63 S.B.	1.50 P.B.	34.70	53.2
					120.00	36	10.52	73.48			–	–	–		65.23	
Single	130	3380	1565	–	25.00		7.50	17.50	–	–	9.30	2.77	3.63 S.B.	1.50 P.B.	34.70	48.6
					130.00	39	11.40	79.60			–	–	–		71.35	
Single	140	3640	1565	–	25.00		7.50	17.50	–	–	9.30	2.77	3.63 S.B.	1.50 P.B.	34.70	44.8
					140.00	42	12.27	85.73			–	–	–		77.48	
Single	150	3900	1565	–	25.00		7.50	17.50	–	–	9.30	2.77	3.63 S.B.	1.50 P.B.	34.70	41.5
					150.00	45	13.15	91.85			–	–	–		83.60	
Single	160	4160	1565	–	25.00		7.50	17.50	–	–	9.30	2.77	3.63 S.B.	1.50 P.B.	34.70	38.7
					160.00	48	14.02	97.98			–	–	–		89.73	

TABLE B.4(ii)

Status	Earnings per week	Earnings after 6 months	Tax allowance	Residual allowance	UB for man plus adult dependent/ Earnings	Tax on UB/ Tax, N.I.	Net income Unemployed/ In work	Child allowance (with UB)	Child benefit	Rent rebate	Rate rebate	Other benefits S.B. Sup Ben P.B. Passports	Total (less work expenses)	Replacement ratio
					40.45	–	40.45			10.65	2.97	2.63 3.00	59.70	
Married	50	1300	2445	1145				–	–			S.B. P.B.		118.4
				44.04 pw	50.00	1.79 4.40	43.81			11.88	3.00	–	50.44	
					40.45	2.14	38.31			10.65	2.97	2.63 3.00	57.56	
Married	60	1560	2445	885				–	–			S.B. P.B.		112.7
				34.04 pw	60.00	7.79 5.27	46.94			9.73	2.66	–	51.08	
					40.45	4.92	35.53			10.65	2.97	2.63 3.00	54.78	
Married	70	1820	2445	625				–	–			S.B. P.B.		106.8
				24.04 pw	70.00	13.79 6.15	50.06			7.58	1.91	–	51.30	
					40.45	7.92	32.53			10.65	2.97	2.63 3.00	51.78	
Married	80	2080	2445	365				–	–			S.B. P.B.		99.9
				14.04 pw	80.00	19.79 7.02	53.19			5.64	1.25	–	51.83	
					40.45	10.92	29.53			10.65	2.97	2.63 3.00	48.78	
Married	90	2340	2445	105				–	–			S.B. P.B.		92.6
				4.04 pw	90.00	25.79 7.90	56.31			3.94	0.65	–	52.65	

					40.45		12.14	28.31			10.65	2.97	2.63	3.00	47.56	
Married	100	2600	2445	–					–	–			S.B.	P.B.		85.8
					100.00	30	8.77	61.23			2.24	0.18	–		55.40	
					40.45		12.14	28.31			10.65	2.97	2.63	3.00	47.56	
Married	110	2860	2445	–					–	–			S.B.	P.B.		79.5
					110.00	33	9.65	67.35			0.71	–	–		59.81	
					40.45		12.14	28.31			10.65	2.97	2.63	3.00	47.56	
Married	120	3120	2445	–					–	–			S.B.	P.B.		72.9
					120.00	36	10.52	73.48			–	–	–		65.23	
					40.45		12.14	28.31			10.65	2.97	2.63	3.00	47.56	
Married	130	3380	2445	–					–	–			S.B.	P.B.		66.7
					130.00	39	11.40	79.60			–	–	–		71.35	
					40.45		12.14	28.31			10.65	2.97	2.63	3.00	47.56	
Married	140	3640	2445	–					–	–			S.B.	P.B.		61.4
					140.00	42	12.27	85.73			–	–	–		77.48	
					40.45		12.14	28.31			10.65	2.97	2.63	3.00	47.56	
Married	150	3900	2445	–					–	–			S.B.	P.B.		56.9
					150.00	45	13.15	91.85			–	–	–		83.60	
					40.45		12.14	28.31			10.65	2.97	2.63	3.00	47.56	
Married	160	4160	2445	–					–	–			S.B.	P.B.		53.0
					160.00	48	14.02	97.98			–	–	–		89.73	

TABLE B.4(iii)

Status	Earnings per week	Earnings after 6 months	Tax allowance	Residual allowance	UB for man plus adult dependent/ Earnings	Tax on UB/ Tax, N.I.	Net income Unemployed/ In work	Child allowance (with UB)	Child benefit	Rent rebate	Rate rebate	Other benefits S.P. Sup Ben P.B. Passports H Heating Allow	Total (less work expenses)	Replacement ratio
Married + 1 child	50	1300	2445	1145 44.04 pw	40.45	–	40.45	0.30	5.85	12.00	3.00	3.85SB 7.50PB 1.90H	74.85	96.9
					50.00	1.79 4.40	43.81			9.46	2.50	16.30 7.50 FIS PB	77.17	
Married + 1 child	60	1560	2445	885 34.04 pw	40.45	2.14	38.31	0.30	5.85	12.00	3.00	3.85SB 7.50PB 1.90H	72.71	98.7
					60.00	7.79 5.27	46.94	–		8.21	2.14	11.30 7.50 FIS PB	73.69	
Married + 1 child	70	1820	2445	625 24.04 pw	40.45	4.92	35.53	0.30	5.85	12.00	3.00	3.85SB 7.50PB 1.90H	69.93	99.4
					70.00	13.79 6.15	50.06	–		7.11	1.78	6.30 7.50 FIS PB	70.35	
Married + 1 child	80	2080	2445	365 10.04 pw	40.45	7.92	32.53	0.30	5.85	12.00	3.00	3.85SB 7.50PB 1.90H	66.93	99.5
					80.00	19.79 7.02	53.19	–		6.23	1.45	1.30 7.50 FIS PB	67.27	

Married					40.45		10.92	29.53	0.30		12.00	3.00	3.85SB 7.50PB	63.93	
+	90	2340	2445	105						5.85			1.90H		107.4
1 child				4.04 pw	90.00	25.79	7.90	56.31	–		4.71	0.92	–	59.54	
Married					40.45		12.14	28.31	0.30		12.00	3.00	3.85SB 7.50PB	62.71	
+	100	2600	2445	–						5.85			1.90H		100.9
1 child					100.00	30	8.77	61.23	–		3.01	0.34	–	62.18	
Married					40.45		12.14	28.31	0.30		12.00	3.00	3.85SB 7.50PB	62.71	
+	110	2860	2445	–						5.85			1.90H		94.5
1 child					110.00	33	9.65	67.35	–		1.42	–	–	66.37	
Married					40.45		12.14	28.31	0.30		12.00	3.00	3.85SB 7.50PB	62.71	
+	120	3120	2445	–						5.85			1.90H		88.2
1 child					120.00	36	10.52	73.48	–		–	–	–	71.08	
Married					40.45		12.14	28.31	0.30		12.00	3.00	3.85SB 7.50PB	62.71	
+	130	3380	2445	–						5.85			1.90H		81.2
1 child					130.00	39	11.40	79.60	–		–	–	–	77.20	
Married					40.45		12.14	28.31	0.30		12.00	3.00	3.85SB 7.50PB	62.71	
+	140	3640	2445	–						5.85			1.90H		75.3
1 child					140.00	42	12.27	85.73	–		–	–	–	83.33	
Married					40.45		12.14	28.31	0.30		12.00	3.00	3.85SB 7.50PB	62.71	
+	150	3900	2445	–						5.85			1.90H		70.1
1 child					150.00	45	13.15	91.85	–		–	–	–	89.45	
Married					40.45		12.14	28.31	0.30		12.00	3.00	3.85SB 7.50PB	62.71	
+	160	4160	2445	–						5.85			1.90H		65.6
1 child					160.00	48	14.02	97.98	–		–	–	–	95.58	

TABLE B.4(iv)

Status	Earnings per week	Earnings after 6 months	Tax allowance	Residual allowance	UB for man plus adult dependent/ Earnings	Tax on UB/ Tax, N.I.	Net income Unemployed/ In work	Child allowance (with UB)	Child benefit	Rent rebate	Rate rebate	Other benefits S.P. Sup Ben P.B. Passports H Heating Allow	Total (less work expenses)	Replacement ratio
Married + 2 children	50	1300	2445	1145	40.45	–	40.45	0.60	11.70	12.00	3.00	10.85SB 10.50PB 1.90H	91.00	100.5
				44.04 pw	50.00	1.79 4.40	43.81	–		9.46	2.49	20.80 10.50 FIS PB	90.51	
Married + 2 children	60	1560	2445	885	40.45	2.14	38.31	0.60	11.70	12.00	3.00	10.85SB 10.50PB 1.90H	88.86	101.9
				34.04 pw	60.00	7.79 5.27	46.94	–		8.31	2.14	15.80 10.50 FIS PB	87.14	
Married + 2 children	70	1820	2445	625	40.45	4.92	35.53	0.60	11.70	12.00	3.00	10.85SB 10.50PB 1.90H	86.08	102.6
				24.04 pw	70.00	13.79 6.15	50.06	–		7.30	1.78	10.80 10.50 FIS PB	83.89	
Married + 2 children	80	2080	2445	365	40.45	7.92	32.53	0.60	11.70	12.00	3.00	10.85SB 10.50PB 1.90H	83.08	103.0
				10.04 pw	80.00	19.79 7.02	53.19	–		6.28	1.44	5.80 10.50 FIS PB	80.66	

Married					40.45	10.92		29.53	0.60		12.00	3.00	10.85SB 10.50PB	80.08	
+	90	2340	2445	105						11.70			1.90H		103.3
2 children				4.04 pw	90.00	25.79	7.90	56.31	–		5.34	1.14	0.80 10.50 FIS PB	77.54	
Married					40.45	12.14		28.31	0.60		12.00	3.00	10.85SB 10.50PB	78.86	
+	100	2600	2445	–						11.70			1.90H		114.2
2 children				–	100.00	30	8.77	61.23	–		3.77	0.59	–	69.04	
Married					40.45	12.14		28.31	0.60		12.00	3.00	10.85SB 10.50PB	78.86	
+	110	2860	2445	–						11.70			1.90H		108.0
2 children				–	110.00	33	9.65	67.35	–		2.07	0.13	–	73.00	
Married					40.45	12.14		28.31	0.60		12.00	3.00	10.85SB 10.50PB	78.86	
+	120	3120	2445	–						11.70			1.90H		102.5
2 children				–	120.00	36	10.52	73.48	–		–	–	–	76.93	
Married					40.45	12.14		28.31	0.60		12.00	3.00	10.85SB 10.50PB	78.86	
+	130	3380	2445	–						11.70			1.90H		94.9
2 children				–	130.00	39	11.40	79.60	–		–	–	–	83.05	
Married					40.45	12.14		28.31	0.60		12.00	3.00	10.85SB 10.50PB	78.86	
+	140	3640	2445	–						11.70			1.90H		88.4
2 children				–	140.00	42	12.27	85.73	–		–	–	–	89.18	
Married					40.45	12.14		28.31	0.60		12.00	3.00	10.85SB 10.50PB	78.86	
+	150	3900	2445	–						11.70			1.90H		82.7
2 children				–	150.00	45	13.15	91.85	–		–	–	–	95.30	
Married					40.45	12.14		28.31	0.60		12.00	3.00	10.85SB 10.50PB	78.86	
+	160	4160	2445	–						11.70			1.90H		77.7
2 children				–	160.00	48	14.02	97.98	–		–	–	–	101.43	

TABLE B.4(v)

Status	Earnings per week	Earnings after 6 months	Tax allowance	Residual allowance	UB for man plus adult dependent/ Earnings	Tax on UB/ Tax, N.I.	Net income Unemployed/ In work	Child allowance (with UB)	Child benefit	Rent rebate	Rate rebate	Other benefits S.P. Sup Ben P.B. Passports H Heating Allow	Total (less work expenses)	Replacement ratio
Married					40.45	–	40.45	0.90		12.00	3.00	13.45SB 13.50PB	102.75	
+	50	1300	2445	1145					17.55			1.90H		100.3
3 children				44.04 pw	50.00	1.79 4.40	43.81	–		8.31	2.51	25.00 13.50	102.43	
												FIS P.B.		
Married					40.45	2.14	38.31	0.90		12.00	3.00	13.45SB 13.50PB	100.61	
+	60	1560	2445	885					17.55			1.90H		101.2
3 children				34.04 pw	60.00	7.79 5.27	46.94	–		7.25	2.14	20.30 13.50	99.43	
												FIS P.B.		
Married					40.45	4.92	35.53	0.90		12.00	3.00	13.45SB 13.50PB	97.83	
+	70	1820	2445	625					17.55			1.90H		101.7
3 children				24.04 pw	70.00	13.79 6.15	50.06	–		6.25	1.78	15.30 13.50	96.19	
												FIS PB		
Married					40.45	7.92	32.53	0.90		12.00	3.00	13.45SB 13.50PB	94.83	
+	80	2080	2445	325					17.55			1.90H		101.9
3 children				14.04 pw	80.00	19.79 7.02	53.19	–		5.28	1.44	10.30 13.50	93.01	
												FIS PB		

Married					40.45	10.92		29.53	0.90		12.00	3.00	13.45SB 13.50PB	91.83	
+	90	2340	2445	105						17.55			1.90H		102.1
3 children				4.04 pw	90.00	25.79	7.90	56.31	–		4.42	1.14	5.30 13.50 FIS PB	89.97	
Married					40.45	12.14		28.31	0.90		12.00	3.00	13.45SB 13.50PB	90.61	
+	100	2600	2445	–						17.55			1.90H		102.1
3 children					100.00	30	8.77	61.23	–		3.58	0.84	0.30 13.50 FIS PB	88.75	
Married					40.45	12.14		28.31	0.90		12.00	3.00	13.45SB 13.50PB	90.61	
+	110	2860	2445	–						17.55			1.90H		114.9
3 children					110.00	33	9.65	67.35	–		1.93	0.31	–	78.89	
Married					40.45	12.14		28.31	0.90		12.00	3.00	13.45SB 13.50PB	90.61	
+	120	3120	2445	–						17.55			1.90H		108.8
3 children					120.00	36	10.52	73.48	–		0.48	–	–	83.26	
Married					40.45	12.14		28.31	0.90		12.00	3.00	13.45SB 13.50PB	90.61	
+	130	3380	2445	–						17.55			1.90H		101.9
3 children					130.00	39	11.40	79.60	–		–	–	–	88.90	
Married					40.45	12.14		28.31	0.90		12.00	3.00	13.45SB 13.50PB	90.61	
+	140	3640	2445	–						17.55			1.90H		95.3
3 children					140.00	42	12.27	85.73	–		–	–	–	95.03	
Married					40.45	12.14		28.31	0.90		12.00	3.00	13.45SB 13.50PB	90.61	
+	150	3900	2445	–						17.55			1.90H		89.6
3 children					150.00	45	13.15	91.85	–		–	–	–	101.15	
Married					40.45	12.14		28.31	0.90		12.00	3.00	13.45SB 13.50PB	90.61	
+	160	4160	2445	–						17.55			1.90H		84.5
3 children					160.00	48	14.02	97.98	–		–	–	–	107.28	

TABLE B.4(vi)

Status	Earnings per week	Earnings after 6 months	Tax allowance	Residual allowance	UB for man plus adult dependent/ Earnings	Tax on UB/ Tax, N.I.	Net income Unemployed/ In work	Child allowance (with UB)	Child benefit	Rent rebate	Rate rebate	Other benefits S.P. Sup Ben P.B. Passports H Heating Allow	Total (less work expenses)	Replacement ratio
Married + 4 children	50	1300	2445	1145 44.04 pw	40.45 50.00	– 1.79 4.40	40.45 43.81	1.20 –	23.40	12.00 7.74	3.00 2.65	20.45SB 16.50PB 1.90H FIS P.B. 27.00 16.50	118.90 112.85	105.4
Married + 4 children	60	1560	2445	885 34.04 pw	40.45 60.00	2.14 7.79 5.27	38.31 46.94	1.20 –	23.40	12.00 6.18	3.00 2.11	20.45SB 16.50PB 1.90H FIS P.B. 24.80 16.50	116.76 111.68	104.5
Married + 4 children	70	1820	2445	625 24.04 pw	40.45 70.00	4.92 13.79 6.15	35.53 50.06	1.20 –	23.40	12.00 5.22	3.00 1.75	20.45SB 16.50PB 1.90H FIS P.B. 19.80 16.50	113.98 108.48	105.1
Married + 4 children	80	2080	2445	325 14.04 pw	40.45 80.00	7.92 19.79 7.02	32.53 53.19	1.20 –	23.40	12.00 4.37	3.00 1.42	20.45SB 16.50PB 1.90H FIS P.B. 14.80 16.50	110.98 105.43	105.3

Married					40.45	10.92		29.53	1.20		12.00	3.00	20.45SB 16.50PB	107.98	
+	90	2340	2445	105						23.40			1.90H		105.4
4 children				4.04 pw	90.00	25.79	7.9	56.31	–		3.52	1.12	FIS P.B.	102.40	
													9.80 16.50		
Married					40.45	12.14		28.31	1.20		12.00	3.00	20.45SB 16.50PB	106.76	
+	100	2600	2445	–						23.40			1.90H		105.5
4 children					100.00	30	8.77	61.23	–		2.65	0.82	FIS P.B.	101.15	
													4.80 16.50		
Married					40.45	12.14		28.31	1.20		12.00	3.00	20.45SB 16.50PB	106.76	
+	110	2860	2445	–						23.40			1.90H		125.9
4 children					110.00	33	9.65	67.35	–		1.78	0.51	–	84.79	
Married					40.45	12.14		28.31	1.20		12.00	3.00	20.45SB 16.50PB	106.76	
+	120	3120	2445	–						23.40			1.90H		119.7
4 children					120.00	36	10.52	73.48	–		0.49	0.07	–	89.19	
Married					40.45	12.14		28.31	1.20		12.00	3.00	20.45SB 16.50PB	106.76	
+	130	3380	2445	–						23.40			1.90H		112.7
4 children					130.00	39	11.40	79.60	–		–	–	–	94.75	
Married					40.45	12.14		28.31	1.20		12.00	3.00	20.45SB 16.50PB	106.76	
+	140	3640	2445	–						23.40			1.90H		105.8
4 children					140.00	42	12.27	85.73	–		–	–	–	100.88	
Married					40.45	12.14		28.31	1.20		12.00	3.00	20.45SB 16.50PB	106.76	
+	150	3900	2445	–						23.40			1.90H		99.8
4 children					150.00	45	13.15	91.85	–		–	–	–	107.00	
Married					40.45	12.14		28.31	1.20		12.00	3.00	20.45SB 16.50PB	106.76	
+	160	4160	2445	–						23.40			1.90H		94.3
4 children					160.00	48	14.02	97.98	–		–	–	–	113.13	

TABLES B.5(i)–B.5(x) *Marginal Tax Rates for Married Women (1)*

TABLE B.5(i)

Status	*Earnings per week*	*Net earnings*	*Husband's earnings or UB*	*Husband's net earnings*	*FIS*	*Child benefit*	*Child allowance*	*Rate + rent rebates*	*Work expenses*	*Child minding*	*Others*	*Total*	*Difference*	*MRT*
Married woman	50	39.63	130	93.71	–	–	–	–	16.50	–	–	116.84	–	–
Married woman	60	45.76	130	93.71	–	–	–	–	16.50	–	–	122.97	6.13	38.7
Married woman	70	51.88	130	93.71	–	–	–	–	16.50	–	–	129.09	6.12	38.7
Married woman	80	58.01	130	93.71	–	–	–	–	16.50	–	–	135.22	6.13	38.7
Married woman	90	64.13	130	93.71	–	–	–	–	16.50	–	–	141.34	6.12	38.7
Married woman	100	70.26	130	93.71	–	–	–	–	16.50	–	–	147.47	6.13	38.7
Married woman	110	76.38	130	93.71	–	–	–	–	16.50	–	–	153.59	6.12	38.7
Married woman	120	82.51	130	93.71	–	–	–	–	16.50	–	–	159.72	6.13	38.7
Married woman	130	88.63	130	93.71	–	–	–	–	16.50	–	–	165.84	6.12	38.7
Married woman	140	94.76	130	93.71	–	–	–	–	16.50	–	–	171.97	6.13	38.7
Married woman	150	100.88	130	93.71	–	–	–	–	16.50	–	–	178.09	6.12	38.7
Married woman	160	107.01	130	93.71	–	–	–	–	16.50	–	–	184.22	6.13	38.7

TABLE B.5(ii)

Status	*Earnings per week*	*Net earnings*	*Husband's earnings or UB*	*Husband's net earnings*	*FIS*	*Child benefit*	*Child allowance*	*Rate + rent rebates*	*Work expenses*	*Child minding*	*Others*	*Total*	*Difference*	*MRT*
Married woman	50	45.60	25.00 UB	–	–	–	–	1.56 6.50	8.25	–	–	70.41	–	–
Married woman	60	52.42	25.00	–	–	–	–	0.95 4.79	8.25	–	–	74.91	4.50	55.0
Married woman	70	58.54	25.00	–	–	–	–	0.35 3.09	8.25	–	–	78.73	3.82	61.8
Married woman	80	64.67	25.00	–	–	–	–	– 1.39	8.25	–	–	82.81	4.08	59.2
Married woman	90	70.79	25.00	–	–	–	–	–	8.25	–	–	87.54	4.73	52.7
Married woman	100	76.92	25.00	–	–	–	–	–	8.25	–	–	93.67	6.13	38.7
Married woman	110	83.04	25.00	–	–	–	–	–	8.25	–	–	99.79	6.12	38.7
Married woman	120	89.17	25.00	–	–	–	–	–	8.25	–	–	105.92	6.13	38.7
Married woman	130	95.29	25.00	–	–	–	–	–	8.25	–	–	112.04	6.12	38.7
Married woman	140	101.42	25.00	–	–	–	–	–	8.25	–	–	118.17	6.13	38.7
Married woman	150	107.54	25.00	–	–	–	–	–	8.25	–	–	124.29	6.12	38.7
Married woman	160	113.67	25.00	–	–	–	–	–	8.25	–	–	130.42	6.13	38.7

TABLE B.5(iii)

Status	Earnings per week	Net earnings	Husband's earnings or UB	Husband's net earnings	FIS	Child benefit	Child allowance	Rate + rent rebates	Work expenses	Child minding	Others	Total	Difference	MRT
Married woman + 1 child	50	39.63	130	93.71	–	5.85	–	–	16.50	5.00	–	117.69	–	–
Married woman + 1 child	60	45.76	130	93.71	–	5.85	–	–	16.50	5.00	–	123.82	6.13	38.7
Married woman + 1 child	70	51.88	130	93.71	–	5.85	–	–	16.50	5.00	–	129.94	6.12	38.7
Married woman + 1 child	80	58.01	130	93.71	–	5.85	–	–	16.50	5.00	–	136.07	6.13	38.7
Married woman + 1 child	90	64.13	130	93.71	–	5.85	–	–	16.50	5.00	–	142.19	6.12	38.7
Married woman + 1 child	100	70.26	130	93.71	–	5.85	–	–	16.50	5.00	–	148.32	6.13	38.7
Married woman + 1 child	110	76.38	130	93.71	–	5.85	–	–	16.50	5.00	–	154.44	6.12	38.7
Married woman + 1 child	120	82.51	130	93.71	–	5.85	–	–	16.50	5.00	–	160.57	6.13	38.7
Married woman + 1 child	130	88.63	130	93.71	–	5.85	–	–	16.50	5.00	–	166.69	6.12	38.7
Married woman + 1 child	140	94.76	130	93.71	–	5.85	–	–	16.50	5.00	–	172.82	6.13	38.7
Married woman + 1 child	150	100.88	130	93.71	–	5.85	–	–	16.50	5.00	–	178.94	6.12	38.7
Married woman + 1 child	160	107.01	130	93.71	–	5.85	–	–	16.50	5.00	–	185.07	6.13	38.7

TABLE B.5(iv)

Status	*Earnings per week*	*Net earnings*	*Husband's earnings or UB*	*Husband's net earnings*	*FIS*	*Child benefit*	*Child allowance*	*Rate + rent rebates*	*Work expenses*	*Child minding*	*Others*	*Total*	*Difference*	*MRT*
Married woman + 1 child	50	45.60	25.00 UB	–	3.75	5.85	0.30	1.59 6.63	8.25	–	7.50 passported	87.97	–	–
Married woman + 1 child	60	52.42	25.00	–	–	5.85	0.30	1.21 5.53	8.25	–	–	82.06	– 5.91	159.1
Married woman + 1 child	70	58.54	25.00	–	–	5.85	0.30	0.61 3.80	8.25	–	–	85.85	3.79	62.1
Married woman + 1 child	80	64.67	25.00	–	–	5.85	0.30	0.15 2.13	8.25	–	–	89.85	4.00	60.0
Married woman + 1 child	90	70.79	25.00	–	–	5.85	0.30	– 0.62	8.25	–	–	94.31	4.46	55.4
Married woman + 1 child	100	76.92	25.00	–	–	5.85	0.30	–	8.25	–	–	99.82	5.51	44.9
Married woman + 1 child	110	83.04	25.00	–	–	5.85	0.30	–	8.25	–	–	105.94	6.12	38.7
Married woman + 1 child	120	89.17	25.00	–	–	5.85	0.30	–	8.25	–	–	112.07	6.13	38.7
Married woman + 1 child	130	95.29	25.00	–	–	5.85	0.30	–	8.25	–	–	118.19	6.12	38.7
Married woman + 1 child	140	101.42	25.00	–	–	5.85	0.30	–	8.25	–	–	124.32	6.13	38.7
Married woman + 1 child	150	107.54	25.00	–	–	5.85	0.30	–	8.25	–	–	130.44	6.12	38.7
Married woman + 1 child	160	113.67	25.00	–	–	5.85	0.30	–	8.25	–	–	136.57	6.13	38.7

TABLE B.5(v)

Status	*Earnings per week*	*Net earnings*	*Husband's earnings or UB*	*Husband's net earnings*	*FIS*	*Child benefit*	*Child allowance*	*Rate + rent rebates*	*Work expenses*	*Child minding*	*Others*	*Total*	*Difference*	*MRT*
Married woman + 2 children	50	39.63	130	93.71	–	11.70	–	–	16.50	5.00	–	123.54	–	–
Married woman + 2 children	60	45.76	130	93.71	–	11.70	–	–	16.50	5.00	–	129.67	6.13	38.7
Married woman + 2 children	70	51.88	130	93.71	–	11.70	–	–	16.50	5.00	–	135.79	6.12	38.7
Married woman + 2 children	80	58.01	130	93.71	–	11.70	–	–	16.50	5.00	–	141.92	6.13	38.7
Married woman + 2 children	90	64.13	130	93.71	–	11.70	–	–	16.50	5.00	–	148.04	6.12	38.7
Married woman + 2 children	100	70.26	130	93.71	–	11.70	–	–	16.50	5.00	–	154.17	6.13	38.7
Married woman + 2 children	110	76.38	130	93.71	–	11.70	–	–	16.50	5.00	–	160.29	6.12	38.7
Married woman + 2 children	120	82.51	130	93.71	–	11.70	–	–	16.50	5.00	–	166.42	6.13	38.7
Married woman + 2 children	130	88.63	130	93.71	–	11.70	–	–	16.50	5.00	–	172.54	6.12	38.7
Married woman + 2 children	140	94.76	130	93.71	–	11.70	–	–	16.50	5.00	–	178.67	6.13	38.7
Married woman + 2 children	150	100.88	130	93.71	–	11.70	–	–	16.50	5.00	–	184.79	6.12	38.7
Married woman + 2 children	160	107.01	130	93.71	–	11.70	–	–	16.50	5.00	–	190.92	6.13	38.7

TABLE B.5(vi)

Status	Earnings per week	Net earnings	Husband's earnings or UB	Husband's net earnings	FIS	Child benefit	Child allowance	Rate + rent rebates	Work expenses	Child minding	Others	Total	Difference	MRT
Married woman + 2 children	50	45.60	25.00 UB	–	8.30	11.70	0.60	1.56 6.67	8.25	–	10.50 passported	101.68	–	–
Married woman + 2 children	60	52.42	25.00	–	3.30	11.70	0.60	1.26 5.66	8.25	–	10.50 passported	102.19	0.51	94.9
Married woman + 2 children	70	58.54	25.00	–	–	11.70	0.60	0.86 4.52	8.25	–	–	92.97	− 9.22	192.2
Married woman + 2 children	80	64.67	25.00	–	–	11.70	0.60	0.30 2.82	8.25	–	–	96.84	3.87	61.3
Married woman + 2 children	90	70.79	25.00	–	–	11.70	0.60	– 1.12	8.25	–	–	100.96	4.12	58.8
Married woman + 2 children	100	76.92	25.00	–	–	11.70	0.60	–	8.25	–	–	105.97	5.01	49.9
Married woman + 2 children	110	83.04	25.00	–	–	11.70	0.60	–	8.25	–	–	112.09	6.12	38.7
Married woman + 2 children	120	89.17	25.00	–	–	11.70	0.60	–	8.25	–	–	118.22	6.13	38.7
Married woman + 2 children	130	95.29	25.00	–	–	11.70	0.60	–	8.25	–	–	124.34	6.12	38.7
Married woman + 2 children	140	101.42	25.00	–	–	11.70	0.60	–	8.25	–	–	130.47	6.13	38.7
Married woman + 2 children	150	107.54	25.00	–	–	11.70	0.60	–	8.25	–	–	136.59	6.12	38.7
Married woman + 2 children	160	113.67	25.00	–	–	11.70	0.60	–	8.25	–	–	142.72	6.13	38.7

TABLE B.5(vii)

Status	*Earnings per week*	*Net earnings*	*Husband's earnings or UB*	*Husband's net earnings*	*FIS*	*Child benefit*	*Child allowance*	*Rate + rent rebates*	*Work expenses*	*Child minding*	*Others*	*Total*	*Difference*	*MRT*
Married woman + 3 children	50	39.63	130	93.71	–	17.55	–	–	16.50	5.00	–	129.39	–	–
Married woman + 3 children	60	45.76	130	93.71	–	17.55	–	–	16.50	5.00	–	135.52	6.13	38.7
Married woman + 3 children	70	51.88	130	93.71	–	17.55	–	–	16.50	5.00	–	141.64	6.12	38.7
Married woman + 3 children	80	58.01	130	93.71	–	17.55	–	–	16.50	5.00	–	147.77	6.13	38.7
Married woman + 3 children	90	64.13	130	93.71	–	17.55	–	–	16.50	5.00	–	153.89	6.12	38.7
Married woman + 3 children	100	70.26	130	93.71	–	17.55	–	–	16.50	5.00	–	160.02	6.13	38.7
Married woman + 3 children	110	76.38	130	93.71	–	17.55	–	–	16.50	5.00	–	166.14	6.12	38.7
Married woman + 3 children	120	82.51	130	93.71	–	17.55	–	–	16.50	5.00	–	172.27	6.13	38.7
Married woman + 3 children	130	88.63	130	93.71	–	17.55	–	–	16.50	5.00	–	178.39	6.12	38.7
Married woman + 3 children	140	94.76	130	93.71	–	17.55	–	–	16.50	5.00	–	184.52	6.13	38.7
Married woman + 3 children	150	100.88	130	93.71	–	17.55	–	–	16.50	5.00	–	190.64	6.12	38.7
Married woman + 3 children	160	107.01	130	93.71	–	17.55	–	–	16.50	5.00	–	196.77	6.13	38.7

TABLE B.5(viii)

Status	*Earnings per week*	*Net earnings*	*Husband's earnings or UB*	*Husband's net earnings*	*FIS*	*Child benefit*	*Child allowance*	*Rate + rent rebates*	*Work expenses*	*Child minding*	*Others*	*Total*	*Difference*	*MRT*
Married woman + 3 children	50	45.60	25.00 UB	–	12.80	17.55	0.90	1.54 5.55	8.25	–	13.50 passport	114.19	–	–
Married woman + 3 children	60	52.42	25.00	–	7.80	17.55	0.90	1.24 4.70	8.25	–	13.50	114.86	0.67	93.3
Married woman + 3 children	70	58.54	25.00	–	2.80	17.55	0.90	0.94 3.85	8.25	–	13.50	114.83	– 0.03	100.3
Married woman + 3 children	80	64.67	25.00	–	–	17.55	0.90	0.51 2.66	8.25	–	–	103.04	– 11.79	217.9
Married woman + 3 children	90	70.79	25.00	–	–	17.55	0.90	0.07 0.93	8.25	–	–	106.99	3.95	60.5
Married woman + 3 children	100	76.92	25.00	–	–	17.55	0.90	–	8.25	–	–	112.12	5.13	48.7
Married woman + 3 children	110	83.04	25.00	–	–	17.55	0.90	–	8.25	–	–	118.24	6.12	38.7
Married woman + 3 children	120	89.17	25.00	–	–	17.55	0.90	–	8.25	–	–	124.37	6.13	38.7
Married woman + 3 children	130	95.29	25.00	–	–	17.55	0.90	–	8.25	–	–	130.49	6.12	38.7
Married woman + 3 children	140	101.42	25.00	–	–	17.55	0.90	–	8.25	–	–	136.62	6.13	38.7
Married woman + 3 children	150	107.54	25.00	–	–	17.55	0.90	–	8.25	–	–	142.74	6.12	38.7
Married woman + 3 children	160	113.67	25.00	–	–	17.55	0.90	–	8.25	–	–	148.87	6.13	38.7

TABLE B.5(ix)

Status	Earnings per week	Net earnings	Husband's earnings or UB	Husband's net earnings	FIS	Child benefit	Child allowance	Rate + rent rebates	Work expenses	Child minding	Others	Total	Difference	MRT
Married woman + 4 children	50	39.63	130	93.71	–	23.40	–	–	16.50	5.00	–	135.24	–	–
Married woman + 4 children	60	45.76	130	93.71	–	23.40	–	–	16.50	5.00	–	141.37	6.13	38.7
Married woman + 4 children	70	51.88	130	93.71	–	23.40	–	–	16.50	5.00	–	147.49	6.12	38.7
Married woman + 4 children	80	58.01	130	93.71	–	23.40	–	–	16.50	5.00	–	153.62	6.13	38.7
Married woman + 4 children	90	64.13	130	93.71	–	23.40	–	–	16.50	5.00	–	159.74	6.12	38.7
Married woman + 4 children	100	70.26	130	93.71	–	23.40	–	–	16.50	5.00	–	165.87	6.13	38.7
Married woman + 4 children	110	76.38	130	93.71	–	23.40	–	–	16.50	5.00	–	171.99	6.12	38.7
Married woman + 4 children	120	82.51	130	93.71	–	23.40	–	–	16.50	5.00	–	178.12	6.13	38.7
Married woman + 4 children	130	88.63	130	93.71	–	23.40	–	–	16.50	5.00	–	184.24	6.12	38.7
Married woman + 4 children	140	94.76	130	93.71	–	23.40	–	–	16.50	5.00	–	190.37	6.13	38.7
Married woman + 4 children	150	100.88	130	93.71	–	23.40	–	–	16.50	5.00	–	196.49	6.12	38.7
Married woman + 4 children	160	107.01	130	93.71	–	23.40	–	–	16.50	5.00	–	202.62	6.13	38.7

TABLE B.5(x)

Status	Earnings per week	Net earnings	Husband's earnings or UB	Husband's net earnings	FIS	Child benefit	Child allowance	Rate + rent rebates	Work expenses	Child minding	Others	Total	Difference	MRT
Married woman + 4 children	50	45.60	25.00 UB	–	17.30	23.40	1.20	1.50 4.59	8.25	–	16.50 passport	126.84	–	–
Married woman + 4 children	60	52.42	25.00	–	12.30	23.40	1.20	1.20 3.74	8.25	–	16.50	127.51	0.67	93.3
Married woman + 4 children	70	58.54	25.00	–	7.30	23.40	1.20	0.90 2.89	8.25	–	16.50	127.48	– 0.03	100.3
Married woman + 4 children	80	64.67	25.00	–	2.30	23.40	1.20	0.60 2.04	8.25	–	16.50	127.46	– 0.02	100.2
Married woman + 4 children	90	70.79	25.00	–	–	23.40	1.20	0.23 0.73	8.25	–	–	113.10	– 14.36	243.6
Married woman + 4 children	100	76.92	25.00	–	–	23.40	1.20	– 0.04	8.25	–	–	118.31	5.21	47.9
Married woman + 4 children	110	83.04	25.00	–	–	23.40	1.20	–	8.25	–	–	124.39	6.08	39.2
Married woman + 4 children	120	89.17	25.00	–	–	23.40	1.20	–	8.25	–	–	130.52	6.13	38.7
Married woman + 4 children	130	95.29	25.00	–	–	23.40	1.20	–	8.25	–	–	136.64	6.12	38.7
Married woman + 4 children	140	101.42	25.00	–	–	23.40	1.20	–	8.25	–	–	142.77	6.13	38.7
Married woman + 4 children	150	107.54	25.00	–	–	23.40	1.20	–	8.25	–	–	148.89	6.12	38.7
Married woman + 4 children	160	113.67	25.00	–	–	23.40	1.20	–	8.25	–	–	155.02	6.13	38.7

TABLES B.6(i)–B.6(v) *Marginal Tax Rates for Married Women (2)*

TABLE B.6(i)

Status	*Wife's earnings per week*	*Net earnings*	*Husband's supplement benefit*	*Husband's net earnings*	*FIS*	*Child benefit*	*Child allowance*	*Rate + rent rebate*	*Work expenses*	*Child minding*	*Others*	*Total*	*Difference*	*MRT*
Married	50	45.60	–	–	–	–	–	3.00 11.88	8.25	–	–	52.23	–	
Married	60	54.73	–	–	–	–	–	9.73 2.66	8.25	–	–	58.87	6.64	33.6
Married	70	63.85	–	–	–	–	–	1.91 7.58	8.25	–	–	65.09	6.22	37.8
Married	80	72.11	–	–	–	–	–	1.25 5.64	8.25	–	–	70.75	5.66	43.4
Married	90	78.23	–	–	–	–	–	3.94 0.65	8.25	–	–	74.57	3.82	61.8
Married	100	84.35	–	–	–	–	–	0.18 2.24	8.25	–	–	78.53	3.96	60.4
Married	110	90.48	–	–	–	–	–	0.71 –	8.25	–	–	82.94	4.41	55.9
Married	120	96.61	–	–	–	–	–	–	8.25	–	–	88.36	5.42	45.8
Married	130	102.73	–	–	–	–	–	–	8.25	–	–	94.48	6.12	38.7
Married	140	108.86	–	–	–	–	–	–	8.25	–	–	100.61	6.13	38.7
Married	150	114.98	–	–	–	–	–	–	8.25	–	–	106.73	6.12	38.7
Married	160	121.11	–	–	–	–	–	–	8.25	–	–	102.86	6.13	38.7

TABLE B.6(ii)

Status	Wife's earnings per week	Net earnings	Husband's supplement benefit	Husband's net earnings	FIS	Child benefit	Child allowance	Rate + rent rebate	Work expenses	Child minding	Others	Total	Difference	MRT
Married + 1 child	50	45.60	–	–	16.30	5.85	–	250 9.46	8.25	–	7.50 passported	78.96	–	–
Married + 1 child	60	54.73	–	–	11.30	5.85	–	2.14 8.21	8.25	–	7.50	81.48	2.52	74.8
Married + 1 child	70	63.85	–	–	6.30	5.85	–	1.78 7.11	8.25	–	7.50	84.14	2.66	73.4
Married + 1 child	80	72.11	–	–	1.30	5.85	–	6.23 1.30	8.25	–	7.50	86.04	1.90	81.0
Married + 1 child	90	78.23	–	–	–	5.85	–	– 4.71	8.25	–	–	80.54	– 5.5	155.0
Married + 1 child	100	84.35	–	–	–	5.85	–	– 3.01	8.25	–	–	84.97	4.43	55.7
Married + 1 child	110	90.48	–	–	–	5.85	–	– 1.42	8.25	–	–	89.50	4.53	54.7
Married + 1 child	120	96.61	–	–	–	5.85	–	–	8.25	–	–	94.21	4.71	52.9
Married + 1 child	130	102.73	–	–	–	5.85	–	–	8.25	–	–	100.33	6.12	38.7
Married + 1 child	140	108.86	–	–	–	5.85	–	–	8.25	–	–	106.46	6.13	38.7
Married + 1 child	150	114.98	–	–	–	5.85	–	–	8.25	–	–	112.58	6.12	38.7
Married + 1 child	160	121.11	–	–	–	5.85	–	–	8.25	–	–	118.71	6.13	38.7

TABLE B.6(iii)

Status	*Wife's earnings per week*	*Net earnings*	*Husband's supplement benefit*	*Husband's net earnings*	*FIS*	*Child benefit*	*Child allowance*	*Rate + rent rebate*	*Work expenses*	*Child minding*	*Others*	*Total*	*Difference*	*MRT*
Married + 2 children	50	45.60	–	–	20.80	11.70	–	2.49 9.46	8.25	–	10.50 passported	92.30	–	–
Married + 2 children	60	54.73	–	–	15.80	11.70	–	2.14 8.31	8.25	–	10.50	94.93	2.63	73.7
Married + 2 children	70	63.85	–	–	10.80	11.70	–	1.78 7.30	8.25	–	10.50	97.68	2.75	72.5
Married + 2 children	80	72.11	–	–	5.80	11.70	–	1.44 6.28	8.25	–	10.50	99.58	1.90	81.0
Married + 2 children	90	78.23	–	–	0.80	11.70	–	1.14 5.34	8.25	–	10.50	99.46	− 0.12	101.2
Married + 2 children	100	84.35	–	–	–	11.70	–	0.59 3.77	8.25	–	–	92.17	− 7.29	172.9
Married + 2 children	110	90.48	–	–	–	11.70	–	0.13 2.07	8.25	–	–	96.13	3.96	60.4
Married + 2 children	120	96.61	–	–	–	11.70	–	–	8.25	–	–	100.06	3.93	60.7
Married + 2 children	130	102.73	–	–	–	11.70	–	–	8.25	–	–	106.18	6.12	38.7
Married + 2 children	140	108.86	–	–	–	11.70	–	–	8.25	–	–	112.31	6.13	38.7
Married + 2 children	150	114.98	–	–	–	11.70	–	–	8.25	–	–	118.43	6.12	38.7
Married + 2 children	160	121.11	–	–	–	11.70	–	–	8.25	–	–	124.46	6.13	38.7

TABLE B.6(iv)

Status	Wife's earnings per week	Net earnings	Husband's supplement benefit	Husband's net earnings	FIS	Child benefit	Child allowance	Rate + rent rebate	Work expenses	Child minding	Others	Total	Difference	MRT
Married + 3 children	50	45.60	–	–	25.00	17.55	–	2.51 8.31	8.25	–	13.50	104.22	–	–
Married + 3 children	60	54.73	–	–	20.30	17.55	–	2.14 7.25	8.25	–	13.50	107.22	3.00	70.0
Married + 3 children	70	63.85	–	–	15.30	17.55	–	1.78 6.25	8.25	–	13.50	109.98	2.76	72.4
Married + 3 children	80	72.11	–	–	10.30	17.55	–	1.44 5.28	8.25	–	13.50	111.93	1.95	80.5
Married + 3 children	90	78.23	–	–	5.30	17.55	–	1.14 4.42	8.25	–	13.50	111.89	– 0.04	100.4
Married + 3 children	100	84.35	–	–	0.30	17.55	–	0.84 3.58	8.25	–	13.50	111.88	– 0.01	100.1
Married + 3 children	110	90.48	–	–	–	17.55	–	0.31 1.93	8.25	–	–	102.02	– 9.86	198.6
Married + 3 children	120	96.61	–	–	–	17.55	–	– 0.48	8.25	–	–	106.36	4.37	56.3
Married + 3 children	130	102.73	–	–	–	17.55	–	–	8.25	–	–	112.03	5.64	43.6
Married + 3 children	140	108.86	–	–	–	17.55	–	–	8.25	–	–	118.16	6.13	38.7
Married + 3 children	150	114.98	–	–	–	17.55	–	–	8.25	–	–	124.28	6.12	38.7
Married + 3 children	160	121.11	–	–	–	17.55	–	–	8.25	–	–	130.41	6.13	38.7

TABLE B.6(v)

Status	Wife's earnings per week	Net earnings	Husband's supplement benefit	Husband's net earnings	FIS	Child benefit	Child allowance	Rate + rent rebate	Work expenses	Child minding	Others	Total	Difference	MRT
Married + 4 children	50	45.60	–	–	27.00	23.40	–	2.65 7.74	8.25	–	16.50 passported	114.64	–	–
Married + 4 children	60	54.73	–	–	24.80	23.40	–	2.11 6.18	8.25	–	16.50	119.47	4.83	51.7
Married + 4 children	70	63.85	–	–	19.80	23.40	–	1.75 5.22	8.25	–	16.50	122.27	2.80	72.0
Married + 4 children	80	72.11	–	–	14.80	23.40	–	1.42 4.37	8.25	–	16.50	124.35	2.08	79.2
Married + 4 children	90	78.23	–	–	9.80	23.40	–	1.12 3.52	8.25	–	16.50	124.32	– 0.03	100.3
Married + 4 children	100	84.35	–	–	4.80	23.40	–	0.82 2.65	8.25	–	16.50	124.28	– 0.04	100.4
Married + 4 children	110	90.48	–	–	–	23.40	–	0.51 1.78	8.25	–	–	107.92	– 16.36	263.6
Married + 4 children	120	96.61	–	–	–	23.40	–	0.07 0.49	8.25	–	–	112.32	4.40	56.0
Married + 4 children	130	102.73	–	–	–	23.40	–	–	8.25	–	–	117.88	5.56	44.4
Married + 4 children	140	108.86	–	–	–	23.40	–	–	8.25	–	–	124.01	6.13	38.7
Married + 4 children	150	114.98	–	–	–	23.40	–	–	8.25	–	–	130.13	6.12	38.7
Married + 4 children	160	121.11	–	–	–	23.40	–	–	8.25	–	–	136.26	6.13	38.7

TABLES B.7(i)–B.7(v) *Married Couple, Both Initially Working (1)*

TABLE B.7(i)

Status	*Employment situation*	*Wife's earnings*	*Wife's earnings after tax and NI*	*Husband's earnings*	*Husband's earnings after tax and NI*	*Rent rebate*	*Rate rebate*	*FIS*	*Child benefit*	*Wife's unemployment benefit*	*Husband's unemployment benefit*	*Work and child minding expenses*	*Total net income*
Married	Both working	85	61.08	140	99.84	–	–	–	–	–	–	16.50	144.42
Married	Wife working Man unemp.	85	67.68	–	–	0.71	–	–	–	–	25.00	8.25	85.14
Married	Wife unemp. Man working	–	–	140	99.84	–	–	–	–	25.00	–	8.25	116.59
Married	Both unemployed	–	–	–	–	8.60	2.25	–	–	25.00	25.00	–	60.85
Married	Both working	64	48.21	105	78.41	–	–	–	–	–	–	16.50	110.12
Married	Wife working Man unemp.	64	54.81	–	–	4.11	0.71	–	–	–	25.00	8.25	76.38
Married	Wife unemp. Man working	–	–	105	78.41	–	–	–	–	25.00	–	8.25	95.16
Married	Both unemployed	–	–	–	–	8.60	2.25	–	–	25.00	25.00	–	60.85

TABLE B.7(ii)

Status	Employment situation	Wife's earnings	Wife's earnings after tax and NI	Husband's earnings	Husband's earnings after tax and NI	Rent rebate	Rate rebate	FIS	Child benefit	Wife's unemployment benefit	Husband's unemployment benefit	Work and child minding expenses	Total net income
Married + 1 child	Both working	85	61.08	140	99.84	–	–	–	5.85	–	–	21.50	145.27
Married + 1 child	Wife working Man unemp.	85	67.68	–	–	–	–	–	5.85	–	25.00 0.30 child	8.25	90.58
Married + 1 child	Wife unemp. Man working	–	–	140	99.84	–	–	–	5.85	25.00	–	8.25	122.44
Married + 1 child	Both unemployed	–	–	–	–	9.65	2.56	–	5.85	25.00	25.00 0.30	–	68.36
Married + 1 child	Both working	64	48.21	105	78.41	–	–	–	5.85	–	–	21.50	110.97
Married + 1 child	Wife working Man unemp.	64	54.81	–	–	4.82	0.37	–	5.85	–	25.00 0.30	8.25	82.90
Married + 1 child	Wife unemp. Man working	–	–	105	78.41	–	–	–	5.85	25.00	–	8.25	101.01
Married + 1 child	Both unemployed	–	–	–	–	9.65	2.56	–	5.85	25.00	25.00 0.30	–	68.36

TABLE B.7(iii)

Status	Employment situation	Wife's earnings	Wife's earnings after tax and NI	Husband's earnings	Husband's earnings after tax and NI	Rent rebate	Rate rebate	FIS	Child benefit	Wife's unemployment benefit	Husband's unemployment benefit	Work and child minding expenses	Total net income
Married + 2 children	Both working	85	61.08	140	99.84	–	–	–	11.70	–	–	21.50	151.12
Married + 2 children	Wife working Man unemp.	85	67.68	–	–	1.97	–	–	11.70	–	25.00 0.60 child	8.25	98.70
Married + 2 children	Wife unemp. Man working	–	–	150	99.84	–	–	–	11.70	25.00	–	8.25	128.29
Married + 2 children	Both unemployed	–	–	–	–	12.00	3.00	–	11.70	1.90 heat 25.00 1.30 SB	3.00 dental 1.50 milk 25.60 6.00 meals	–	91.00
Married + 2 children	Both working	64	48.21	105	78.41	–	–	–	11.70	–	–	21.50	116.82
Married + 2 children	Wife working Man unemp.	64	54.81	–	–	5.32	0.54	1.30 10.50 PB	11.70	–	25.00 0.60	8.25	101.52
Married + 2 children	Wife unemp. Man working	–	–	105	78.41	–	–	–	11.70	25.00	–	8.25	106.86
Married + 2 children	Both unemployed	–	–	–	–	12.00	3.00	–	11.70	1.90 heat 25.00 1.30 SB	3.00 dental 1.50 milk 25.60 0.60 6.00 meals	–	91.00

TABLE B.7(iv)

Status	*Employment situation*	*Wife's earnings*	*Wife's earnings after tax and NI*	*Husband's earnings*	*Husband's earnings after tax and NI*	*Rent rebate*	*Rate rebate*	*FIS*	*Child benefit*	*Wife's unemployment benefit*	*Husband's unemployment benefit*	*Work and child minding expenses*	*Total net income*
Married + 3 children	Both working	85	61.08	140	99.84	–	–	–	17.55	–	–	21.50	156.97
Married + 3 children	Wife working Man unemp.	85	67.68	–	–	1.78	0.27	–	17.55	–	25.00 0.90 child	8.25	104.93
Married + 3children	Wife unemp. Man working	–	–	140	99.84	–	–	–	17.55	25.00	–	8.25	134.14
Married + 3 children	Both unemployed	–	–	–	–	12.00	3.00	–	17.55	3.90 SB 25.00 9.00 meals	3.00 dental 1.50 milk 25.00 0.90 1.90 heat	–	102.75
Married + 3 children	Both working	64	48.21	105	78.41	–	–	–	17.55	–	–	21.50	122.67
Married + 3 children	Wife working Man unemp.	64	54.81	–	–	4.51	1.17	5.80 13.50 PB	17.55	–	25.90	8.25	114.99
Married + 3 children	Wife unemp. Man working	–	–	105	78.41	–	–	–	17.55	25.00	–	8.25	112.71
Married + 3 children	Both unemployed	–	–	–	–	12.00	3.00	–	17.55	3.90 SB 25.00 9.00 meals	3.00 dental 1.50 milk 25.00 0.90 1.90 heat	–	102.75

TABLE B.7(v)

Status	*Employment situation*	*Wife's earnings*	*Wife's earnings after tax and NI*	*Husband's earnings*	*Husband's earnings after tax and NI*	*Rent rebate*	*Rate rebate*	*FIS*	*Child benefit*	*Wife's unemployment benefit*	*Husband's unemployment benefit*	*Work and child minding expenses*	*Total net income*
Married + 4 children	Both working	85	61.08	140	99.84	–	–	–	23.40	–	–	21.50	162.82
Married + 4 children	Wife working Man unemp.	85	67.68	–	–	1.58	0.44	–	23.40	–	25.00 1.20 child	8.25	111.05
Married + 4 children	Wife unemp. Man working	–	–	140	99.84	–	–	–	23.40	25.00	–	8.25	139.99
Married + 4 children	Both unemployed	–	–	–	–	12.00	3.00	–	23.40	12.00 meals 3.00 dental 25.00 1.50 milk 1.90 heat	10.90 sup 25.00 1.20	–	118.90
Married + 4 children	Both working	64	48.21	105	78.41	–	–	–	23.40	–	–	21.50	128.52
Married + 4 children	Wife working Man unemp.	64	54.81	–	–	3.40	1.08	10.30 16.50 PB	23.40	–	25.00 1.20	8.25	127.44
Married + 4 children	Wife unemp. Man working	–	–	105	78.41	–	–	–	23.40	25.00	–	8.25	118.56
Married + 4 children	Both unemployed	–	–	–	–	12.00	3.00	–	23.40	12.00 meals 3.00 dental 25.00 1.50 milk 1.90 heat	10.90 SB 25.00 1.20	–	118.90

TABLES B.8(i)–B.8(v) *Married Couple, Both Initially Working (2)*

TABLE B.8(i)

Status	*Employment situation*	*Wife's earnings*	*Wife's earnings after tax and NI*	*Husband's earnings*	*Husband's earnings after tax and NI*	*Rent rebate*	*Rate rebate*	*FIS*	*Child benefit*	*Wife's supplementary benefit*	*Husband's supplementary benefit*	*Work and child minding expenses*	*Total net income*
Married	Both working	85	61.08	140	99.84	–	–	–	–	–	–	16.50	144.42
Married	Wife working Man unemp.	85	75.18	–	–	4.79	0.95	–	–	–	–	8.25	72.67
Married	Wife unemp. Man working	–	–	140	99.84	–	–	–	–	–	–	8.25	91.59
Married	Both unemployed	–	–	–	–	12.00 SB	3.00 SB	–	–	–	41.70 3.00 passported	–	59.70
Married	Both working	64	48.21	105	78.41	–	–	–	–	–	–	16.50	110.12
Married	Wife working Man unemp.	64	58.38	–	–	8.87	2.34	–	–	–	–	8.25	61.34
Married	Wife unemp. Man working	–	–	105	78.41	1.39	–	–	–	–	–	8.25	71.55
Married	Both unemployed	–	–	–	–	12.00 SB	3.00 SB	–	–	–	41.70 scale 3.00 passported	–	59.70

TABLE B.8(ii)

Status	*Employment situation*	*Wife's earnings*	*Wife's earnings after tax and NI*	*Husband's earnings*	*Husband's earnings after tax and NI*	*Rent rebate*	*Rate rebate*	*FIS*	*Child benefit*	*Wife's supplementary benefit*	*Husband's supplementary benefit*	*Work and child minding expenses*	*Total net income*
Married + 1 child	Both working	85	61.08	140	99.84	–	–	–	5.85	–	–	21.50	145.27
Married + 1 child	Wife working Man unemp.	85	75.18	–	–	5.58	1.22	–	5.85	–	–	8.25	79.58
Married + 1 child	Wife unemp. Man working	–	–	140	99.84	–	–	–	5.85	–	–	8.25	97.44
Married + 1 child	Both unemployed	–	–	–	–	12.00	3.00	–	5.85	–	41.70 scale 7.50 passport 1.90 heat 2.90 child	–	74.85
Married + 1 child	Both working	64	48.21	105	78.41	–	–	–	5.85	–	–	21.50	110.97
Married + 1 child	Wife working Man unemp.	64	58.38	–	–	7.71	2.00	9.30 + 7.50 passported	5.85	–	–	8.25	82.49
Married + 1 child	Wife unemp. Man working	–	–	105	78.41	2.17	0.16	–	5.85	–	–	8.25	78.34
Married + 1 child	Both unemployed	–	–	–	–	12.00	3.00	–	5.85	–	41.70 scale 7.50 passport 1.90 heat 2.90 child	–	74.85

TABLE B.8(iii)

Status	*Employment situation*	*Wife's earnings*	*Wife's earnings after tax and NI*	*Husband's earnings*	*Husband's earnings after tax and NI*	*Rent rebate*	*Rate rebate*	*FIS*	*Child benefit*	*Wife's supplementary benefit*	*Husband's supplementary benefit*	*Work and child minding expenses*	*Total net income*
Married + 2 children	Both working	85	61.08	140	99.84	–	–	–	11.70	–	–	21.50	151.12
Married + 2 children	Wife working Man unemp.	85	75.18	–	–	5.77	1.29	3.30 10.50 passported	11.70	–	–	8.25	99.49
Married + 2 children	Wife unemp. Man working	–	–	140	99.84	–	–	–	11.70	–	–	8.25	103.29
Married + 2 children	Both unemployed	–	–	–	–	12.00	3.00	–	11.70	–	41.70 scale 10.50 passport 1.90 heat 10.20 child	–	91.00
Married + 2 children	Both working	64	48.21	105	78.41	–	–	–	11.70	–	–	21.50	116.82
Married + 2 children	Wife working Man unemp.	64	58.38	–	–	7.91	1.99	13.80 10.50 passported	11.70	–	–	8.25	96.03
Married + 2 children	Wife unemp. Man working	–	–	105	78.41	2.92	0.32	–	11.70	–	–	8.25	85.10
Married + 2 children	Both unemployed	–	–	–	–	12.00	3.00	–	11.70	–	41.70 scale 10.50 passport 1.90 heat 10.20 child	–	91.00

TABLE B.8(iv)

Status	*Employment situation*	*Wife's earnings*	*Wife's earnings after tax and NI*	*Husband's earnings*	*Husband's earnings after tax and NI*	*Rent rebate*	*Rate rebate*	*FIS*	*Child benefit*	*Wife's supplementary benefit*	*Husband's supplementary benefit*	*Work and child minding expenses*	*Total net income*
Married + 3 children	Both working	85	61.08	140	99.84	–	–	–	17.55	–	–	21.50	156.97
Married + 3 children	Wife working Man unemp.	85	75.18	–	–	4.85	1.26	7.80 13.50 passported	17.55	–	–	8.25	111.89
Married + 3 children	Wife unemp. Man working	–	–	140	99.84	–	–	–	17.55	–	–	8.25	109.14
Married + 3 children	Both unemployed	–	–	–	–	12.00	3.00	–	17.55	–	41.70 scale 13.50 passport 1.90 heat 13.10 child	–	102.75
Married + 3 children	Both working	64	48.21	105	78.41	–	–	–	17.55	–	–	21.50	122.67
Married + 3 children	Wife working Man unemp.	64	58.38	–	–	6.82	1.99	18.30 13.50 passported	17.55	–	–	8.25	108.29
Married + 3 children	Wife unemp. Man working	–	–	105	78.41	2.78	0.66	–	17.55	–	–	8.25	91.15
Married + 3 children	Both unemployed	–	–	–	–	12.00	3.00	–	17.55	–	41.70 scale 13.50 passport 1.90 heat 13.10 child	–	102.75

TABLE B.8(v)

Status	*Employment situation*	*Wife's earnings*	*Wife's earnings after tax and NI*	*Husband's earnings*	*Husband's earnings after tax and NI*	*Rent rebate*	*Rate rebate*	*FIS*	*Child benefit*	*Wife's supplementary benefit*	*Husband's supplementary benefit*	*Work and child minding expenses*	*Total net income*
Married + 4 children	Both working	85	61.08	140	99.84	–	–	–	23.40	–	–	21.50	162.82
Married + 4 children	Wife working Man unemp.	85	75.18	–	–	3.94	1.27	12.30 16.50 passported	23.40	–	–	8.25	124.34
Married + 4 children	Wife unemp. Man working	–	–	140	99.84	–	–	–	23.40	–	–	8.25	114.99
Married + 4 children	Both unemployed	–	–	–	–	12.00	3.00	–	23.40	–	41.70 scale 16.50 passport 1.90 heat 20.40 child	–	118.90
Married + 4 children	Both working	64	48.21	105	78.41	–	–	–	23.40	–	–	21.50	128.52
Married + 4 children	Wife working Man unemp.	64	58.38	–	–	5.73	1.97	22.80 16.50 passported	23.40	–	–	8.25	120.53
Married + 4 children	Wife unemp. Man working	–	–	105	78.41	2.24	0.67	2.30 16.50 passported	23.40	–	–	8.25	115.27
Married + 4 children	Both unemployed	–	–	–	–	12.00	3.00	–	23.40	–	41.70 scale 16.50 passport 1.90 heat 20.40 child	–	118.90

TABLE B.9 *Replacement ratios from Table B.7 and B.8*

Status	*Initial earnings*		*Replacement ratio if husband working*		*Replacement ratio if husband unemployed*	
			Col. 1	*Col. 2*	*Col. 3*	*Col. 4*
Married	Husband Wife	140 85	80.7% 1st year	63.4% Thereafter	71.5% 1st year	82.2% Thereafter
Married	Husband Wife	105 64	86.4% 1st year	64.9% Thereafter	79.7% 1st year	97.3% Thereafter
Married + 1 child	Husband wife	140 85	84.3% 1st year	67.1% Thereafter	75.5% 1st year	94.1% Thereafter
Married + 1 child	Husband wife	105 64	91.0% 1st year	70.6% Thereafter	82.5% 1st year	90.7% Thereafter
Married + 2 children	Husband wife	140 85	84.9% 1st year	68.3% Thereafter	92.2% 1st year	91.5% Thereafter
Married + 2 children	Husband wife	105 64	91.5% 1st year	72.8% Thereafter	89.6% 1st year	94.8% Thereafter
Married + 3 children	Husband wife	140 85	85.5% 1st year	69.5% Thereafter	97.9% 1st year	91.8% Thereafter
Married + 3 children	Husband wife	105 64	91.9% 1st year	74.3% Thereafter	89.4% 1st year	94.8% Thereafter
Married + 4 children	Husband wife	140 85	85.9% 1st year	70.6% Thereafter	107.1% 1st year	95.6% Thereafter
Married + 4 children	Husband wife	105 64	92.3% 1st year	89.7% Thereafter	93.3% 1st year	98.6% Thereafter

APPENDIX C

Empirical Evidence on the Effect of Taxation Upon Labour Supply

There are two major approaches which have been used in estimating the effects of income tax upon the supply of labour services. First, the survey approach in which a randomly selected group are asked questions about their work behaviour and implicitly/explicitly about the perceived effect of taxation upon their supply of labour. The second approach involves econometric techniques. Here the relevant elasticities are measured from actual work–leisure decisions of workers, the chief advantage being that the researcher is not so much concerned about workers' statements on the perceived effects of taxation upon their supply decisions, but with their actual (observed) behaviour in response, *inter alia*, to taxation or changes therein.

THE SURVEY EVIDENCE

For purposes of expositional clarity and elucidation of the evidence underlying the proposed reforms, one can usefully distinguish between the impact of taxation upon lower income (or manual worker) families and higher income groups.

Lower Income Families

A number of interesting studies carried out in the 1950–60s have to be ignored since the tax rate structure and other factors affecting labour supply decisions have so altered as to make them at best of historical interest and at worst positively misleading. Brown and Levin (1974) collected and analysed data from more than 2,000 weekly paid workers, and after a large number of factual and attitudinal questions about work, in which tax was not mentioned by the interviewer (so as not to elicit only desired answers), the respondents were asked if income tax had made them work more or less overtime, or whether it had no effect on their supply decisions. The results were as follows:

	More overtime %	*No effect* %	*Less overtime* %
Replies for men	15	74	11
Replies for women	2	93	6

To check the plausibility of these claims, Brown and Levin examined how many actual hours overtime the respondents had worked. To simplify the matters we consider the position of men only:

Claim	*All men* %	*Actual average overtime worked* (hours)
Neither	74	4.2
Work less	11	3.5
Work more	15	9.0

Those who claimed they worked more as a result of tax did indeed work more overtime than average; and those who claimed less overtime did work less than the average. In addition to plausibility there is also the question of constraints. First, the authors recognized that employees may not be free to choose the amount of overtime they would like to work e.g. employment may stipulate a shorter/longer working week as a condition of employment and some 30 per cent of the men in the sample were estimated constrained in this way. Second, pay constraints – 9 per cent of men had such a constraint, and third, personal constraints e.g. work supply determined by health or family commitments etc. – 6 per cent of men were estimated to have such a constraint. The re-estimated figures show:

Claim	*All men*	*Highly plausible*	*Highly plausible and unconstrained*
Neither	74	79	69
Work more	15	14	22
Work less	11	7	9

The most dramatic change came in the increased number of those prepared to work more, if unconstrained – this was particularly true of married men with children who had formerly claimed to be unaffected by tax. Brown and Levin concluded the aggregate effect of tax on supply of overtime hours amounts to about 1 per cent of the total hours worked, tax inducing slightly more people to work.

Survey on Higher Income Groups

There are two surveys in the UK of the effects of income tax on higher paid individuals. They are particularly interesting since both study the same professions – self-employed solicitors and accountants. Break (1957) randomly selected 306 self-employed solicitors and accountants, this group being chosen as 'tax sensitive' categories, in that, first, being self-employed they determined their own hours of work, and so were less constrained than other workers and, second, professionally they would be more aware of tax rates than less informed workers. The generally reported result is that 13 per cent of the sample reported definite disincentive effects, whilst 10 per cent of the sample reported definite incentive effects. As for those experiencing disincentive effects, nearly half said they had turned down work offered to them in the past. Of this group a third (i.e. one sixth total disincentive) reported tax had been a crucial factor – all these individuals had faced tax rates of 60 per cent or more. However, those in the lowest income bracket did not regard the tax as being paramount. The middle-income group tended to take on all work which came their way, but reported being less actively involved in seeking new business than they would have been under lower tax rates. A third type of disincentive practice was to shift the workload to other persons within the firm; about one quarter of those experiencing disincentives turned over work to partners or staff because of their own tax rates. Of those experiencing definite incentive results, about half reported that tax considerations were the chief reason for delaying their retirement. The other half found themselves having to work harder on a day-to-day basis, because high taxes prevented them from being able to employ further staff to reduce their own workload. Break then went on to consider whether higher marginal tax rates increased the disincentive effect, and reported as follows:

	Total Taxable Income		
Reaction	Under £2000	£3000–5000	Over £5000
Disincentive	6 per cent	14 per cent	30 per cent
Incentive	11 per cent	10 per cent	13 per cent

Whilst this indicates that higher marginal rates increased the disincentive, for lower income groups the results are less convincing.

Indeed, taken overall the net disincentive effect is 'not large enough to be of great economic or sociological importance . . . the chorus of complaints against penal taxation echoed by the vast majority of respondents was surprisingly infrequently translated into action'. Fields & Stanbury (1972) attempted to repeat Break's survey with a random sample of 285 solicitors and accountants. On average, 19 per cent of the sample experienced disincentives (rising to 30 per cent for those on top rates), whilst 11 per cent experienced incentive effects. Unlike Break they find the net effect is statistically significant and suggest the disincentive effect is growing stronger over time. Moreover, there appears to have been a substantial shift in the type of disincentive effect. However, there are important differences between the two survey studies, especially the interviewing techniques so the two studies may not be directly comparable as at first appears.

As for the methodological difficulties which may be encountered using this approach see Moser and Kalton (1971). The principal difficulties lie in a number of areas. First in framing the questionnaire in as objective a form as possible, so as not to elicit only 'desired' answers, and even if steps are taken to mitigate implausible answers, there is still the difficulty of interpreting and evaluating the importance of the variables under consideration. One has seen Break's point about the chorus of complaints against penal taxation being infrequently translated into action. The plausibility aspect also arises insofar as non-tax factors play a part in the supply of labour services. The isolation and quantifications of those factors causes difficulty, and cannot really be satisfactorily dealt with by simplifying assumptions, as in Break's survey. The second area of difficulty already noted concerns whether the interviewers determine their own hours of work. Note the Brown and Levin estimates of unconstrained workers and Break's choice of self-employed workers. The third question concerns how 'representative' the sample is. Some researchers have pointed out that those who are really dissuaded may already have emigrated and chosen less demanding occupations, so the tax induced distortions come out in career choice, rather than sampling means (see ORC Survey 1976). As a result of these and other problems, Fields and Stanbury concluded future research seems to be in the direction of econometrics, and it is to this area that we shall now confine our attention.

THE ECONOMETRIC EVIDENCE

The earliest estimates of the relations between working hours and hourly earnings were made by Douglas (1934). Using annual time-series data from 1890 to 1926 for a 15 industry sample, he found a strong negative correlation between the two and there was only one weak positive correlation. Similar results followed on an inter-industry cross-sectional basis. Douglas concluded that the elasticity of supply with respect to the wage lay between −0.1 and −0.2, implying a 1 per cent increase in hourly earnings would tend *ceteris paribus* to cause a decrease of between 0.1 per cent and 0.2 per cent in hours normally worked. Subsequently a number of studies using time-series data tested the relationship between working hours and hourly earnings using regression techniques and in most cases the elasticity of labour supply with respect to hourly earnings was confirmed as negative. However, as Feldstein (1968) has pointed out, the problem is one of identifying a labour supply curve from such observations; to overcome this difficulty he suggests two methods. First, one should include variables in addition to wages in the supply equation, so that if these were included – e.g. in an inter-industry study – and if these were the only systematic facts that caused inter-industry differences in the supply function, including them in the regression would have the same effect as using a sample of observations which related to a single supply curve. This leads to his second suggestion, namely to sample observations from a single labour market in which it is more likely to be a single supply curve. (For a criticism of this approach see Rayner, 1969). His results were on the whole insignificant, only 4 out of 11 regression coefficients on hourly earnings were significantly negative, and he concluded that had a more homogeneous sample been taken a positively sloped supply curve would have been estimated.

A second difficulty arises from the progressive nature of taxation. The effect of a tax has been seen to alter the budget constraint, but as progressive tax rates are banded, we must maximize the utility function subject to a non-linear budget constraint. Cain and Watts (1973) reviewed many of the earlier studies and have commented on the notable lack of unanimity in the signs of the income and substitution effects, and as Haveman and Watts (1977) point out, this lack of agreement weakens confidence in any of their findings. However, as a result of improved techniques (e.g. Kosters' 1969 pioneering work) and specifications, more general agreement has been reached in later studies. To give a general idea of the gross uncompensated wage elasticities which have been obtained in the USA refer to Table C.1.

TABLE C.1

Study	*Uncompensated wage elasticity*	*Data*
Finegan (1962)	− 0.25 to − 0.35	Inter-occupational
Rosen (1969)	− 0.07 to − 0.30	Inter-industry
Owen (1971)	− 0.11 to − 0.24	Time-series
Abbot and Ashenfelter (1976)	− 0.07 to − 0.14	Time-series

This later study is particularly interesting since Abbot and Ashenfelter have provided compensated elasticities for prime age married males, the substitution elasticity being +0.12 and the income elasticitiy being −0.27. This clearly points to a backward-bending supply curve with the income effect dominant, as the income elasticity has a larger absolute value than the substitution elasticity. The relatively small substitution elasticity implies that higher marginal tax rates may have only a small disincentive at least on the supply of hours for all but the higher wage earners. Moreover, as many of the studies point to the income elasticity having a much larger value than the substitution elasticity, this is consistent with the observed secular decline in the supply of hours offered by males as real wages have increased. However, this observation needs to be qualified in a number of ways. In particular we must consider the effects of trades unions on shortening the standard working week, which to some extent has generated a black economy and secondary working systems (Board of Inland Revenue, 1982). The disincentive effects may well have increased over recent years, as the real burden of taxation has increased. From a policy implication viewpoint, if these estimates of a small substitution elasticity are accepted, then high marginal rates (given our assumption of no social security) may have only a weak disincentive effect on the supply of hours for the majority of the labour force (lower income end).

Up to now, US evidence has been considered; let us turn to the leading study in the UK carried out by Brown, Levin and Ulph (1976). They regressed actual hours worked on net marginal wage rate and other factors hypothesized to shift the supply schedule. It will be seen that as the net marginal wage rate rises, the supply of hours fall. But whilst the authors reported a negative elasticity with respect to the marginal wage, their model implies that this elasticity varies with the wage rate, and because their model is quadratic the elasticity eventually becomes positive. The overall implication is that the income effect dominates the substitution effect for lower paid workers, and conversely for the higher paid.

COMMENTS AND EVIDENCE ON THE NEGATIVE INCOME TAX PROPOSALS

We have already surveyed the empirical evidence on the benefits–earnings literature, and considered the impact of income tax upon labour supply decisions, but these are in a policy prescription context mere preliminaries to the central question as to how to induce increased supply of services, given the existing or proposed tax-transfer systems.

It is widely recognized that both the tax and benefits system have failings in their own right, and whilst these need not detain us here, it should be noted that some of the main problems, such as the question of low take-up rates, multiple benefit entitlements and claims as well as low tax thresholds are considered in the main body of the report. Here we are primarily concerned with the additional and what may be considered the central problem which arises from the interaction between the social welfare system and the present system of taxing low-paid workers. In the present context this is illustrated most clearly in poverty trap situations, where individuals who desire to render additional labour services are dissuaded both by the high marginal rates of tax on extra earnings and by the withdrawal of means-tested benefits (e.g. FIS) at an implicit rate starting at 50 per cent or considerably more, so that the worker as a result of additional work effort can end up with a lower disposable income than formerly. The reasons are that the positive rate of income tax when coupled with the (implicit) rate of benefit withdrawal occasions a total marginal tax rate on the extra earnings in excess of 100 per cent.

The causes of this 'excessive' marginal tax rate are seen as arising principally from the low level of tax threshold when compared with the level of welfare benefits, and in particular from the level of prescribed income for FIS; the fact that FIS is calculated on 'gross' rather than net income basis; and the exacerbation of these by the passported benefits scheme. The case for a better integrated and more co-ordinated tax-transfer scheme has been recognized and recommended for many years and is overwhelming, yet means of achieving it are far from agreed.

THE TAX CREDIT PROPOSALS 1972

The aims of the 1972 proposals were, first, to simplify the tax system and in particular the allowances scheme by replacing it with a system of tax credits (and also changing the collection of income tax under the PAYE provisions), and second, to harmonize the tax-transfer system by reducing avoidable complexities and duplications, and at the same time providing an automatic minimum level of income support. The scheme was intended to cover a wide variety of income recipients, including those employees earning over £8 per week (at that time representing one quarter average earnings), all those in receipt of the main national insurance benefits and old age pensions (etc). It was estimated that the scheme would cover 90 per cent of the working population, but specifically excluded were those earning less than £8 p.w., the self-employed and those in receipt of supplementary benefit. By excluding those on the lowest earnings, the proposals came in for severe criticism – indeed it seemed that whilst income maintenance schemes sought to provide a minimum income level, these proposals excluded the very groups who would most need income support.

The proposed income tax changes need not detain us, since most of them have already been effected or are about to be implemented. Moreover the tax simplification would not, *per se*, improve the interaction of the tax–benefits system. However, the numerous tax allowances which were then available would be replaced by three tax credits, illustrated in the Green Paper as:

A single person's credit	=	£*X* per week
Married couple's credit	=	£*Y* per week
For each child	=	£*Z* per week

such amounts being calculated as corresponding to just over the equivalent tax allowance at that time. The significance of the tax credit as an instrument of co-ordinating the tax-transfer system lay in the fact that if the credits exceeded the tax due on other income, the excess would be immediately and automatically repayable. For example, a single man on a weekly income of £10 (in 1972 terms) would be entitled to a tax credit of £4 and liable to income tax at 30 per cent, so that:

tax payable on £10 ⓐ 30 per cent = £3
tax actually paid = £3 *less* tax credited £4
= £1 refund

so the taxpayer's disposable income is £10 plus £1 cash refund, namely £11 – as such the tax credit provides a rational tax-transfer system for those covered by the scheme. Moreover by bringing into charge all the main national insurance benefits, unemployment and sickness benefit were now to be brought into charge to tax. Once again this aspect of the reforms has been superseded by the Government's taxation of these benefits since July 1982.

However appealing these changes may appear there were a number of difficulties which were apparent even at that time. As Polanyi and Polanyi (1974) noted the scheme was not comprehensive in scope; leaving aside those on SB, those on less than one quarter average earnings were excluded. In evidence given to the

Select Committee it was estimated that about half a million people with incomes below the poverty line would not receive tax credits since they would have insufficient earnings. By comparison, our own scheme of negative income tax with the exception of supplementary benefit claimants will cover all those on low incomes and so is more comprehensive in nature than the scheme formerly advocated. This will therefore obviate many of the complexities and inefficiencies perpetuated by the 1972 type proposals and result in reduced administrative and compliance costs. Apart from the coverage aspect, the other major objection to the earlier scheme as a means of low-income support for those covered by it, lies in the fact that there was only one level of tax and one level of credit for a given size of family, irrespective of income. As such the scheme represented an insensitive instrument by which to concentrate help where it was most needed. For example, if it was intended to reduce the burden of taxation for those with low earnings, the tax credit would have to be increased significantly and whilst this may raise the poor out of poverty, it would also assist everyone else. The proposal would result in a combination of credits inadequate to raise the poor out of poverty and benefits widely dispersed over 'non-poor' households, resulting in excessive costs if the credits were to be raised to more adequate levels. Polanyi and Polanyi (1974) have quantified the distributional ineffectiveness of the proposals in the following terms: although the scheme distributes some £1,300 million of net benefits per annum, this goes mainly to 'non-poor' recipients. Only about £155 million (12 per cent) actually goes to people who can broadly be classified as poor. Moreover of the 2.8 million persons regularly receiving SB, only 1 million would have their incomes raised to the level at which they no longer needed this support. This means that about 3 million people (including claimants' dependents) would still be relying on this form of assistance. In addition a further 2 million (including dependents) who at present fail or are ineligible to claim SB will remain in poverty.

The general structure of the 1972 proposals is such that they fail to concentrate income support on those who most need it; as such their cost-effectiveness is in doubt. In considering the cost-effectiveness of the proposals, we may also note from an efficiency viewpoint that tax credits, being a lump sum rather than an allowance against earnings, may actually have a disincentive effect for low income earners, since they receive less cash refund the higher their earnings. Although the Green Paper stated that the marginal rates would be reduced for the low paid, calculations show that they could be significant (see Lees, 1967; Beckerman (1979) *Economic Journal*, pp. 261–79).

By comparison, our own proposals for alleviating poverty amongst low-income families provides a far more sensitive and concentrated means of income support. Being based upon the existing schemes of poverty support in both child benefit and FIS terms, we have widely accepted base criteria upon which to build. Moreover, whereas the 1972 proposals operated solely through the 30 per cent basic rate for all income groups, occasioning spillover effects, our proposals concentrate solely on those in the lower income groups, thereby minimizing this consequence. The present proposals represent a more sensitive means of support in several respects. For example, whereas the 1972 proposals with the insensitivity to variation in regional housing costs (etc.) could only be remedied by increased complexity or excessive and indiscriminate expenditure, our proposals are based on the existing means-tested criteria of FIS, thereby concentrating assistance where it is most needed. In addition to the difficulties which were evident in the tax credit proposals at that time, there are a number of additional difficulties which would be encountered if such a scheme were to be introduced at the present time. Perhaps the most interesting in the present context concerns the means of quantifying the tax credit, and level of qualifying income. Coverage apart, what values should be given to the tax credit? Clearly if we were to use the value of present tax allowances, this would not only provide an inadequate level of income support, but also represent a serious inconsistency with current levels of social security; as such the value of tax allowances cannot be used. Clearly the SB scale could be used if a highly restricted coverage were accepted, but this defeats the main objective of negative income tax schemes. Clearly if the type of proposals put forward in 1972 were to be applied to the existing tax-transfer scheme, an entirely new and arbitrary basis for quantification would be required. In contrast, our proposals for a negative income tax builds upon the existing structure and requires only minor technical adjustments. In particular, whereas the 1972 proposals lead us back to the problem of lack of synchronization between benefit levels and the value of tax allowances, our proposals directly confront this problem in such away as to emphasize work incentives rather than income support, thereby encouraging workers to help themselves back into prosperity.

We have already seen that if tax thresholds are so low that tax is levied on families which are officially acknowledged as having inadequate income to meet their needs, then increased tax thresholds *vis à vis* benefit levels will be one way of alleviating the difficulties associated with low wage earners. And from an equity viewpoint the increase in thresholds will, in itself, take many poor families out of tax altogether. Whilst this may be an expensive and not particularly cost-effective means of directing relief to those in most need, if some greater degree of cohesion between thresholds and benefit levels is not sought, the problem of the poverty trap (and the unemployment trap) is likely to increase as the gap between the two enlarges. If social security benefits are indexed whilst tax allowances are eroded there will be an increasing overlap between the tax and social security system exacerbating the existing difficulties.

More positively, our proposals for calculating Family Income Supplement on a 'net' rather than a 'gross' incomes basis obviates the tax induced distortions for those in receipt of welfare benefit; in essence it breaks the principal characteristic of the poverty trap, namely its additive nature resulting from the coupling of positive tax rates with the implicit tax rates of welfare withdrawals. In effect we have an integrated tax-transfer scheme for those in work or business.

The proposed increases in child benefit may be linked up similarly, for under the existing scheme, those in work receive substantially less financial support than those out of work; by increasing non-taxable child benefit those in work would benefit relative to those out of work since the latter would receive a *pro tanto* reduction in the child allowance element of supplementary benefit.

It may be thought that calls for an extension of the existing NIT element in the present system represent calls for disincentives to be increased. We would reject this contention given the exact nature of the proposals we have formulated, but for purposes of completeness we may be interested to review the empirical evidence on other negative income tax schemes, which are particularly different from our own.

Evidence of NIT Experiments

One of the main obstacles to adopting NIT is the popular fear that the provision of higher incomes might lead to a fall in willingness to work. The theory behind this is similar to that put forward in our analysis of the benefits–earnings surveys. To test this, negative income tax schemes were introduced experimentally in several places in the USA – perhaps the best known being that carried out in New Jersey.

The New Jersey Experiment

To be eligible a family must have an able bodied male of working age and an income not in excess of 150 per cent of the official poverty line. Nearly 1400 people were enrolled, 724 were classified as 'experimental' families, and 650 as 'controlled'.

The former were allocated to one of eight separate NIT schemes combining four guarantee levels (at 125 per cent, 100 per cent, 75 per cent and 50 per cent of the poverty line) and three tax rates (30 per cent, 50 per cent and 70 per cent).

Before considering the results, some of the weaknesses of the scheme should be mentioned. How can inferences about a permanent NIT be drawn on the basis of a three-year experiment; the breaking up of families and people dropping out of the plan meant 41 per cent of the experimental families and 45 per cent of the control families lacked continuous structure and data throughout the experimental period. This high attrition rate was in part the result of New Jersey instituting a welfare programme (AFDC-UP) that produced higher benefits than several of the programmes. Another unexpected factor was that different ethnic groups behaved very differently. These and other difficulties mean the results should be treated with caution. The size of the payment received varied between the various experimental groups and Haveman and Watts have concluded that 'there are no findings here to indicate a significant reduction in labour supply'.

As an example the hours by (white) husbands were, in the pre-experimental period: experimental group 34.1, controls 34.8; during experimental period: experimental group 31.8, controls 34.4.

We can see little difference in the pre-experimental period, but during the experiment the difference between the two groups is largely accounted for by reduced accurate working in the case of the experimental group.

Hall (1975), disagreeing with earlier conclusions has argued that the results for white husbands do in fact show a significant reduction in labour supply, pointing to the 2.3 fewer hours worked by the experimental group after the experiment came into force; and an increased differential between the two groups, amounting to some 2.6 hours during the experiment compared with 0.7 before it. These and other measures, he argues, all show a significant reduction in hours for the experimental group.

The Seattle and Denver Experiments

Unlike the New Jersey experiments, these results are consistent with the predictions of economic theory, and are broadly in agreement with the econometric estimates of the effects of taxation on labour supply.

These experiments provided for three levels of guaranteed income – \$3800, \$4800 and \$5600 (1971 dollars) and four tax rates. The researchers estimated the effects of the experiment by comparing hours worked prior to the experiment with those worked in the second year of the experiment.

Details of the results are not given here, but they imply a total reduction in hours of 5.3 per cent for husbands and 22 per cent for wives, and 11.2 per cent for female heads of households.

These results lend support to Hall's interpretation of the New Jersey Experiment, and tend to cast doubt on Haveman and Watts' interpretation of the results.

We have seen in the New Jersey experiment that the NIT programme ran for three years, and the question is whether on this basis inferences can be made about a permanent NIT. In the Seattle and Denver experiments some enrolled for three years, others for five years. There were no significant differences in the labour responses between the two groups in the second year of the experiment.

CONCLUSIONS

There can be little doubt that income tax does have disincentive effects on the supply of labour services; more accurately, these effects increase the higher the marginal rate of tax encountered at each level of earnings.

Whilst the evidence is most apparent when explicit tax rates are considered as in the case of higher income groups, the distortionary effect will in all probability be encountered in its most severe form by those at the lowest income levels, since it is here that the very highest marginal rates of tax are encountered. We have considered the failings of the previous Conservative administration's tax credit scheme and drawn out lessons used in our own proposals, which are a practical move towards negative income tax utilizing *existing* mechanisms. While the US evidence of NIT experiments confirms some disincentive effects of NIT, the social objectives involved are better met by NIT than by the present nexus of tax/benefit provisions which yield the poverty trap.

APPENDIX D

The History and Present State of Union Legislation

The purpose of this appendix is to examine British trades union power in relation to its effect on employment (Minford, 1982a) and the extent to which it impinges on the efficient operation of the labour market (Kochin, 1980). We attempt to do this by examining the two major areas of union power. These are trades union immunities and the closed shop. The following two sections are our interpretations of the history and present state of the law as it touches on these two areas. It is of course not intended as a definitive exegesis but rather as an introduction to the complexities of the subject.

TRADES UNION IMMUNITIES

The law governing strikes and other industrial action is based on legal immunity (as opposed to positive rights) which protects those who organize and participate in trade disputes from certain action which would otherwise be unlawful. In the greater part of the last century trades union activity was governed by the criminal law. Workers who went on strike or were involved in other industrial action did so under the penalty of prosecution for such offences as intimidation and conspiracy. The Trade Union Act 1871 and the Conspiracy and Protection of Property Act 1875, save for picketing, removed criminal liability for criminal conspiracy, in restraint of trade, if a combination of two or more persons acted in contemplation or furtherance of a trade dispute. (See Section 1 of the Criminal Law Act 1977 for the present law pertaining to criminal conspiracy.)

Following this legislation, a succession of civil liabilities in tort, (i.e. civil non-contractual wrongs – as opposed to criminal wrongs – which are redressed by an injunction restraining the action and/or compensated by damages for the loss suffered), were developed by the common law judges. Examples were: (a) the tort of inducing (by union officials) breach of contracts of employment (by workers) enabling the employer to seek the above redress; and (b) the tort of civil conspiracy whereby a person (an employer) could sue any other person (a worker or union official) who had conspired with others to cause damage (e.g. resulting from strike) which the courts perceived as other than in pursuance of their legitimate interest.

The development of civil liabilities in industrial relations culminated in the famous Taff Vale case (*Taff Vale Railway Co.* v. *Amalgamated Society of Railway Servants* 1901, AC 426, HL) in which the highest appellate court in the land (The House of Lords) held, for the first time, that a trades union as a distinct and separate entity from its officials could be liable for the unlawful action of its members. The Taff Vale decision, on trades union liability, was rendered redundant by the provision of immunity in the Trades Dispute Act 1906 (hereinafter referred to as the 1906 Act) from which flowed the underpinnings of the present day legal structure of trades union immunities. The Act was repealed by the Industrial Relations Act 1971 (hereafter referred to as the 1971 Act) but its provisions form the basis of the Trades Union and Labour Relations Act 1974 (hereafter referred to as the 1974 Act) as amended by the Trades Union and Labour Relations (Amendment) Act 1976. Section 4 gave trades unions complete immunity from actions in tort.

Individuals (union officials and workers) were afforded immunity, if they acted in contemplation or furtherance of a trade dispute, from actions in civil conspiracy and interference with a person's freedom to use his capital and labour. In addition s.3 stated that an act done by a person, (for example the leader of a strike calling out workers), in contemplation or furtherance of a trade dispute would not be actionable (by the employer) on the grounds that it induced some other person (the workers called out), to break their contracts of employment. The workers actually breaking their contracts could, however, be sued (as they can to the present date) by their employer in contract for damages, but the section afforded immunity to any person, whether an official or not, for inducing that breach, which but for the immunity would be actionable in tort.

The Act also provided the first definition of lawful picketing. Immunity was not furnished for inducing breach of commercial contracts, that is, a direct inducement by a worker or union official persuading his employer to break his commercial contract with his supplier or customer. There was some judicial confusion concerning whether indirect inducement to break a commercial contract had s.3 immunity. Indirect inducement occurred when a person (a union official) had immunity for calling out workers on strike, in breach of their contracts of employment, but where such action had the indirect effect of causing the employer of the strikers to break his commercial contracts.

In the case of *Rookes* v. *Barnard* 1964, (AC 1129, 1 ALL ER 367 HL (E)) the House of Lords held that s.3 did not confer immunity on union officials who threatened that there would be strike action against a failure to dismiss a non-union member. The union officials were sued for the tort of intimidation, which constitutes the threat of an unlawful act, the unlawful act being that contracts of employment would be broken. Section 3 of the 1906 Act gave protection only to a person inducing a breach of a contract of employment and not to one actually threatening or intimidating an employer that the same would occur.

The Trades Disputes Act 1965 enlarged the protection in the 1906 Act to cover the tort of intimidation by conferring immunity on threats to break a contract of employment or to induce others to do the same.

The Donovan Commission reporting in June 1968 (HMSO, Cmnd. 3623) concluded that the immunities conferred by the 1906 Act through judicial interpretation constituted a legal maze. The report recommended that one of the methods of clarifying the law was by extending immunity, for inducing breach of contracts of employment, to all contracts.

The Labour Government's White Paper, *In Place of Strife* (1969) endorsed the above recommendation. The Paper's other proposals were, however, more contentious. These were for the resolution of recognition disputes between unions; for compulsory ballots in official strikes; for union registration; and for a statutory cooling-off period where unconstitutional stoppages or unofficial action occurred. In each case there was to be provision for the Secretary of State to refer cases to a newly constituted industrial board, which would have had power to impose financial penalties on individuals, trades unions and employers in breach of its orders. There was hostility from unions and under pressure the government withdrew its proposals, at the same time obtaining an undertaking from the TUC that it would intervene in unofficial strikes. The Government subsequently introduced a Bill stripped of its penal clause, but the Bill was overtaken by a General Election which returned a Conservative Government who enacted the 1971 Act.

The 1971 Act was an innovatory and wide ranging statute which changed the face of industrial law and sought to bring industrial relations within the scope of *positive* judicial control. The Act repealed the 1906 Act returning to the Taff Vale position, in that a trade union as distinct from its members or officers could once again be liable under the provisions of the Act. Immunity was furnished, however, if the union was registered under the Act, and it acted in contemplation or furtherance of a trade dispute. Its members and officials had additionally to act with the authority or on behalf of the registered trades union to attract immunity. These provisions had the direct effect of making unofficial strikes unlawful – in 1980 about 90 per cent of strikes were unofficial (HMSO, Cmnd. 8128). The 1971 Act also gave individual rights to workers, such as the right to belong or not to belong to a trades union. The Act also introduced an implied legal presumption that written collective agreements were to have contractual status (i.e. legally binding on both parties) unless the agreement expressly excluded this. The 1971 Act encountered severe union opposition. The TUC instructed trades unions not to register under the Act, thereby foregoing the provisions and the immunity contained in them. The 1971 Act led to a number of fierce and controversial court cases before being repealed by the Labour Government's 1974 Act. (See for example: *Churchman and others* v. *Port of London Shop Stewards' Committee and others* 1972, ICR 222 CA; *Con-Mech Engineering Ltd.* v. *AUEW* 1973, ICR 620 NIRC; *Heatons Transport (St Helens) Ltd.* v. *TGWU* 1972, ICR 308 HL (E); *Midlands Cold Storage Ltd.* v. *Turner and others* 1972, ICR 230 NIRC.)

The 1974 Act

Section 13 of the 1974 Act as amended substantially re-enacted the immunities contained in the 1906 Act in an extended form. In broad terms, s.13 conferred widespread immunity on individuals (whether acting officially or otherwise), against the industrial torts of (i) intimidation; (ii) inducing breaches of contracts, (commercial as well as contracts of employment); (iii) civil conspiracy; (iv) interference with the trade, business or employment of another.

The immunity conferred on individuals is dependent on the acts being done in contemplation or furtherance of a trade dispute as defined in s.29 of the 1974 Act. If there is no trade dispute then immunity is lost. If there is a trade dispute, but a person is deemed not to be acting in contemplation or furtherance of the same, immunity is also lost. In addition, s.29 lays down prescribed categories into which a dispute must fall to retain immunity, for example terms and conditions of employment or the physical conditions in which any workers are required to work.

Section 14 of the 1974 Act was based upon and re-instated the immunity originally conferred on trade unions by s.4 of the 1906 Act. Section 14 conferred almost total immunity on trades unions for actions in tort whether or not action was taken in contemplation or furtherance of a trade dispute or was taken on its behalf or instruction by its officials or members.

Employment Act 1980

Secondary Picketing. Section 16 of the 1980 Act, in broad terms, takes away the previous immunity granted to pickets to attend lawfully other than at their own place of work in a trade dispute. Lawful industrial picketing may only be carried out by a person at or near his own place of work (subject to limited exceptions).

Secondary Industrial Action. Secondary industrial action is action taken by employees of an employer who is not a party to a trade dispute. Such action may take the form of a sympathy strike, blacking or secondary picketing.

Section 17 of the 1980 Act has the effect of removing immunity for secondary industrial action that induces the breach of a commercial contract, unless permitted by the section. In broad terms s.17 permits secondary action during the currency of the dispute only, if the principal purpose is directly to prevent or disrupt the supply, under a subsisting contract, of goods or services to an employer who is party to the dispute, by an employer not in dispute, whose employees are taking secondary action in breach of their contracts. (See *Marina Shipping Ltd.* v. *Laughton* 1982, ICR CA 215.) The secondary action must be directly targeted – and likely – to interfere with the supply of goods or services, to the employer in dispute, from his immediate suppliers or customers. Also where a person pickets at his own place of work in contemplation or furtherance of a trade dispute to which his employer is not a party, then such picketing must also adhere to the provisions in s.17.

The effect of s.17 is to curtail severely immunities previously conferred on secondary industrial action.

Summary of Trade Union Immunities after 1980 Act. An individual who is in breach of his contract of employment by taking strike, or other industrial, action may be sued by his employer and dismissed without notice. Legal immunity is not granted to a worker in breach of his contract of employment. Rather, the organizers (who may or may not be officials of the union), who induced that breach, by calling a strike or other industrial action, have immunity from being sued by an employer for what would otherwise be an actionable civil wrong, or tort redressed by damages and/or an injunction. Immunity also extends to other industrial torts: civil conspiracy, inducing breach of commercial contracts, intimidation or interference with trade, business or employment of another. Such immunity, however, is only conferred if a person is acting in contemplation or furtherance of a trade dispute. Immunity is also removed from pickets unless they picket at their own place of work; from most forms of secondary industrial action, unless it is targeted specifically to interfere with the supply of goods or services to or from the employer in dispute, with his first supplier or first customer; and from industrial action to compel trades union membership, except where employees work for the same employer or at the same work place as those taking such action (Employment Act 1980, s.18).

Organizers of primary industrial action (i.e. a dispute between an employer and his employees) retained widespread immunity and a trades union, as a separate entity from its members, had virtual total immunity for industrial torts carried out on its behalf or instruction.

The Employment Act 1982

This Act, which reached the statute book on 28 October, has radically reforged the liability of a trades union for actions in tort.

The Immunity of Trades Unions. Section 15 repealed s.14 of the 1974 Act, thereby removing the anomalous blanket immunity enjoyed by trades unions thus far. Henceforth trades unions may be sued for such torts as nuisance, negligence or breach of duty, and if such torts result in personal injury or if the union is sued for breach of duty in connection with the ownership, occupation, possession, control or use of property, the damages claimable are unlimited. If, however, no personal injury results only limited damages may be claimed. Trades union liability in this respect will be brought into line with that of the individual, save that an individual always faces unlimited damages.

In addition, a trades union will be liable in tort where proceedings are brought against it on certain grounds specified in s.13 of the 1974 Act, as amended e.g. inducing breach of contracts, intimidation and civil conspiracy, if the acts in question do not attract immunity under s.13, so that a trades union now has immunities parallel to those of an individual. An example of when a trades union is liable might be where an act is not in contemplation or furtherance of a trade dispute, or where union officials have induced breach of contracts of employment for the purpose of secondary action not permitted by s.17 of the 1980 Act.

However for the purpose of determining in proceedings whether a trades union (as distinct from its officials) is liable in respect of the act (or tort) in question, that act (under s.15) shall be taken to have been done by the union only if it was authorized or endorsed by a responsible person.

A union will therefore be liable only, for the unlawful and unprotected acts of its officials under s.13, where such acts have been authorized or endorsed by: (a) the principal executive committee of the union; or (b) by any person empowered by the written rules of the union to authorize or endorse acts of the kind in question; or (c) the president or general secretary, defined as officials of the union who hold office in that position or, if there is no such office, who hold the office which is equivalent or nearest equivalent to the said offices; or (d) by an employed official of the union; or (e) by any committee of the union to whom an employed official regularly reports.

But an act endorsed or authorized by an employed official or by any committee to which he regularly reports, will not be taken to have been authorized or endorsed by a responsible person – thereby freeing the union from liability – if (i) the employed official or any committee to which he regularly reports, at the time in question, was prevented by the written rules of the union from authorizing or endorsing acts of the kind in question; or (ii) the act has been repudiated by the principal executive committee or by the president or general secretary. However, such an act will not be treated as repudiated unless it is repudiated as soon as is reasonably practicable after the purported authorization or endorsement of the act has come to the knowledge of the principal executive committee, or the president or general secretary, and the person who purported to authorize or endorse the act has been notified in writing without delay that it has been repudiated. In any event an act will not be treated as repudiated if at any time after the union concerned purported to repudiate it, the principal executive committee, the general secretary or the president has behaved in such a manner which is inconsistent with the purported repudiation.

Section 15 is, in the main, concerned with the vicarious liability of a trades union, i.e. where it is being sued for actions carried out on its behalf or instruction by its members or officials. This does not mean that an employer must sue only the trades union, he may still sue the individuals or officials concerned, as he could prior to the Act. Such a course of action would obviously be prudent where the union is not deemed responsible, for its officials' unlawful acts, under s.15. An employer may also sue both the union and the officials in a joint action. Also, since in future trade disputes must be 'between workers and their employer' (see s.18 post), a dispute purely between a union and an employer, not involving any of the employer's workers, will no longer have immunity conferred for the industrial torts of its officials under s.13. Therefore, a trades union could be liable in these circumstances under s.15, having lost immunity under repealed s.14, and s.13 immunity not applying.

Section 16 limits the amount of damages which may be awarded against a trades union in an action in tort, except in the following cases where the damages may be unlimited: negligence, nuisance or breach of duty resulting in personal injury or breach of duty in connection with the ownership, occupation, possession, control, or use of property. For all other torts (including industrial torts) the limits in any one action are:

Trades Union Membership	*Maximum Limit of Damages (£)*
Less than 5,000	10,000
5,000–25,000	50,000
25,000–100,000	125,000
100,000 or more	250,000

In deciding on the size of union membership, where a trades union consists wholly or mainly of organizations or their representatives, the members of such organizations, as have their headquarters' main office in Great Britain shall be treated as members of the union.

Under s.17 damages, costs and expenses awarded against a trades union in any proceedings cannot be recovered from certain 'protected' union property, e.g. property held in a political fund or a provident benefits fund. In general terms a union fund will only be at risk if the union is responsible by procuring or supporting action which is unlawful, and in any event it is for an aggrieved employer to institute legal proceedings. He is under no legal compulsion to do so, and in many cases may prefer to 'keep the peace', and abrogate his rights. The underlying government policy behind s.15 (apart from removing the blanket immunity previously conferred on unions) can be inferred from the Green Paper (HMSO, Cmnd. 3888) as curbing unofficial strikes and persuading unions to use more power at a central level by changing their 'rule books'.

Summary of the Practical Implications of Section 15. Section 15 removes the blanket immunity hitherto enjoyed by trades unions in tort, leaving individuals free to sue them for unlawful tortious acts. In the case of industrial torts, however, a trades union will have the same immunities as those conferred on individuals, under s.13 of the 1974 Act as amended. The scope of such immunity was reduced by ss.16 and 17 of the 1980 Act, and is further cut back by s.18 (restricting the ambit of a 'trade dispute') and s.14 (removing immunity where there is pressure to impose union membership or recognition requirements). Where an action in tort is brought against a trades union, for inducing a breach of contract, intimidation or civil conspiracy, then in broad terms a union will only be deemed liable if a 'responsible person' authorizes or endorses such action, or such action is not repudiated by the union or not forbidden by the union rules. Where a union is liable, an employer may jointly sue the official (or individual) and the union, or alternatively any of the forementioned alone. In all other torts (e.g. negligence) it will be for the courts to determine when a union is responsible for the unlawful acts of its officials or members.

Trade Disputes. Section 18 amends and restricts the meaning and ambit of a 'trade dispute' in s.29 of the 1974 Act, with an attendant reduction in immunity for individuals and trades unions.

A 'trade dispute' henceforth will be restricted to cover only disputes 'between workers and their employers'. This change in definition has two implications: (i) a dispute purely between an employer and a union will fall outside the definition of a trade dispute thereby, in such circumstances, removing any immunity previously available, under s.13 of the 1974 Act as amended, for the tortious acts of the union's officials; (ii) a union, its officials or workers, cannot fall within the definition of 'a trade dispute' where they are in 'actual' dispute with an employer other than their own. It is still lawful for secondary action to be taken, which is permitted by s.17 of the 1980 Act, where another employer is in dispute with his workers. But, where no such dispute exists, a union, its officials, or workers employed by a different employer cannot 'create' a trade dispute with that other employer and then take secondary action under the umbrella of s.17, in contemplation or furtherance of the same. This provision therefore further curtails the restricted immunity furnished by s.17 of the 1980 Act to take secondary industrial action. The Employment Secretary said of this change:

> a trades union outside the company cannot declare that it is in dispute with that company, because it does not like the way that company runs its

business, or because none of the employees is in a trades union. The effect will be that they cannot organize blacking or other secondary action against him (*Hansard*, 1982)

Disputes 'between workers and workers' are also omitted from the definition of a trade dispute, thereby removing immunity from disputes which do not involve an employer, e.g. demarcation disputes and disputes between unions relating to union membership. (See *Taff Vale Railway Co.* v. *Amalgamated Society of Railway Servants* 1901.) This is a return to the wording of the 1971 Act.

Section 18 also substitutes 'relates wholly or mainly to' in place of 'is connected with' into the definition of a trade dispute. The rationale of this change (which is also a return to the wording of the 1971 Act) is to remove immunity from disputes which only have a tenuous connection with the prescribed subject matter of a trade dispute in s.29. For example, in the 'Nawala' case (*NWL Ltd.* v. *Nelson and Woods* 1979, ICR 867, 3 ALL ER 614 HL), which concerned the blacking of a ship by a union in support of its campaign against flags of convenience, the House of Lords held that if there was a genuine connection between the dispute and the matters listed in s.29, then predominance of subject matter (such as political or personal disputes) is irrelevant. Purely political strikes such as the TUC's day of action against Conservative Government policy on 14 May 1980, have always been outside the ambit of s.29 and lost immunity (*The Times*, 1982a). The substitution of 'relates wholly or mainly to' will put many disputes, which are political or personal in content, outside the definition of trade disputes, thus removing immunity from tortious acts relating to them.

Section 18 also restricts the definition of a trade dispute in s.29 relating to matters occurring outside the UK. The clause will in effect exclude immunity from disputes relating to matters occurring outside the UK unless the action, taken in the UK in contemplation or furtherance of a trade dispute, is likely to affect, by the outcome of the dispute, the persons carrying out the action in the UK in respect of one or more matters specified in s.29.

Section 18 narrows the definition of 'a worker' in a trade dispute, with the effect that a worker in relation to a dispute with an employer means a worker employed by that employer, or a person who has ceased to be employed by that employer where his employment was terminated in connection with the dispute or the termination of his employment was one of the circumstances giving rise to the dispute. Formerly any worker not employed by an employer could be party to a dispute. But henceforth, there cannot be a trade dispute between an employer and workers *not* employed by him, except in the limited circumstances outlined above. The provisions in s.18 relating to trade disputes will further squeeze the scope of immunity available to trades unions, their officials and individuals.

The Repeal of s.13 (2) of the Trades Union and Labour Relations Act 1974. Section 19 repeals s.13 (2), which stated 'for the avoidance of doubt it is hereby declared that an act done by a person in contemplation or furtherance of a trade dispute is not actionable in tort on the ground only that it is an interference with the trade, business or employment of another person, or with the right of another person to dispose of his capital or his labour as he wills'.

Dismissal In Connection With a Lock-Out, Strike or Other Industrial Action. Section 9 substantially amends s.62 of the Employment Protection (Consolidation) Act 1978 — hereafter 1978 Act. As we explained earlier, an employer has the right to dismiss, without notice, all his employees who are on strike. Hitherto however, under s.62 an employer could leave himself open to claims for unfair dismissal for 'victimization' if he dismissed only certain workers on strike and kept 'the others' in his employ (and this applied even where 'the others' were employees who had returned to work before the employer dismissed those continuing the strike), or he re-engaged a worker or workers who had been on strike, but not others. Another difficulty in this area was highlighted in a recent court of Appeal case (*Coates and another* v. *Modern Methods and Material Ltd*, CA, *The Times*, July 7, 1982) where it was held that an industrial tribunal was entitled to hold that an employee *intending* to go to work, but then witholding her labour by refusing to pass pickets because she did not wish to be abused by them, was herself taking part in the strike. This decision was crucial as she was the only employee *not* to be dismissed thus entitling other strikers to pursue claims for unfair dismissal.

Section 9 has now made substantive amendments to s.62 with the following consequences: an employer may henceforth dismiss all strikers (or those engaged in other industrial action) – from his 'establishment' at or from which the strikers work – 'who were taking part in the action' at the date of dismissal (as opposed to the wording 'who took part' previously in s.62). In effect an employer will not leave himself open to face unfair dismissal claims if some strikers have returned to work, and he keeps them in his employ but dismisses those still 'taking part' in the strike. An employer will therefore be able to give an ultimatum to his striking workforce that those who do not return to work by a certain date will be dismissed and, in such circumstances, he can continue to employ those who return and dismiss those continuing the strike without being subsequently liable to face unfair dismissal claims. It should be noted, however, that an employer could still risk facing such claims if he dismissed only some of those actually 'taking part' in the strike.

Section 9 further amends s.62 with the effect that an employer may re-engage an employee(s) who was 'taking part' in a strike, where he has not re-engaged others, without facing unfair dismissal claims, provided he re-engages the employee(s) after the expiry of a period of three months following the date of dismissals. If he re-engages only some strikers within a three-month period of dismissal, he would again leave himself open to unfair dismissal claims. The amendments made by s.9 will have a substantial impact in future industrial relations, for although an employer's common law right to dismiss workers on strike without notice has remained intact, despite s.62, henceforth the ability of employers to take such a course of action, without having to consider the compensation element of unfair dismissals, will obviously have significant implications in situations such as that pertaining in the recent ASLEF drivers strike.

Union Membership Requirement in Contracts and Related Industrial Action. Section 18 of the 1980 Act (acts to compel trades union membership), is repealed and replaced by more extensive provisions in the 1982 Act. These complex provisions are examined in more detail in relation to 'the closed shop and related practices'. A brief summary of the new provisions follows.

(1) Section 12 renders void (and without legal effect) any term or condition of a contract for the supply of goods or services insofar as it requires that work under the contract is performed

only by union (or non-union) labour. Similarly a term or condition is void if it requires a party to the contract to recognize a trades union (whether or not named in the contract) for the purposes of negotiating on behalf of workers, or to negotiate or consult with any official of a trades union (s.13).

(2) A new (non-criminal) statutory duty is created, which is actionable in tort by an aggrieved party, where in broad terms a person on the grounds of union membership (or non-union membership) or union exclusion, (i.e. where a person's ground of action is that the person against whom it is taken does not, or is not likely to, recognize, negotiate or consult as outlined in s.13) (a) fails to include a person in a maintained list of approved suppliers of a tender list; (b) terminates a contract for the supply of goods or services; (c) excludes a person from a group of tenderers of fails to permit a person to submit a tender.

(3) Section 14 (1) removes immunity (in tort) conferred under s.13 of the 1974 Act as amended, from persons (e.g. a trades union or its officials) who induce the inclusion by another person (e.g. an employer) of a term or condition rendered void by ss. 12 or 13 or induces a person to contravene the new statutory duties.

Section 14 (2) in general terms removes immunity (in tort under s.13) from persons who induce certain industrial action (e.g. breach of contracts of employment, or threats of same etc.) interfering with the supply of goods or services (whether or not under a contract), and taken for either of the following reasons:

(1) work done or to be done in connection with the supply of goods or services, has been or is likely to be performed by persons not employed by the employer of those taking the industrial action, who are (or are not) members of a trade union;

(2) the supplier of the goods or services (not being the employer of those taking industrial action in breach of their contracts, etc.) does not or is not likely to recognize, negotiate or consult as outlined in s.13.

It should be noted that immunity is retained under s.14 (2) in the circumstances outlined, where such action is aimed against the employer (of those taking the action), on the grounds that fellow employees are not members of a trades union (etc.). Section 14 (2) in effect restricts the ambit of immunity conferred on tortious acts in two areas.

(1) Primary industrial action (disputes between workers and their employer) – an example might be where workers are induced to black the supply of goods to a firm ('and one of the reasons for so doing' is that work in connection with the supply of those goods will be done by non-union labour), in 'furtherance' of a primary dispute with their own employer concerning for example the 'facilities for officials of trades unions' (see s.29 of the 1974 Act).

(2) Secondary industrial action (which is the area where s.14 (2) will mainly apply), where such action is taken by employees (not in dispute with their own employer) but in contemplation or furtherance of a dispute between another employer and his workers. The severely curtailed immunity for the organizers of such action in tort under s.17 of the 1980 Act is totally removed where s.14 (2) pertains.

Summary. The immunity of trades unions, officials and individuals against actions in tort was enshrined in the Trade Disputes Act 1906. These immunities were cut back by the Industrial Relations Act 1971, but subsequently re-emerged and were re-enacted in a more extended form in the 1974 Act as amended. The Employment Act 1980 took the first major step in curbing these immunities by removing immunity in tort from pickets, unless they picket at their own place of work, and from the organizers of secondary industrial action unless it is directly targeted against the immediate suppliers or customers of the employer in dispute, to prevent or disrupt the supply of goods or services under a contract subsisting between them.

The provisions in the Employment Act 1982 have taken another major step in curbing these immunities. The hitherto blanket immunity enjoyed by trades unions in tort is removed. Unions henceforth may be sued on the same terms as any other individual save for certain limits on the amount of damages recoverable. In addition, a trades union will be liable in tort and its funds put in jeopardy where it is deemed legally responsible for certain specified (unprotected) industrial tortious acts of its officials. Section 13 (2) of the 1974 Act is repealed and the immunity conferred thereunder is removed for the tort of '. . . an interference with the trade business or employment of another', though it should be noted that there has been judicial doubt as to whether such a tort has in fact ever actually existed.

Henceforth a 'trade dispute' is restricted to cover only disputes 'between workers and their employer'. A trades union and its officials will lose immunity in tort where the dispute is solely between a trades union and an employer. The limited immunity to take secondary industrial action is further curbed in that a union, its officials or individuals who organize (induce) secondary action against an employer, not in dispute with his own employees, cannot 'create' a 'dispute' with that employer; and as a consequence have no immunity for secondary action even if it is 'permitted' by s.17 of the 1980 Act. Nor is immunity conferred on tortious acts where certain secondary action is taken on the grounds of non-union membership (or union membership), and union exclusion. Disputes between workers and workers (e.g. a demarcation dispute) are now excluded from the ambit of tortious immunity, as those with specified workers who have ceased to be employed by an employer and certain disputes occurring outside the UK.

Wide immunity is still furnished in tort for organizers of workers taking primary industrial action against their own employer, e.g. strikes, blackings, work to rule, a go slow. The Act will, however, curb immunity in tort for organizers of primary action where a dispute is not taken to relate wholly or mainly to the prescribed industrial matter in s.29 of the 1974 Act. Thus disputes which are political or personal, or any other dispute not relating wholly or mainly to the matters prescribed, will not attract immunity. In addition, those who organize primary action on the grounds of non-union membership (or union membership), and 'union exclusion', subject to certain exceptions, will also lose immunity for tortious acts.

Finally, in general terms, an employer will be able to dismiss striking employees without facing unfair dismissal claims for 'victimization', where some strikers have returned to work and have been retained in employment prior to such dismissals. The efficacy of the Act's provisions, as with those contained in the 1980 Act, depend entirely on an employer's willingness to pursue his legal rights. This is especially relevant in the light of recent utterances by trades union leaders which suggest that the provisions in the Employment Acts of 1980 and 1982 offer little deterrent to those intent on flouting them (*The Times*, 1982a).

THE CLOSED SHOP AND RELATED PRACTICES

The Extent of the Closed Shop in the British Economy

A closed shop is generally understood to mean an agreement or some form of arrangement, whereby employees or potential employees can obtain or continue in employment, only if they become or remain members of a specified trades union. In a recent survey (Lennard, Dunn and Wright, 1980) it was found that a minimum of 5.2 million employees in Great Britain were covered by closed shop arrangements in the period 1978–9, representing about 1 in 4 of the total workforce and approximately 2 in 5 of the unionized sector. These results reveal the increasing growth of the closed shop as a feature of Britain's economy, when compared to an earlier survey (McCarthy, 1964) held in the period 1962–4. In this first survey, the closed shop was shown to cover about 3.76 million workers, representing approximately 1 in 6 of the total workforce – an increase over a 15-year period of 1.5 million employees subject to the closed shop.

There has been a significant spread of penetration of the closed shop into white collar employment. In 1979 1.1 million, or 22 per cent, of the closed shop population were non-manual employees compared to 300,000, or 8 per cent, in 1964. Manual workers however are still the dominant class of members, amounting to 4.1 million of the overall total. 1 in 3 blue collar workers were involved in closed shop practices, compared with 1 in 10 of white collar employees. The growth of manual and non-manual membership of closed shop agreements in the public sector is also apparent in the 1978–9 survey (see Tables 3 and 4, Lennard *et al.*, 1980, p. 20).

Closed shops may for practical purposes be divided into two categories. In 'pre-entry closed shops', a union controls the supply of labour to employers by restricting entry to those who hold the 'appropriate union card' prior to their application. In 1979 16 per cent of those covered by closed shop arrangements fell into this category. The remaining 84 per cent fell into the second category of 'post-entry' closed shops. Here the union does not control the supply of labour by making membership a precondition of entry into employment, rather the employee must agree to join a particular trades union at some specified time thereafter.

Summary of Previous Legislation Pertaining to the Closed Shop

Closed shops have existed in one form or another since the latter part of the 19th century, though there was no statutory law dealing with them until the Conservative Government's Industrial Relations Act of 1971. This Act for the first time provided a statutory right not to join a trades union, and also introduced statutory protection against unfair dismissals. Where an employee was dismissed for refusing to become a member of a union subject to a closed shop, that dismissal was automatically unfair, entitling the employee to be redressed by compensation or re-engagement. Pre-entry closed shop agreements were declared void. (Under s.7 of the Industrial Relations Act 1971, pre-entry closed shop agreements were declared void and a worker refused engagement due to such an agreement could seek a declaration from the National Industrial Relations Court, that such an agreement was void. Such a declaration was the only remedy available to prospective employees.) However, a trades union registered under the Act could enter into a voluntary 'agency shop' with an employer. If the employer refused to co-operate, an 'agency shop' could be enforced against his wishes, if a ballot of the relevant employees showed that either two thirds of those voting or a majority of those eligible to vote were in favour.

Where an 'agency shop' was implemented, a worker's right not to join the trades union was extinguished. Consequently he could be dismissed without redress unless, while remaining a non-member of the union, he paid union dues or, if he objected on the grounds of conscience to making such contributions, he paid them to charity. In addition a registered trades union was permitted to implement an 'approved closed shop'. Such approval was only forthcoming if certain provisions in the Act were strictly adhered to. In an 'approved closed shop' a worker had his right not to be a member of a trade union reinstated only if he was a conscientious objector.

The crux of the efficacy of the provisions in dealing with 'approved closed shops', 'agency shops' and legal immunities, within a controlled framework, depended on trades unions registering under the Act. The TUC instructed unions not to register (those who did were subsequently expelled) and led an orchestrated campaign against the Act, rendering many of its provisions inoperable.

In retrospect the Act, during its relatively short lifetime of three years, appeared to have little or no impact in either existing closed shop practices or in abating the growth and implementation of new closed shop agreements. This result is thought to be largely attributable to unions and employers acting in concert to circumvent the Act's provisions. (For a fuller discussion of this observation, see Hanson, Jackson & Miller, 1982.) The 1971 Act was repealed by the Labour Government's 1974 legislation.

The formation and implementation of a closed shop is a purely voluntary agreement or arrangement reached by employers and unions in which the law does not directly intervene. The law pertaining to closed shops is, in the main, concerned with an individual's statutory rights not to be unfairly dismissed, or to have action short of dismissal taken against him for refusing to join, or remain a member of, a union. Under the provisions of the 1974 Act, if a 'Union Membership Agreement' (UMA) – a statutorily defined closed shop agreement or arrangement – was operating, such that it was the practice for all employees to belong to a specified trades union, an employer could fairly dismiss an employee (so that he had no legal redress) should he refuse to become or remain a member of that union. However, protection was available if he genuinely objected on grounds of 'religious belief' to being a member of any trades union whatsoever, or on any 'reasonable grounds' to being a member of a particular trade union. Where a worker's employment was terminated under these circumstances the dismissal was regarded as unfair, and the employee could seek redress.

The 1976 Amendment Act curtailed the limited protection afforded to individuals who objected to joining a closed shop, to that based upon 'religious belief' only.

The Labour Government's legislation of 1974–6 was seen as a fundamental attack on individual freedom and has been referred to as 'vicious legislation', 'an utterly deplorable situation . . . which eliminated the conscience clause and led to several hundred non-union employees being dismissed without compensation' (Hanson, 1982). (See also the Employment Act 1982, s.2).

Following the introduction in 1975 of a closed shop agreement between British Rail and the NUR, more than 40 British Rail employees were subsequently dismissed in 1976 for refusing to join the union. They had no redress since their objections were not on grounds of 'religious belief', the only protection afforded under the 1976 Amendment Act.

Three dismissed employees took their case to the European Commission of Human Rights who found that the Labour Government's 1976 Amendment Act had breached the European Convention on Human Rights by furnishing restricted protection for employees who objected to joining a closed shop. The matter was then referred to the European Court of Human Rights and in the case of *Young, James and Webster* v. *United Kingdom*, the Court delivered judgment on 13 August 1981 and held by a majority vote of 18–3 that there had been a breach of Article 11 of the Convention, by the UK Government. Article 11(i) states: 'everyone has the freedom of personal assembly and to freedom of association with others, including the right to form and to join trades unions for the protection of his interests'.

In addition, the Court was of the opinion that, although the proximate cause of the dispute was the 1975 agreement between British Rail and the unions, the nub of the complaint was 'the domestic law' (the 1976 Amendment Act). 'Hence the UK was responsible for any violation of the rights and freedoms under the Convention which were thus made lawful.' The Court also held, on the assumption that Article 11 does not guarantee a right not to be compelled to join a particular union and would not necessarily infringe the rights and freedoms guaranteed by the Convention, that:

'a threat of dismissal involving a loss of livelihood, particularly when directed against employees engaged before the closed shop was introduced, constitutes a most serious form of compulsion which strikes at the very substance of the freedom guaranteed by Article 11 . . . Pluralism, tolerance and broadmindedness, are hallmarks of a democratic society' (*European Human Rights Reports*, 1982).

The outcome of the case may be interpreted as a castigation of the 1976 Amendment Act's provisions on the closed shop, as being undemocratic and impinging on individual freedom.

Summary of the Law Pertaining to the Closed Shop and Related Issues Prior to the Employment Act 1982

What follows is a brief description of the law prior to the Employment Act 1982, which has made substantial amendments and repeals extending the scope of these provisions.

The Closed Shop. The 1980 Act to a large extent restored and widened an individual's right not to be unfairly dismissed where he objected to being a member of a union subject to a closed shop agreement.

Section 7 (which is now repealed), made such a dismissal automatically unfair where:

(1) an employee genuinely objected on the grounds of conscience or other deeply held personal conviction to being a member of any trades union whatsoever, or of a particular trades union; or

(2) an employee belonged to a class of workers prior to the implementation of a closed shop agreement relating to that class of workers, and he had not at any time since the introduction of the closed shop been a member of a trades union in accordance with that agreement; or

(3) a UMA took effect after 14 August 1980 and the agreement had not been approved in a secret ballot by not less than 80 per cent of those entitled to vote; or

(4) a UMA had been approved in a ballot in which the dismissed employee was entitled to vote, but the employee had not at any time since the ballot was held been a member of a trades union

in accordance with that agreement. (In general terms a UMA means an agreement or arrangement between an independent trades union (not being under the control or domination, or liable to interference by an employer, e.g. by the provision of financial or material support), and an employer which relates to employees of an identifiable class. A UMA must have the effect in practice of requiring such employees, for the time being of that class, (whether or not there is a condition to that effect in their contracts of employment) to be or become a member of the union (s.30 of the 1974 Act).)

The provisions of the 1980 Act, together with (Hepple and Higgins) Code of Practice on Closed Shop Agreements and Arrangements, substantially widened the scant protection afforded to individuals under previous legislation. The above provisions have been adopted in an extended form by the Employment Act 1982.

Related Provisions of the 1980 Act. Section 18 removed immunity in tort when certain industrial action was taken for the purpose of compelling workers to become members of a particular trades union, unless those workers worked at the same place or for the same employer as those taking the industrial action.

Section 10 in simple terms enabled an employer, who was induced by industrial action to dismiss unfairly an employee for not joining a trades union, to join the trades union or other person as a party to any subsequent proceedings. The union was then partly or wholly liable to meet any compensation award. Section 10 also enabled a sub-contractor to join a contractor in proceedings who had insisted on a union-only contract which resulted in the unfair dismissal of his employee.

Section 15 confers the right on an employee not to have action 'short of dismissal' taken against him by his employer, for the purpose of compelling him to become a member of a trades union. This right is only applicable, where a closed shop exists, if, had the action amounted to a dismissal, it would be unfair. The provisions as to joinder in s.10 applied equally to s.15.

Section 4 (which remains unaltered by the 1982 Act) introduced a new right pertaining solely to the closed shop, whereby every person who is, or is seeking to be in employment, has the right not to have an application for membership of the union unreasonably refused or to be unreasonably expelled from the same. Section 4 affords some protection against unions arbitrarily refusing an individual's application for membership of a union where a pre-entry closed shop is in operation, thereby depriving him of a 'right to work'. (The protection extends equally to post-entry closed shops and to existing members of either form.)

The Employment Act 1982

The Under-Secretary of State for Employment has said (*Journal of the Institute of Personnel Management*, 1982), when referring to the railwaymen's case before the European Court of Human Rights '. . . as a result of the 1980 Act we are now in compliance with article 11. . . .' (*Hansard*, 1982, p. 818). If there were any doubts about the validity of this assertion or of the Government's view that 'the 1980 Act had put matters right . . .' (p. 738) then the provisions in the Employment Act 1982 dealing with the closed shop and related practices will allay them.

Retrospective Compensation for Employees Dismissed under Previous Legislation in Relation to UMAs. Section 2 is unique in industrial law in that it retrospectively compensates as '. . . an act of belated justice' . . . 'about 400 people who were dismissed between 1974 and 1980 under the Labour Government's [closed shop] legislation. . . .' (*Hansard*, 1982, p. 817).

In simple terms s.2 empowers the Secretary of State at his discretion to make payments of compensation to persons previously dismissed from employment for non-membership of a trades union where a UMA operated. To qualify for compensation, an individual must have been dismissed on or after 16 September 1974, when the Labour Government's closed shop provisions came into force (which were so openly criticized by the European Court of Human Rights), and before 15 August 1980, when the extended rights conferred by s.7 of the Employment Act 1980 came into operation.

An individual must further show that between the above periods he did not bring, or brought but did not succeed in a complaint of unfair dismissal. In addition, he must show that if the 1980 amendments had been force in relation to his dismissal, he would have been entitled by virtue of those amendments to succeed in a complaint of unfair dismissal. The amount of compensation which may be awarded is subject to a maximum, together with interest, being that which would have been awarded at the date of dismissal had the employee brought a successful complaint. It is a criminal offence, under s.2, punishable with a maximum fine of £1000, for a person to make, for the purpose of obtaining compensation for himself or another, a statement which is false in a material particular and which that person knows to be false.

It is estimated that the once and for all expenditure involved under s.2 could be £2 million over 18 months, with total staff costs and administrative expenses of the order of £250,000 over the same period. The Employment Secretary said that s.2 is a direct response to the suffering caused by the last Labour Government's closed shop legislation (*Hansard*, 1982, p. 740). The section has also been seen as an indication of the present Conservative Government's 'regret' that it did not enter into a 'friendly settlement' (Hanson, 1982) with the railwaymen, provided by the rules of the European Commission on Human Rights but, instead, contested the case before the European Court of Human Rights.

Considerable controversy has reigned over whether there is retrospective legislation in s.2. The Employment Secretary, commenting on this criticism said:

> it does not retrospectively declare unfair what the law then said was fair, it simply provides a power to be exercised at the Secretary of State's discretion to compensate from public funds people sacked between 1974 and 1980, who would have been entitled to compensation if the main provisions of the 1980 Act had been in force (*Hansard*, 1982, p. 768).

The Under-Secretary, in endorsing the above view, said: 'it is not (retrospective) because it will not make any employer or individual subject to any *new* proceedings in respect of past dismissals.'

The European Court of Human Rights commenting on the railwaymen's case said: 'although individual interests may on occasions be subordinated to those of a group, democracy does not simply mean that the views of the majority must always prevail. A balance must be achieved which ensures the fair and proper treatment of minorities and avoids any abuse of dominant position'. The effect of ss. 3–8 and ss. 10–14 would now appear to strike this balance.

Dismissal for Non-Membership of a Union In Accordance With a UMA. Section 3 extends and amplifies the protection, originally found in s.7 in the 1980 Act to all closed shops. Dismissal for non-membership of a UMA will automatically be unfair for all existing closed shops, unless within five years before the dismissal a ballot has been held (in accordance with s.58A) in which not less than 80 per cent of those entitled to vote, or not less than 85 per cent of those who voted, were in favour of the UMA. If, however, a UMA came into force after 14 August 1980, and has not previously been balloted, then not less than 80 per cent of those entitled to vote must be in favour. It is clear, therefore, that pre-1980 closed shops will have a less rigorous first balloting requirement. On a second or subsequent ballot, however, which logically will have to be held at minimum five-yearly periods, in what amounts to a periodic review, the balloting requirement becomes much more severe. Both a minimum 80 per cent of those entitled to vote *and* 85 per cent of those voting must be in favour of the UMA.

Where a ballot is not held, or does not attain the requisite majority, the dismissal of an employee, who refuses to become or remain a member of the union, for whatever reason, will automatically be unfair thus entitling the employee to seek greatly enhanced levels of compensation (see ss. 4 and 5). Where the balloting requirements are met, such a dismissal would be fair unless an employee can bring himself within one of the other categories discussed earlier in relation to s.7 of the 1980 Act.

Section 7 is repealed by the Act but its provisions are mirrored in s.3 with minor amendments, and with important additions in relation to s.4 of the 1980 Act and in relation to a 'written code'.

Dismissal of an employee for non-membership of a UMA is automatically unfair under the 1982 Act.

(a) Where the employee 'genuinely objects on grounds of conscience or other deeply held personal conviction . . .'.
(b) Where the UMA took effect after 14 August 1980 and the employee was entitled to vote in the ballot through which the agreement was approved (if it were not approved the employee

would have redress under the new provision in s.3) and the employee has not, at any time since the date of the ballot, been a member of a trades union in accordance with that agreement.

(c) Where the existing employee has not at any time been a member of a trades union to which the UMA relates, since its introduction.

(d) (Subject to certain conditions) where, at the time of the dismissal for non-membership of a UMA, there was a declaration made under s.4 of the 1980 Act, of unreasonable exclusion or expulsion from a trades union, or proceedings on such a complaint are pending.

In a case where (a) or (d) above does not apply (so that a dismissal would not be unfair), then an employee may have redress if (a) he holds qualifications which are relevant to his employment, (b) he is subject to a written code which governs the conduct of those persons who hold those qualifications and (c) he has: (i) been expelled from a trades union for refusing to take part in a strike or other industrial action; or (ii) refused to become or remain a member of a trades union. If the above requirements are met, then a person may make a claim for unfair dismissal, if the principal reason for his refusal, in the case of (c)(i) is that his taking part in the action would be in breach of the code; or, in the case of (c)(ii) that if he became or remained a member he would be required to take part in a strike, or other industrial action, which would be in breach of that code.

Parallel protection to that outlined above is available to an employee who is dismissed where a UMA operates, for not complying with a requirement (whether or not imposed in his contract of employment) that he will make 'one or more payments' or his employer is entitled to deduct 'one or more sums from his remuneration', in the event of his failure to become or on his ceasing to remain, a member of the trades union. An example might be where an employee has 'promised' to pay his union dues or pay the same to charity if he does not remain a member of the union.

The Balloting Requirement Under Section 58A. The ballot must be conducted to ensure that, so far as is reasonably practicable, all those entitled to vote have an opportunity of voting and of so doing in secret. The persons entitled to vote in a ballot in relation to the application of a UMA to any class of employees shall be all those who belong to that class who: (a) in the case of a ballot in which votes may be cast only on one day are in the employment of the employer and (b) in any other case are in employment on the day specified by the person conducting the ballot. In the latter case, no day can be specified which falls after the last day on which votes may be cast or so long before that date as to be unreasonable.

Enhanced Rates of Compensation where Dismissal for Non-union Membership in a Closed Shop is Held to be Unfair. Section 4 provides in broad terms that where an employee is found to be unfairly dismissed by virtue of his non-membership of a trades union in accordance with a UMA any basic award is subject to a minimum of £2000. The maximum award under this head, which is calculated as if the dismissed employee was redundant, is currently £4050. In addition, there is a compensatory award payable (maximum £7000).

According to s.5, where an employee is unfairly dismissed by virtue of his non-membership of a trades union in accordance with a UMA, and he requests that an order by the tribunal is made for his reinstatement or re-engagement, a new special award must be made in addition to the basic award and compensatory award. Where no order is made for reinstatement or re-engagement, the amount of the special award is subject to a minimum of £10,000 and a maximum of £20,000. The maximum amount of compensation is:

basic award	£4050
compensatory award	£7000
special award	£20,000
	£31,050

Where an order is made for reinstatement or re-engagement but the order is not complied with, then, unless the employer satisfies the tribunal that it was not practicable to comply with the order, the amount of the special award must be increased to one week's pay multiplied by 156 or £15,000 whichever is the greater (and subject to no maximum).

An employee unfairly dismissed for non-membership of a closed shop under the Act's provisions would, as a minimum receive £12,000 if there was no order for reinstatement or re-engagement, or £17,000 if such an order were not complied with. This contrasts with the median award for unfair dismissal in 1980 of £598 (Neal, 1982).

However, these awards may be reduced in certain circumstances. For example: (i) where the tribunal considers that any conduct of the complainant before the dismissal was such that it would be just and equitable to reduce or further reduce the special award, it must do so; (ii) where the tribunal finds that the complainant has unreasonably prevented an order for reinstatement or re-engagement from being complied with, or refused an offer by the employer (made otherwise than in compliance with such an order) which, if accepted, would have the effect of reinstating the complainant as if he had not been dismissed, then the tribunal must reduce or further reduce the amount of the special award as it considers just and equitable.

Section 6 sets out matters to be disregarded by a tribunal when considering the reduction of an award. The tribunal must disregard any conduct or action of the complainant, where, in broad terms, it constitutes a breach of a requirement: (i) to become or be a member of a trades union or to cease to be or refrain from becoming a member of the same; or (ii) it constitutes a refusal to make payments or an objection to deductions from remuneration as outlined in s.3.

The new provisions relating to balloting all existing closed shops, although not rendering the closed shop illegal for non-compliance, will lead to fewer 'fair' dismissals for non-union membership. In addition, it is highly probable that there will be fewer actual dismissals bearing in mind the new special award, and the fact that compensation may in certain instances be met solely out of trades union funds (s.7).

The new provisions have led to criticism that high levels of compensation will encourage 'bounty hunters', 'free riders' and 'free loaders'. Others have countered these arguments saying that those in the closed shop 'could agree to allow the individual not to belong to the union and work alongside him' (*Hansard*, 1982, pp. 768–9). In any event, there are provisions in the Act for compensation to be reduced in such circumstances. It should be noted, however, that the Secretary of State may order that the new provisions, in s.3 relating to existing closed shops, shall not come into operation for 'such period as may be specified', save only for a UMA taking effect after 14 August 1980 (s.22).

An intimation of the length of period over which the Employment Secretary will postpone the 'review of existing closed shops', was given in a speech, at the Financial Times Seventh Industrial Relations Conference, when he stated he was 'minded to give one or two years after Royal Assent for proper preparation for ballots' (*Journal of the Institute of Personnel Management*, 1982).

Awards Against Third Parties. Section 10 of the 1980 Act is repealed and replaced by more extensive provisions in s.7. An employee, complaining to a tribunal that his dismissal was unfair (e.g. from a closed shop), will have a new 'right of joinder'. He may require that any person (in most cases a trades union) who exerted pressure on his employer to dismiss him for not being a member of a trades union, by calling or threatening industrial action, is joined in the proceedings. The tribunal then has power to make the award wholly against the trades union or partly against the employer and the union. It should be noted that the employer still retains his right to 'join in' a trades union. But the nub of the new provision is that previously only the employer could 'join in' a union, which he may have been reluctant to do where there was 'a threat to good industrial relations'. In future a complainant employee, under his own volition, may 'join in' a union and recover his compensation directly from its funds.

Section 7 is likely to dissuade unions from taking action, (outlined above) for, in the case of an unfair dismissal from a closed shop, the union might find itself ordered to pay compensation in excess of £30,000.

Interim Relief. Section 8 extends the right of certain complainants to apply to industrial tribunals for interim relief, i.e. an order for the continuation of their contracts of employment until the determination of their complaint, or, with the employer's approval, reinstatement or re-engagement. The relief available, under s.77 of the 1978 Act, now includes employees who claim they have been unfairly dismissed for non-membership of a trades union *including* non-membership of a closed shop agreement.

Action Short of Dismissal. Section 10 extends the relief of s.15 of the 1980 Act (not to have action short of dismissal taken against an employee by his employer to compel him to be a trades union member) to the new provisions in section 3. Included in this extended relief are the provisions relating to the making of payments or deductions from remuneration where an employee ceases to become or remain a member of a trades union, and also included are employees subject to written codes.

Related Practices: Prohibition of Union Membership Requirements in Contracts. S.10 of the 1980 Act and its limited joinder facility in relation to 'union only' contracts is repealed and replaced by greatly extended provisions in s.12. Section 12 provides that any terms or conditions of a contract for the supply of goods or services (hereafter referred to as a commercial contract) is void (and of no legal effect) insofar as it purports to require that the whole or part of the work done is to be done 'only' by workers who are members of a trades union. It should be noted, that the provisions in ss. 12 and 14 apply equally to requirements that work is done only by non-union members.

An example of the effect of s.12 would be where a sub-contractor signed a commercial contract with a 'union only' clause. Such a clause would be void and of no legal effect. The sub-contractor could use non-union labour without being in breach of contract. If the contractor then terminated the contract as a consequence of the use of non-union labour, the sub-contractor could sue the contractor for breach of contract, and, under s.12 (2) (b), he may have an additional right to sue in tort for breach of statutory duty.

Section 12 (2) (a) (as supplemented) provides, in general terms, that it is a breach of statutory duty for a person to exclude a supplier from a list of approved suppliers or a tender list, on the ground that work under a subsequent contract would, or would be likely to, be performed by non-union labour. Section 12 (2) (b) (as supplemented) provides that it is a breach of statutory duty for a person to terminate a commercial contract on the ground that work done or to be done, or which is likely to be done, is performed by non-union labour.

Section 12 (2) (c) (as supplemented) provides in general terms, that a breach of statutory duty occurs where a person in relation to a proposed commercial contract: (i) excludes a person from a group from whom tenders are invited; (ii) fails to permit a person to submit such a tender; (iii) otherwise determines not to enter into a commercial contract with that person; and the reason for the above acts is if the proposed contract were entered into, work to be done would be, or would likely to be, performed by non-union labour.

The breach of statutory duty does not create a criminal offence, but an aggrieved party may sue the person responsible for damages in tort. It should also be noted that an aggrieved party under s.12 (2) (b) may have the additional remedy of suing in contract. The rationale behind s.12 can be inferred from the Employment Secretary's comments, when he said, in relation to union-only labour requirements in contract:

> these are widely used to extend the closed shop into firms where neither employer nor employees want it . . . some Labour controlled local authorities . . . have been most blatant in their refusal to award contracts to firms unless their work force is 100 per cent unionized. In some cases they have refused to allow non-union firms even to tender for contracts. There is no doubt also a cost to the ratepayer of deliberately stifling competition . . . like all uncompetitive practices, the end result can be only loss of jobs (*Hansard*, 1982, p. 743).

It is interesting to note in this context, that Aims of Industry, the advocate for private enterprise, claimed to have found a loophole in the Bill during its passage through Parliament, whereby councils insisted 'that contractors sign recognition and procedural agreements' with unions, in effect ensuring union negotiated contracts. Aims quoted a letter to contractors from East Kilbride District Council, stating that from 1 October they will have to have signed a recognition and procedure agreement if they want to remain on the council's approved list (*Financial Times*, 1982). The Government closed this loophole by adding a new clause to the Bill in the committee stage of the House of Lords, to prevent companies or councils requiring firms tendering for contracts to recognize or have agreements with trades unions if they are to gain contracts (*The*

Times, 1982b) Lord Mackay, the Lord Advocate, had told peers that the move was aimed mainly at abuse by local authorities who sought to force contractors to recognize or negotiate with unions as a condition of eligibility for tendering or receiving contracts (*Guardian*, 1982).

These new provisions form s.13 of the Act, which mirrors s.12 as follows: s.13 (1) states that any term or condition of a contract for the supply of goods or services is void insofar as it purports to require any party to the contract (a) to recognize a trades union (whether or not named in the contract) for the purposes of negotiating on behalf of workers, or any class of workers employed by him; (b) to negotiate or consult with, or with any official of, one or more trades unions (whether or not so named). A person is also liable for breach of statutory duty if on the ground of 'union exclusion' he acts in a manner falling within para. (a) (b) or (c) of s.12 (2) (above).

A person acts on the ground of union exclusion if the ground, or one of the grounds, for his action is that the person against whom it is taken does not, or is not likely to recognize, negotiate or consult, as outlined in (a) and (b) above.

Related Practices: Pressure to Impose Union Membership Requirements. Section 14 (1) in simple terms removes immunity from actions in tort furnished by s.13 of the 1974 Act as amended, from any person who attempts to induce any other person to include in a contract a provision rendered void by ss. 12 and 13, or to contravene the new statutory duties. Section 14 (1) is aimed at removing immunity from trades unions who try to frustrate the provisions in ss. 12 and 13 by putting 'pressure' on their employer, thereby inducing him to contravene the same. In addition, s.14 (b) removes immunity in tort under s.13 where, in general terms, certain industrial action is taken on the grounds of non-union membership (or union membership) or union exclusion 'which interferes with the supply (whether or not under a contract) of goods or services or can reasonably be expected to have such an effect'.

Section 14 (2) takes away immunity (in respect of both primary and secondary action) from the organizers of industrial action. The reasons for this more extensive restriction on trades union immunities than that furnished in s.18 of the 1980 Act (which is repealed by the Act) is found in the Government's Green Paper. The paper argues that where companies are blacked, with the purpose of compelling workers to join a particular trades union, the organizers have no immunity. But blacking is commonly used, not to compel workers to join a union, but 'to prevent them from doing work which has traditionally been the preserve of union members'. In such cases the organizers of action would continue to have immunity. 'The question is whether immunity should be removed from all industrial action of this kind' (HMSO, Cmnd. 8128). The Government have answered this question in the Act. Section 14, together with the restricted ambit of a 'trade dispute' and the extensive provisions relating to 'prohibition of union membership requirements' and 'union recognition requirements', have provided substantial protection against those who take industrial action, or seek to discriminate commercially, on such grounds.

Summary of the 1982 Act's Provisions on The Closed Shop and Related Practices. Section 2 retrospectively compensates individuals, at the discretion of the Employment Secretary, who were dismissed between 1974 and 1980. The individuals who may claim compensation are those who were dismissed, without redress, under the Labour Government's closed shop legislation, but whose dismissals would have been unfair under the provisions of the 1980 Act, save for those relating to balloting requirements.

Section 3 provides wide ranging rights for employees dismissed for non-union membership of a closed shop. It reinforces and extends the balloting requirement for new closed shops (in the 1980 Act), to all existing closed shops.

A dismissal, for non-union membership of a closed shop will, in general, be automatically unfair unless the UMA is approved by the requisite majority in a secret ballot. The closed shop must be approved, within 'five years ending with the time of dismissal', by a minimum of 80 per cent of those entitled to vote or 85 per cent of those who voted. In effect a five yearly 'periodic review' is imposed, with the requisite approval being more severe on a second or subsequent ballot.

Sections 4 and 5 introduce a new framework of compensation at greatly enhanced rates. A person unfairly dismissed from a closed shop can expect minimum compensation of £12,000 if the tribunal order re-engagement or reinstatement and a minimum of £17,000 if an employer refuses to comply with such an order. The maximum claim for compensation will be in excess of £30,000.

Section 7 extends to a complainant, in an unfair dismissal case (including alleged unfair dismissal where a closed shop pertains), the right to require that there be joined in the proceedings, any person (including a trades union) who he claims exerted pressure on his employer to dismiss him, by calling or threatening industrial action because he was not a member of a trades union. Such an employee can claim compensation directly from a trades union's funds. Hitherto 'joinder' was only available to an employer.

Section 8 extends interim relief to those unfairly dismissed for non-membership of a trade union, including those in a closed shop as well as those dismissed for membership or activities in a trades union. The relief available is reinstatement, re-engagement or an order for continuation of their contracts of employment.

Section 10 extends an employee's right not to have action short of dismissal taken against him, in order to force him to become a union member, to the new provisions in s.3 (dismissal for non-membership of a union).

Section 11 introduces changes in respect of joinder in cases of action short of dismissal, which are parallel to the changes introduced by s.7 in relation to joinder in unfair dismissal cases.

Section 12 declares void any term in a commercial contract which requires only the use of union labour or only the use of non-union labour. It makes it unlawful to exclude non-union or union firms from tendering lists, and it makes it unlawful to award or terminate a commercial contract on the ground that union or non-union labour will perform the work under that contract.

Section 13 introduces parallel provisions, to those in s.12 in relation to union recognition requirements and 'union exclusion'. Section 14 removes immunity from a person in tort (including a trades union) who induces another person (an employer) to include in a contract provisions rendered void by ss. 12 and 13 or to breach the statutory duties thereunder. Immunity is also removed where action is taken against an employer, other than an employer of those taking the action, on the grounds that work is, or is likely to be, done by workers who are, or are not, members of a trades union (or on the grounds of union recognition in defined circumstances).

The Act's provisions have greatly increased the statutory protection afforded to an individual dismissed for non-membership of a closed shop and where action short of dismissal is taken against him. In addition enterprises employing non-union labour receive protection against commercial discrimination and industrial action on such grounds. The balloting provisions will render closed shops less efficacious in achieving their desired ends. In some instances the closed shop may prove inoperable.

However, protection is afforded only to a person who is 'dismissed'; therefore, no protection is provided for those seeking employment. The fact that no remedy is available for prospective employees is particularly pertinent where a pre-entry closed shop operates. All closed shops remain 'lawful' even if they do not have the requisite support under the Act's balloting provisions.

APPENDIX E

The European Tax-transfer System in 1981

BELGIUM

The Concept of Taxable Income

Impôt des personnes physiques is levied on the world-wide income of resident individuals, subject to the relevant double taxation arrangements.

There is in effect a 'schedular' type system whereupon income from the various sources are aggregated to arrive at total chargeable income. Confining our attention to employment income only, the following points need be noted: if no statement of actual expenses is produced, there is a standard deduction of up to BF75,000, the flat rate deduction being 20 per cent of the income up to BF150,000, 10 per cent of the income from 150,000 to 300,000, and 5 per cent of that portion exceeding 300,000 up to the maximum. There is relief (up to certain limits) for pension and superannuation contributions, including social security payments, and reimbursement of travelling to and from work (max. BF5,000). It should be noted that wages, salaries and other emoluments are paid under deduction at source, the amount so withheld being fully credited against final liability.

As indicated in our analysis of the UK tax system the treatment of dependents and housing costs is particularly important, so most of our attentions are confined to these areas.

Allowances for dependents are calculated as percentages of the tax up to fixed limits. As such the tax relief is considered in the notes on tax liability, rather than tax relief in determining taxable income. Mortgage interest payments in connection with the acquisition or construction of a dwelling place may in certain circumstances be allowed.

Social Security Income and Contributions

Certain social security benefits (including allowances for children) are exempt from income tax. Details of the taxation of benefits are considered later.

Both employers and employees pay social security contributions, and two points are particularly worth noting; first, that payments by the employer can amount to as much as 45 per cent of the payroll cost for wage earners; and second, payments by employees are (within limits) allowable deductions for tax purposes, being calculated on gross wages, but with ceilings which vary with the cost of living.

Local Taxes

Apart from the municipal surcharge (*taxe communale additionelle à l'impôt des personnes physiques*) which may not exceed 6 per cent of the resident individual income tax, there are no other major local taxes on income.

Tax Rates and Liability

Although the top marginal rate is 72 per cent payable on taxable income in excess of BF4 million, there is a ceiling so that the effective tax burden cannot exceed 67.5 per cent of taxable income.

Let us now consider the domestic rates in more detail. No tax is payable on net income less than BF100,000. For net taxable incomes up to BF750,000, the tax tables in force from 21 January 1981 are used. However, it should be noted that when the family's earned income does not exceed BF1,050,000 for the year 1982, only 80 per cent of the occupational income is taken into account for the determination of the tax rate (splitting system) provided this system is more favourable to the taxpayer.

As mentioned earlier there are reductions for dependents based on the tax itself as follows:

(1) for taxpayers with a dependent wife: BF4,618;
(2) for those with one dependent child: 5 per cent plus BF500 with a minimum of BF2,809 and a maximum of BF5,118;
(3) for those with 2 dependent children: 15 per cent plus BF1,250 with a minimim of BF8,177 and a maximum of BF15,104;
(4) for those with 3 dependent children: 25 per cent plus BF2,250, with a minimum of BF16,337 and a maximum of BF30,424;
(5) for those with 4 dependent children: 45 per cent plus BF3,500, with a minumum of BF32,772 and a maximum of BF62,043;
(6) for those with 5 dependent children: 65 per cent plus BF47,500, with a minimum of BF52,804 and a maximum of BF100,859;
(7) for those with 6 dependent children: 90 per cent plus BF6,000, with a minimum of BF76,894 and a maximum of BF147,788.

Unemployment Benefit

This is paid at a fixed percentage (60 per cent) of previous average gross earnings to those who have been in full-time employment and are capable of, available for and registered for work, and must not have refused suitable employment. Unemployment must not have been due to voluntary leaving, misconduct or strike action.

The 60 per cent of previous average gross earnings (*GY*) may be received indefinitely by heads of families, those who have worked for at least 20 years and those with a '33 per cent incapacity for work'. From January 1981, all other claimants have their benefit reduced to 40 per cent of *GY* after one year. The above is subject to both a minimum (BF600 a day) and a maximum (BF786 a day) for heads of households. Family allowances are paid in addition to unemployment benefit.

There is a public assistance scheme for low-income earners which is available on a local basis. Claims vary from case to case – payments are dependent on individual needs and the system is thought to be of minor significance.

There do not seem to be any benefits related to income – housing subsidies or free school meals, for example. Unemployment benefit is not taxable.

FRANCE

The Concept of Taxable Income

Impôt sur le revenu des personnes physiques is levied on the total (global) aggregated schedular income as described earlier in relation to Belgium. As regards employment income the following points may be noted:

Leaving aside the *déduction supplémentaire* which applies to only certain trades, there is a *déduction normale* of 10 per cent given in respect of the expenses of employment, unless the taxpayer can substantiate higher expenses. This deduction is limited to F40,000. Secondly, there is an earned income relief of 20 per cent (*abbatement spécial applicable au montant net des traitements et salaires*) on salaries up to F360,000. It should be noted that earned income relief is given after the *déduction normale*, hence the tax applies to a maximum of 72 per cent of earnings. In addition other deductions include pension, superannuation and social security contributions.

Having computed taxable earnings in this way there are a number of allowances which may be claimed. Housing costs are allowed in the case of owner-occupiers in much the same way as for Belgium. So too the tax treatment of dependents is calculated on an income-splitting basis, as we shall see shortly.

Social Security Income and Contributions

Certain social security benefits, family and maternity allowances are exempt from income tax. Both employees and employers pay social security contributions: employee 12.9 per cent, employer 41 per cent in 1981.

Tax Rates and Income-splitting

The rates of tax range from a minimum of 5 per cent, to a maximum of 60 per cent. For married taxpayers and those with dependents relief from tax is not given by way of relief, but by means of the income-splitting (*quotient familial*) system. Here the income of the family is divided into a number of parts, according to the number of dependents. The tax attributable to each part is calculated and then multiplied by the total number of parts, to give the total tax payable. The number of parts into which income is divided is given by the application of the following coefficients:

Size of Family Unit	*Number of Parts (Coefficients)*
Single person (no dependents)	1
Married couple (no dependents)	2
Married with one dependent	2.5
Each additional dependent child	0.5

The tax as computed in this way is then subjected to certain deductions (*réductions*) and surcharges (*majorations*) and marginal relief is available for those on small incomes.

Unemployment Benefit

This is available to those who are available and registered for, and capable of work and free from disqualification. There are three types of benefit: (i) special unemployment benefit; (ii) basic unemployment benefit; and (iii) end of entitlement benefit.

Special Unemployment Benefit. This is granted to those made redundant for economic reasons before the age of 60. Rates are as follows: (*Q* denotes quarter, *GY* = insurable earnings)

F25 per day +	*Q*1 65 per cent *GY*	or	*Q*1 75 per cent *GY*
	*Q*2 60 per cent *GY*		*Q*2 70 per cent *GY*
	*Q*3 55 per cent *GY*		*Q*3 65 per cent *GY*
	*Q*4 50 per cent *GY*		*Q*4 60 per cent *GY*

whichever is the more beneficial, also subject to the minimum benefit, first F25 + 70 per cent of minimum wage (SMIC) or as in the second case 90 per cent of minimum wage/SMIC, again whichever is the more beneficial. The maximum benefit allowed is 90 per cent of insurable earnings. Special unemployment benefit may be claimed for 365 days (426 days if aged 50–4, 547 days for those aged over 55). Thereafter those made redundant move onto basic unemployment benefit.

Basic Unemployment Benefit. The amount payable here if F25 + 42 per cent of insurable earnings per day, subject to the minimum F57 per day and maximum 90 per cent of insurable earnings. For those aged under 50 this benefit may be claimed for 365 days; 50–5 year olds for 791 days; and 912 days for those over 55. Once this benefit is exhausted, an end of entitlement benefit is claimed.

End of Entitlement Benefit. This is F25 per day. Those aged over 50 may claim this for 274 days; 50–4 year olds for 365 days; and those over 55 for 465 days.

Family allowances are paid in addition to all the above benefits. Public aid is available on a local basis but there are no tied subsidies to income levels and, as in Belgium, the system seems to be of negligible importance. Unemployment benefit is taxable.

WEST GERMANY

Here taxable income is income from all sources except sources of income which include, *inter alia*, (i) compulsory social security payments made by employer up to certain limits; (ii) removal, travelling and other expenses subject to ceiling; and (iii) payments by the employer. Husband and wife may elect to submit a joint return, in which case the tax is calculated at twice the amount payable on half the joint income.

Allowable Deductions

In computing taxable income the following are allowable: (i) church taxes; (2) health, accident and employment insurance; (3) an earned income relief of DM2,214; and (4) social security contributions paid by employees.

This is 9.25 per cent of employees' gross earnings up to a maximum of DM52,800 + 1.5 per cent unemployment insurance. Manual workers and other employees earning less than DM39,600 pay health insurance premiums at 11–16.4 per cent.

Child Benefits

Upon application, a monthly cash allowance of DM50 for the first child, DM100 for the second and DM220 for each additional child is payable. This is tax free, and is not included in the total income computation.

Tax Rates and Liability

Tax is levied at progressive rates commencing at 22 per cent and increasing to about 56 per cent. It should be noted that the majority of religious groups pay church tax imposed by the states at rates of between 8 and 9 per cent of the individual's *tax* liability. But the amount of church tax so paid is then allowed in finalizing the individual's personal tax liability to the Government.

Unemployment Allowance (Arbeitslosengeld)

This is available to those ready and capable for work and who have not refused suitable employment. Unemployment must not be due to voluntary leaving or misconduct. Claimants must have had at least six months' insured work during the last three years. The amount paid is 68 per cent of wages after legal deductions subject to a maximum wage of DM980 (1980). Family allowances are payable in addition. *Arbeitslosengeld* is payable for between 78 and 312 days according to employment record. Once this benefit is exhausted the unemployed receive unemployment assistance.

Unemployment Assistance (Arbeitslosenhilfe)

This is 58 per cent of wages after legal deductions, the amount being payable for an unlimited period. Again family allowances are payable in addition.

Social Assistance (Sozialhilfe)

This is available in Germany. It also seems to be the closest equivalent of the supplementary benefits scheme (in the UK), to be found on the Continent. Payments from the scheme are discretionary and on a local basis, and therefore there are no national indices.

Housing Allowances (Wohngeld)

These are available to low-income families. Also low-cost 'social' housing is built and families in such dwellings receive a housing allowance. This is available whether the breadwinner is employed or unemployed. Amounts paid vary according to individual needs. Unemployment and other associated benefits are not taxable.

ITALY

Income from all sources is liable to income tax (IRPEF) after the following allowable deductions: interest on mortgage loans up to L4 million capital amount; social security and welfare contributions (the employee's contributions being 7.8 per cent of gross salary); and a flat rate deduction of 25 per cent of employment income.

In addition, personal allowances are made directly against IRPEF rather than against taxable income. An allowance of L36,000 is granted to each taxpayer, with a further deduction of L228,000 for employees. For resident individuals, there is a further allowance of up to L168,000.

Tax Rates

IRPEF is charged at progressive rates ranging from 10 per cent on taxable income of L3 million rising to 72 per cent on incomes exceeding L550 million. Family allowances are not liable for tax.

Unemployment Benefit

Here there are two types of unemployment compensation, special and normal unemployment benefit.

Special Unemployment Benefit. This scheme started in 1968 and is paid to industrial workers who lose their jobs through redundancy or their firm closing down. The rate of benefit is two thirds of basic wages net of tax and social security contributions and is available for six months, thereafter reviewed every three months. In practice such benefit may be claimed indefinitely. Family allowances are payable also.

Normal Unemployment Benefit. This is payable to those not entitled to special unemployment benefit. It may be claimed indefinitely but (at less than 40p per day) it may be ignored, for all the unemployed, in general, are entitled to special unemployment benefit.

Social Aid

This is available on a local basis. Again it is of a discretionary nature and like the other countries it seems of little importance. Unemployment benefit is not taxable.

References

Abbot, M. and Ashenfelter, O. (1976) 'Labour supply, commodity demand and the allocation of time', *Review of Economic Studies*, 43, pp. 381–411.

Ashenfelter, O. (1978) 'Unemployment as a constraint on labour market behaviour', in M. J. Artis and A. R. Nobay (eds) *Contemporary Economic Analysis*, London, Croom Helm.

Beckerman, W. (1979) 'The impact of income maintenance payments on poverty in Britain 1975', *Economic Journal*, 89.

Benjamin, D. and Kochin, L. (1979) 'Searching for an explanation of unemployment in inter-war Britain', *Journal of Political Economy*, 87, No. 3, pp. 441–70.

Benjamin, D. and Kochin, L. and Critics (1982) 'Unemployment and unemployment benefits in twentieth century Britain: a reply to our critics' and preceding critics' Comments, *Journal of Political Economy*, 90.

Break, G. F. (1957) 'Income taxes and incentives to work: an empirical study', *American Economic Review*, September.

Brown, C. V. and Levin, E. (1974) 'The effects of income taxation on overtime: the results of a national survey', *Economic Journal*, pp. 846–7.

Brown, C. V., Levin, E. and Ulph, D. T. (1976) 'Estimates of labour hours supplied by married male workers in Great Britain', *Scottish Journal of Political Economy*, November.

Cain, G. G. and Watts, W. W. (1973) *Income Maintenance and Labour Supply*, Chicago, Markham.

Douglas, P. H. (1934) *The Theory of Wages*, London, Macmillan.

European Human Rights Reports (1982) Part 13, 13 January, p. 38.

Feldstein, M. S. (1968) 'Estimating the supply curve of working hours' *Oxford Economic Papers* 20, pp. 74–80.

Fields, D. B. and Stanbury, W. T. (1971) 'Income taxes and incentives to work: some additional empirical evidence', *American Economic Review*, June.

Financial Times, (1982) ' "Aims of Industry" warns of Tebbit Bill loophole' 28 May.

Finegan, T. A. (1962) 'Hours of work in the United States: a cross sectional analysis', *Journal of Political Economy*, 70, pp. 452–70.

Godfrey, L. G. (1978) 'Testing against general AR and MA error models when the regressions include lagged dependent variables', *Econometrica*, Vol. 46, No. 6.

Guardian (1982) 'Ban proposed on union-only contracts' 14 July.

Hall, R. E. (1975) 'Effects of experimental negative income tax on labour supply', in J. A. Pechman and P. M. Timpane (eds) *Work Incentives and Income Guarantees: The New Jersey Negative Income Tax Experiment*, Brookings Institution.

Hansard (1982) House of Commons Parliamentary Debates, 8 February. HMSO, Vol. 17, No. 52, pp. 737–832.

Hanson, C. G. (1982) 'Labour law, Tebbit style', *Journal of Economic Affairs*, Vol. 2, No. 3, April, p. 153.

Hanson, C. G., Jackson, S.M. and Miller, D. (1982) *The Closed Shop – a Comparative Study in Public Policy and Trade Union Security in Britain, the USA and West Germany* Aldershot, Gower, Ch. 5.

Haveman, R. H. and Watts, H. W. (1977) 'Social experimentation as policy research: a review of negative income tax experiments' in V. Halberstadt and A. J. Culyer, *Public Economics and Human Resources*, Paris, Editions Cujas.

Hepple, B. A. and Higgins, P. O. (1981) Code of Practice on 'Closed shop agreements and arrangements', *Encyclopedia of Labour Relations Law*, London, Sweet and Maxwell.

HMSO (1968) *Royal Commission on Trades Unions and Employers' Associations Report*, June, Cmnd. 3623.

HMSO (1969) *In Place of Strife – a Policy for Industrial Relations*, January, Cmnd. 3888.

HMSO (1972) *Proposals For A Tax Credit System*, Cmnd. 5116.

HMSO (1981) *Trade Union Immunities*, January, Cmnd. 8128, para. 15.8(a) para. 125, paras. 289–90.

HMSO (1982) *Report of the Commissioners for Year Ended 31 March 1982*, Board of Inland Revenue, Cmnd. 8514.

Holden, K. and Peel, D. A. (1979) 'The Determinants of the unemployment rate: some empirical evidence', *The Statistician*, Vol. 20, No. 2.

Holden, K. and Peel, D. A. (1981) 'Unemployment and the replacement ratio – some reduced form estimates for the UK', *Economics Letters*, 8, pp. 349–54.

Howell, R. (1981) *Why Work? A Radical Solution*, Conservative Political Centre.

Junankar, P. N. (1981) 'An econometric analysis of unemployment in Great Britain, 1952–75', *Oxford Economic Papers*, 33, pp. 387–400.

Kochin, Levis, A. (1980) 'The social cost of union gains', *Statsvetenskaplig Tidskrift* (The Swedish Journal of Political Science), 5.

Kosters, M. H. (1969) 'Effects of an income tax on labour supply' in A. C. Harberger and M. J. Bailey (eds), *The Taxation of Income From Capital*, Washington: Brookings Institution.

Lancaster, T. (1979) 'Econometric methods for the duration of unemployment', *Econometrica*, 47, pp. 939–56.

Lancaster, T. and Chesher, A. (1982) 'An econometric analysis of reservation wages', Hull Economic Research Paper, No. 71 (revised) University of Hull, October.

Layard, R., Metcalf, D. and Nickell, S. (1978) 'The effect of collective bargaining on relative and absolute wages', *British Journal of Industrial Relations*, November.

Lees, D. (1967) 'Poor families and fiscal return' *Lloyds Bank Review*, October.

Lennard, J., Dunn, S. and Wright, M. (1980) 'The extent of closed shop arrangements in British industry', *Department of Employment Gazette*, January, Vol. 88, No. 1, pp. 16–22.

Lewis, H. G. (1963) *Unionism and Relative Wages In The United States*, University of Chicago Press.

Lucas, R. E. and Rapping, L. S. (1969) 'Real wages, employment and inflation', *Journal of Political Economy*, 77.

McCarthy, W. E. J. (1964) *The Closed Shop in Britain*, Oxford, Basil Blackwell.

Mackay, D. I. and Reid, G. L. (1972) 'Redundancy, unemployment and manpower policy', *Economic Journal*, 82, pp. 1256–72.

Maki, D. and Spindler, Z. A. (1975) 'The effect of unemployment compensation on the rate of unemployment in Great Britain', *Oxford Economic Papers*, 27, 3.

Minford, A. P. L. and Hilliard, G. (1978) 'The cost of variable inflation' in M. J. Artis and A. R. Nobay (eds) *Contemporary Economic Analysis*, London, Croom Helm.

Minford, A. P. L. (1980) 'A rational expectations model of the UK under fixed and floating exchange rates', in *The State of Macroeconomics*', Carnegie Rochester Conference Series on Public Policy 12, pp. 293–355.

Minford, A. P. L. (1982a) 'Trade unions destroy a million jobs', *Journal of Economic Affairs*, Vol. 2, January, pp. 73–9.

Minford, A. P. L. (1982b) 'Labour market equilibrium in an urban economy', SSRC Working Paper No. 8103 (revised October 1982), Liverpool University, provisionally forthcoming *Oxford Economic Papers*.

Moser, C. A. and Kalton, G. (1971) *Survey Methods in Social Investigation*, London, Heinemann Educational Books.

Mulvey, C. (1976) 'Collective agreements and relative earnings in UK manufacturing in 1973', *Economica*, 43 (172), pp. 419–27, November.

Muth, J. F. (1961) 'Rational expectations and the theory of price movements', *Econometrica*, 38, 1, pp. 315–35.

Neal, A. (1982) 'Recent developments in unfair dismissal', *New Law Journal*, Vol. 132, 8 April.

'News and notes', (1982) *Journal of the Institute of Personnel Management* June, No. 6, Vol. 14.

Nickell, S. (1979a) 'The effects of unemployment and related benefits on the duration of unemployment', *Economic Journal*, 89, March.

Nickell, S. (1979b) 'Estimating the probability of leaving unemployment; *Econometrica*, 47, pp. 1249–66.

Nickell, S. (1981) 'The demand for labour function in UK manufacturing', Paper presented to Treasury Academic Panel, Centre for Labour Economics, London School of Economics.

ORC (1976) *Tax and Motivation of Management*, London, ORC.

Owen, J. D. (1971) 'The demand for leisure', *Journal of Political Economy*, 79, pp. 56–76.

Parsley, C. J. (1980) 'Labour union effects on wage gains: a survey of recent literature, *Journal of Economic Literature, 18*, pp. 1–31.

Polanyi, G. and Polanyi, C. (1974) 'Tax credits, a missed opportunity', *National Westminster Bank Review*.

Rayner, A. C. (1969) 'On the identification of the supply curve of working hours', *Oxford Economic Papers*, 21, pp. 294–8.

Rosen, S. (1969) 'On the inter industry wage and hours structure', *Journal of Political Economy*, 77, pp. 249–73.

Smith, R. (1982) 'A note on likelihood ratio tests for the independence between a subset of stochastic regressors and disturbances', Discussion Paper in Econometrics, No. ES 118, University of Manchester, February.

Stewart, M. (1976) 'The determinants of earnings in Britain, an occupation specific approach', Centre for Labour Economics, Discussion Paper No. 4, London School of Economics.

The Times (1982a) 'Union choose NHS as the battleground' 13 June.

The Times (1982b) 'Union-only contracts outlawed' 14 July.

Treble, J. G. (1982) 'Does the union/non-union wage differential exist?' Paper given to 1982 AUTE Conference at Surrey University, mimeo, University of Hull.

Author Index

Subject Index